THE ATTACK ON BIG BUSINESS

THE ATTACK ON BIG BUSINESS

BY J. D. GLOVER
Professor of Business Administration

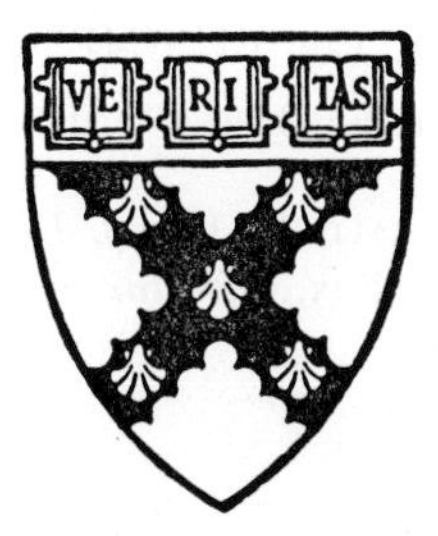

DIVISION OF RESEARCH
GRADUATE SCHOOL OF BUSINESS ADMINISTRATION
HARVARD UNIVERSITY
BOSTON
1954

HARVARD UNIVERSITY
GRADUATE SCHOOL OF BUSINESS ADMINISTRATION
GEORGE F. BAKER FOUNDATION

DONALD K. DAVID, *Dean*
BERTRAND FOX, *Director of Research*

Library of Congress Catalog Card No. 54-11415

PRINTED AT
THE PLIMPTON PRESS
NORWOOD, MASSACHUSETTS, U.S.A.

To the memory of

MY MOTHER

Foreword

THIS BOOK has been written primarily for use by thoughtful business leaders. The writing of it was undertaken at the behest of a group of professors at the Harvard Business School who met together some years ago for a series of discussions concerned with what topics of research in the general area of big business seemed to be especially interesting and important. Professor Glover was a member of that group.

This group recognized that big business had become a key instrumentality for getting things done in America, whether in peace or in war. Yet big business is periodically under attack from one source or another. Accordingly, we felt that it was important for citizens generally, and for businessmen more particularly, to understand the meaning of this seeming contradiction. Why do people so generally patronize big business and yet entertain deep misgivings about it? Professor Glover's book sheds light on this question.

Professor Glover's mission was not to make detailed studies of business practices nor of particular corporations, nor to formulate theories growing out of such studies. His mission was to examine the literature of the attack, to discern any pattern there might be, and to summarize the attack on big business. He has studied a perfectly enormous mass of literature and has spent much time evaluating it. He has endeavored to summarize systematically the attack as he found it, to make clear the themes he found running through the literature, and to give enough by way of examples to convey with accuracy its outline and tenor. He has purposely avoided quantities of footnotes and quotations which he might have used, in order to keep this book within smaller space limits. The extensive bibliography he gives includes numerous items he could easily and well have quoted from. This listing of items should serve those who might like to follow the matter further or to test the representativeness of the samples he does give.

Other publications have already grown out of the inspiration of that discussion group which met to talk about research in the area of big business, such as the volume on *The Growth of Integrated Oil Companies,* by Professors John G. McLean and Robert Wm. Haig[1]; and the articles, "Product Diversification and the Public Interest," by Professor Kenneth R. Andrews, and "The Champion Case: What Is Competition?" by Professor Harry L. Hansen and Mr. Marcell N. Smith, both of which appeared in the *Harvard Business Review.*[2] Other members of this Faculty are continuing to collect data and to ponder its economic and social meaning in terms of theories of a dynamic economy.

I hope that this book will help businessmen to understand the nature and importance of the recurring attacks on business, and enable them to re-examine and where appropriate to redirect their business policies accordingly. In view of the paucity of factual information about how this relatively new social institution — big business — actually carries on its work, and the further fact that it is hard for the average man to evaluate the pros and cons, I hope that businessmen will follow Mr. Glover's suggestion and take initiative in supplying the public with more facts about their own companies than ever before. In addition they can cooperate actively with those who come seeking after facts. In either case, businessmen must adopt a self-confident attitude of willingness to let the chips fall where they may. Thus economists, political and social theorists, moralists, and the people at large will become more fully informed and better prepared to reach their own judgments concerning this vastly important instrumentality of modern life.

EDMUND P. LEARNED
Professor of Business Administration

Soldiers Field
Boston, Massachusetts
June 1954

[1] Boston: Harvard University, Graduate School of Business Administration, Division of Research, 1954.

[2] "Product Diversification and the Public Interest," Volume XXIX, No. 4, July 1951, pp. 91–107; "The Champion Case: What Is Competition?" Volume XXIX, No. 3, May 1951, pp. 89–103.

Preface

WITHIN the alloted span of a human life, America has gone through a revolution. How and where we live; how we work and what we work at; what we make and what we use — all these things have been profoundly changed. Our population has increased more than three-fold. Our material production has increased more than eleven-fold. We *were* mostly a rural, agrarian people. Now we are mostly urban and industrial.

The end of this revolution is not yet in sight.

This revolution of ours may lack the dramatic fireworks of the French or Russian revolutions. Or even of the American Revolution of 1776. But it has had far more immediate, direct, tangible, and pervasive impact on the daily life and mode of living of ordinary individuals than any of them. The chapter in history most nearly comparable is England's Industrial Revolution of the 19th Century. The changes which swept over England captured the imagination of plain folk, politicians, and historians. They were deeply stirred, often shocked, and sometimes frightened by the extent and depth of these changes. But our own departure from things past has been far greater than was theirs.

This revolution of ours has not yet been named.

With no greater oversimplification than is common in historical labels, it *could* be called the Big Business Revolution.

For one of its outstanding distinguishing features has been the rise of the *big* business corporation as a *commonplace.* In mid-century there are thousands upon thousands of companies that are *big* businesses as compared with the "representative firm" of seventy years ago, or to what is common in most other countries today. The large business corporation has emerged as a distinctive, well-nigh typical part of the American scene. More than any other nation — for better or for worse — we have availed ourselves of this means for organizing economic life.

This revolution has been brought about pre-eminently by what large-scale production and large-scale organization have done and made possible. Many factors, of course, have operated to carry this development forward. Government agencies, for example, have played an important part; so have the universities. So, too, has *small* business in vitally important ways. But the home, the office, the classroom and hospital, the farm and the factory all provide concrete evidence that the large business corporation has been the chief vehicle by which this revolution has been carried forward. And that it has been one of the prime movers. We differ markedly from other countries and other times in the way we make and do things, in the way we buy and sell, in the way we develop and exploit technological change. To the extent that we do *differ,* more than anything else this is a direct consequence of our doing so many things through large-scale organization.

From its rapid emergence in the era of the Trusts right down to the present, big business has been under continuous and vigorous attack by a host of varied critics. Throughout its history, "big business" has been deplored, disparaged, decried, and legislated against. It has been denounced by Presidents, and by Senators and Representatives in Congress. Many of the nation's intellectuals have ranged themselves against it. It has been viewed with profound misgivings by ordinary citizens.

In volumes upon volumes of testimony before Congressional committees, in popular novels, in learned treatises and textbooks, in poetry, in sermons, in opinions of Supreme Court Justices, "big business" and its works have been seen as evil and attacked. The literature of the criticism of "big business," and of the civilization it has done so much to bring into being, represents by now a perfectly staggering mass of material.

This book is a survey and a study of that criticism.

This book is an endeavor to put together an accurate and understandable picture of the kinds of things that have been said and written against "big business." I have tried to discern the pattern and essence of this criticism, its principal charges, and its underlying premises. I have tried to reproduce its major lines of argument. I have tried to see and convey what this criticism adds up to, and what it means — especially what it means for the administrators of *big* business.

The widespread hostility, suspicion, and just plain unfriendliness manifested by this criticism is an important element of the environment *all* business operates in. As such, and properly understood, it has a claim to be taken into account. In fact, often it is not. Principally this seems to be because many businessmen do not understand this part of the reality about them as well as they do other parts. Say, the realities of competition and industrial techniques. Considering the mass of this welter of criticism, if nothing else, it is not surprising that this should be so. The purpose of this book is to be of help to businessmen — especially those responsible for *big* businesses — in formulating policies, reaching decisions, and taking actions ever better related to this aspect of the reality that lies about them. If it serves that purpose, I shall be content.

A few words about the contents of this book: It is in four parts. Each of the first three parts deals with one of the major levels on which criticism of big business has been levied. The first part deals with the attack that has been made on economic grounds. The second treats of social and political criticism. The third takes up the criticism that has been advanced on ethical and moral grounds, not so much of "big business" directly and as such, but of the civilization — the industrial civilization — with which "big business" is inevitably and intimately associated. The fourth part consists of interpretation and evaluation, and conclusions as to the significance of all this criticism for businessmen.

Perhaps I should explain why I took up the economic, the social and political, and the ethical and moral criticism in that order. It was my design to start with the kind of material I supposed would be the most familiar, or in any event most understandable to most businessmen, and from there go on to areas less familiar. In that way, it seemed to me, the reader could most easily get a grasp of the whole.

In putting together this survey, I have given many examples and mentioned many people. The ones I chose seemed to me to illustrate best and most interestingly, out of the quantity of material at hand, the particular points of view expressed. Doubtless many better illustrations could have been found. Others doing this same job would surely have chosen a different set of illustrations, in any case. They might, for instance, have referred to Henry George's *Progress and Poverty* or to Edward Bellamy's *Looking Backward.* I could well have quoted from these items, but did not. They might have made more or less use of the view of European critics. That would depend on how important to American thinking they judged them to be, and upon how useful they thought it to be to get across something of the international dimensions of the attack on "big business." These are all matters of purpose and judgment. I have aspired to capture for businessmen an accurate and usable impression of the things that have been said.

My debt to my colleagues of the Faculty of the Harvard University Graduate School of Business Administration is evident at every turn. In their classes, conversations, and books much of what appears here was gleaned. Out of this group of men with whom I have been so long associated it is not easy to single out a few for mention by name. But there are some personal acknowledgments which must be made.

In preparing this work, I have especially had the benefit of the patience, good will, and hard-headed thinking of my friend, Professor Edmund P. Learned. He first encouraged me to undertake this project and he has given me without stint of his assistance all along the way.

The germ of many an idea presented here had its origin in my almost daily talks with my friend, colleague, and fellow-townsman, Professor Ralph M. Hower.

In putting together, interpreting, and presenting this material I have benefited incalculably from ideas and suggestions offered by Professors Melvin T. Copeland, Richard S. Meriam, Bertrand Fox, Charles I. Gragg, Robert W. Austin, Harry L. Hansen, Joseph C. Bailey, George F. F. Lombard, John G. McLean, Kenneth R. Andrews, and Paul R. Lawrence.

I should like, especially, to record my earnest thanks to our Associate Dean, Stanley F. Teele, for making time available to me to carry out this enterprise.

In making these earnest acknowledgments, I wish in no way to involve my friends in culpability for any of the views or shortcomings which appear in this book. They have offered without reservation, but, of course, I was free to choose. More, I was free to merge, develop, and add to their ideas in my own way. In justice, they cannot be held responsible for what has happened to their thoughts after they were adopted by a foster-parent.

I hope Miss Margaret F. Bullwinkel who typed the manuscript and assisted me diligently all along the line knows how much I appreciate her help and cheerfulness. And I should like at long last to express my thanks to Mrs. Harriet L. Williams and Miss Lorna M. Daniells, reference librarians at the Baker Library, for the enormous and unflagging help they have given in suggesting, locating, and getting material, and in checking what seemed at times to be an endless procession of citations. Also, most fortunately, I have had the editorial assistance of Miss Ruth Norton and Miss Margaret C. Williams in preparing the manuscript in its finished form.

Finally — but finally only because of protocol — I must express my affectionate gratitude to my wife, Ruth Adams Glover. To her were delegated many of the responsibilities which ordinarily fall upon the "man of the house" that I might fully devote my attention to this enterprise. She managed these extra duties and burdens along with those involved in bringing up a lively family in the manner becoming to the true Administrator. She also helped me, when my own thoughts failed, over many a difficult spot encountered in producing what the reader finds here. Next autumn, in contrast to the last two years, I must put up the storm windows and doors myself. And take them down the following spring, also.

Of course, full responsibility for the finished product falls without further delegation upon the author.

J. D. GLOVER

Weston, Massachusetts
April 15, 1954

CONTENTS

PART I

The Economic Attack on Big Business

Introduction

RIGHT here at the very outset as the first item on the agenda we'd better take up a matter of definition — What *is* this thing, "big business," the target of all the criticism?

One might suppose that "big business" is something that could be defined precisely and concretely, even if arbitrarily. Conceivably, for instance, it might be defined as companies having, say, assets stated at more than $1,000,000, $10,000,000, $100,000,000, or $1,000,000,000, as the case might be. Given any such definition, one could then list by name all the companies included in the group.

A scattering of critics have attempted to set up exact definitions of this sort. Some have even listed the particular corporations which, for them, comprise "big business." But no such definition commands a preponderant following.

Actually, the matter of defining "big business" isn't nearly so simple as that anyway.

When you take a look at the nouns, the terms, the figures of speech which critics use to describe what it is they are opposed to, it becomes quite clear that it is something more than just an uncertain list of particular corporations. And when you take a look at the nouns, the terms, the concepts which are used to describe what they approve and favor *instead* of "big business," it becomes clearer still.

Here is a sample list of the expressions used by *economic* critics when they are talking about what it is *they* are critical of:

"big business," "Big Business," "bigness," "The Big";
"Trusts";
"Industrial Combinations," "great combinations";
"giant consolidations," "consolidations," "mergers";
"mammoth corporations," "giant corporations," "corporate empires";

"great establishments," "massed capital";
"monopoly," "*prima facie* monopoly," "monopolistic competition," "oligopoly";
"monopoly power," "economic power," "substantial control of the market";
"large business," "large-size in American business";
"large business units";
"large-scale production," "large-scale operations";
"large enterprise";
"large companies," "modern business";
"corporations";
"anyone important enough to affect the prices of the things that he sells and buys . . . almost every businessman . . . the ordinary businessman. . . ."

And here, in contrast, is a sample list of the terms used by critics on the economic plane when they are talking about what it is they are *not* attacking, or about that which they favor instead:

"separate concerns," "independent concerns," "independent companies," "small companies";
"other companies" (as distinguished from "big companies");
"competing corporations," "the competitor," "competition," "pure competition";
"representative firms";
"the small enterpriser," "the small businessman," "smaller units," "smaller firms";
"little workshops," "little establishments";
"the millions of farmers."

When we pass to the critics who attack "big business" on the social and political plane, as we shall in Part II, the collection of terms used changes somewhat. Some of the expressions encountered on the economic plane are carried over, but many new ones are added. Some carry an emotional charge of considerable force close to the surface. And we encounter concepts at even higher levels of abstraction than before.

For example, these are some of the expressions met with on this next plane of criticism:

"big business," "Big Business," "big companies," "bigness";
"trusts," "combinations";
"great corporations," "huge corporations," "giant corporations";
"mammoth financial complexes," "colossi";
"the 200 largest nonfinancial corporations";
"the 250 largest corporations";
"the largest corporations";
"the larger companies";
"industrial concentration," "economic concentration," "big economic power";
"concentration of economic power," "concentration of private power";
"massive concentration of corporate wealth," "unlimited financial power";
"power that controls the economy," "organized economic power";
"the money power";
"short-sighted and muscle-bound private control over the economy";
"the free-wheeling bandwagon of big business";
"political and financial privilege," "the privileged," "privilege";
"the entrenched economic group";
"the special interests," "the vested interests," "business interests";
"the controlling influences," "captains of industry," "the plutocratic circle";
"industrial aristocracy," "industrial oligarchy," "plutocracy";
"the corporate community," "the corporate system";
"large-scale enterprise," "modern machinery," "modern industry";
"giant technology," "functional rationalization";
"the large corporation," "the modern corporation";
"modern business," "modern business organization";
"Industrial Capitalism," "the business system";

"the corporation";
"organized business enterprise";
"businessmen," "the businessman";
"business."

And here is a sample list of the terms put up in contradistinction to "big business" and such like when political and social critics are talking about that which they hold up as something of an "ideal":

"the individual workman . . . the small merchant . . . the petty employer";
"the individual businessman," "individual industry," "independent entrepreneurs";
"small enterprises," "smaller companies," "the small entrepreneur";
"little business, local business";
"small competitive businessmen," "small and independent business";
"the typical business corporation of the last century";
"widely distributed property," "tiny individual economic units";
"resident proprietors beholden to no one";
"classless individualism," "middle class capitalism";
"the naturally harmonious world of the small entrepreneur";
"economic democracy";
"organization of industry in small units";
"the competitive model," "competition";
"a cultural system drenched with the artisan spirit of small enterprise";
"private enterprise," "free enterprise";
"individualism," "liberalism," "laissez-faire," "democratic society," "democracy";
"private business";
"the plain people," "the common people," "the many," "the people";
"the little man," "the common man."

The criticism on the *ethical and moral* plane uses terms which take over where these lists leave off. There, the expressions become even more abstract. We shall take this matter up in due course, when we come to it in Part III.

The target of the criticism is clearly something more than just a particular, if uncertain, group of corporations, be it more or less extensive. Essentially, it seems to me, the common bond among the critics is their opposition to departure from some sort of an "ideal" way of things in which economic life, political life, and social life is based upon independent, unorganized, unrelated, and even isolated individuals. This ideal is embodied in the individual as the economic unit, the political unit, and the social unit. "Colossi," "mammoth corporations," and even "larger companies" are merely the more obvious, outstanding manifestations of deviation. For some critics, all "modern business" and even the "ordinary businessman" represent a deviation from this "ideal." They are an embodiment of this deviation. They are among the principal prime movers of this deviation.

It is the deviation from the "ideal," and everything associated with this deviation — in reality or in fancy — which is the ultimate object of the criticism directed against "big business." This criticism expresses *reaction* against the modern industrial revolution.

Lest any "ordinary businessman" who reads this be in doubt, when it comes right down to it, the critics are not just talking exclusively about "corporate empires," or even "large companies." They are talking about *you*.

In the text of this book, I shall henceforth use the term big business, without initial capitals and without quote marks, to stand for the whole welter of things which critics have in mind.

And now to the first of the three levels of attack, the economic.

The economic attack on big business boils down to two arguments: that it is inefficient; that it is monopolistic. These two propositions run as continuous strands down through the history of the criticism which has been levelled at big business on economic grounds. They are its essence.

The development of the economic attack over the past fifty years or more represents the maturing and the refinement of these two ideas. This is no happenstance. It was a matter of logical, if not of ideological, necessity that these two arguments should have become the crux of the criticism on this plane.

The whole matter goes back to the basic theory and justification of laissez-faire capitalism. This was the doctrine, and still is, in its classical form, that the free unhampered activity of individuals seeking their own private material gain will lead, of automatic necessity, to the best of all possible worlds. This organizational structure of society — or, perhaps, this nonorganization — will lead to results that could be equalled, if at all, only by an infallible, all-wise, all-powerful central control. It leads to the greatest possible national product. To a national product composed ideally of what the people as a whole want most. It leads to a completely fair, objectively determined parcelling out of shares of that product among all individuals. It leads to an ideal use of all resources, natural and human. Since this system leads to results which are ideal in every particular, it obviously cannot be improved upon. Any other arrangement must necessarily be inferior. This was, and is still, the classical rationalization of laissez-faire capitalism.

One of the basic, one of the cardinal, premises of that classical doctrine is that economic activity will be carried on by a *large number* of necessarily *small* units. These units are so small that the activity of any one of them, or even of several of them acting together has no perceptible effect on the sum total of what happens. It has only been within the past twenty years, interestingly enough, that this essential premise has been fully developed in detail. But even the critics of fifty years ago who could not think and express themselves in the elaborated concepts of modern economics seemed to have known intuitively that it was one of the basic premises of this classical theory.

Business units which are *big,* and necessarily *few,* stand opposed to that fundamental premise. Obviously a *big* business is not *minute.* It is self-evident that the number of big corporations necessarily must be *few* as compared to the number of small enterprises. Big corporations do not correspond to the basic unit which the whole classical theory presupposes and is founded upon: the *minute,* absolutely competitive, and — it should be added — the completely irresponsible, economic atom. Among other things — according to this theoretical scheme — it follows, therefore, that they will not, automatically and of necessity, be freely and unreservedly competitive. They will be monopolistic.

From the first days of the Trusts, certainly by 1900, it was generally felt — even if only vaguely and uneasily — by their friends and foes alike, that big corporations did not look very much like the ideal atom of the ideal system. They were bigger than that. Quite apart from whether *big* atoms would be monopolistic or not, or even whether they might be conspiratorial, many of the critics clearly and vigorously opposed these new large companies on the ground that they were a far cry from the free, unassociated, and unbeholden individual. It could not be by such large, new entities as these that the best of all possible worlds was to be brought about.

The defenders of the Trusts, including economists of great prestige in their time, also were aware, if only intuitively, of the disparity between the classical individual atom and these new large units which had so rapidly come upon the scene. Since the classical system led to the *best* of all possible worlds, how could a system made up of such new, contrasting entities lead to anything else than something inferior? The burden of proof that they were not an undesirable deviation from the ideal automatically fell upon them. In hearings before the Industrial Commission of Congress in 1899–1900, it is perfectly clear that witness after witness felt this burden.

They had to offer a justification for the departure from the classical rationalization. They did. They argued that, while, to be sure, big corporations — in those days they were commonly equated with "trusts" and "combinations" — did represent a departure, it was a justified departure. They would be more efficient. Greater efficiency, with greater abundance for everyone, was held out as an end which fully justified the departure from principle.

This vindication on the basis of an expediency, more than anything else, was persuasive. At least, so it would seem, to very many.

Moreover, the defenders of the Trusts, combinations, and big businesses generally, held that, despite their great size, they were not really monopolies. They were not alone in their respective fields. They had competitors. And in any case, there were always *potential* competitors. The readiness of these potential competitors to swarm in if the Trusts exacted too high a toll would always hold them in check. Officers of trusts said so. Eminent economists agreed.

Big business carried the day.

But the attack, beaten off, lived to fight another day.

Voices, increasingly influential voices, began to say, and then to proclaim, that the highly touted efficiency of the Trusts was pure humbug. They were not more efficient. They were *less* efficient. These were persuasive voices.

But the facts didn't seem to bear them out. Trusts — supposedly inefficient — actually prospered. Not only that. Big business generated a growing flood of low-cost, mass-produced goods. Not only old familiar staples, but *new* things, things unknown a generation earlier — like automobiles and electrical appliances. The theory was hard to reconcile with the facts. The explanation offered by critics was that they were only *seemingly* more efficient. Their *real* inefficiency was said to be concealed by the gains they were able to exact by virtue of their monopoly powers. But this argument couldn't be made to stick.

The new big corporations actually *weren't* monopolies in the traditional sense of the word. The traditional sense of a "monopoly" was a literal one: a single seller. But these big companies all had competitors, if only much smaller ones. Also, these large enterprises held no royal or legislative charter which gave them the sole right to engage in their particular line of business. It was a free country. Anyone could go into any business he wanted to. Competitors would swarm in — so it was said — if the big companies exacted too high a profit, or didn't give the best product for the lowest cost. So they weren't monopolistic. And if they weren't monopolistic, *ergo* they must be competitive.

Economic critics had no completely convincing answer to that.

At least, not until the Depression of the Thirties. Then, in the Depression, the pent-up hostility toward big business was unleashed in a torrent. In the Depression, many big corporations looked pretty feeble. Some, especially among the railroads and utilities, had gotten mixed up in pretty curious, not to say odorous, kinds of deals. In the minds of many, these situations reflected discredit on all big business. They didn't look like vigorous, more efficient building blocks of an order of things which was superior even to the classical mechanism. Giving big business a back-handed sort of credit for being a key instrumentality in the American economy, critics said it was responsible for the Depression. The operation of the economy, all too obviously, was far from ideal. That was one thing.

Another, perhaps even more important so far as the criticism was concerned, was the appearance of a new development of economic theory which seemed to show that big corporations *were* like monopolies after all. They weren't "monopolies" in the old sense, to be sure. But they weren't competitive either. They were "monopolistic." And they led to results which looked more like the results of monopoly than the results of competition.

The whole issue was fully re-opened on a grand scale. Big businesses *were* a deviation from the ideal atom after all. An economic mechanism made up of such units *was* inferior to the ideal mechanism of old. And, as for their supposed greater efficiency, it didn't exist. Big business was a deviation from principle which could no longer — critics said — be justified as an expedient leading to more for everyone.

Beginning in 1938 there was a great governmental economic inquiry, the Temporary National Economic Committee. More than anything else, it was preoccupied with bigness in business.[1] Just about at the height of its activity, war in Europe broke out. The Committee ended its work and filed a final report on a note of uncertainty. Maybe big business was saved by the bell. Maybe that particular attack had spent itself. In any case, within a few months, the United States was in the thick of a multifront war. The war gave everyone something else to do besides attack or defend big business. The attack went on, to be sure, but on a far-reduced scale. Such as it was, it was pretty well drowned out by the din of a real battle against foreign enemies.

Since the war, the attack on big business has been twice renewed in full measure. In 1949 by the "Celler Committee"

[1] "Among us today a concentration of private power without equal in history is growing.

"This concentration is seriously impairing the economic effectiveness of private enterprise as a way of providing employment for labor and capital and as a way of assuring a more equitable distribution of income and earnings among the people of the Nation as a whole. . . ."

"Private enterprise is ceasing to be free enterprise and is becoming a cluster of private collectivisms; masking itself as a system of free enterprise after the American model, it is in fact becoming a concealed cartel system, after the European model. . . ."

". . . Men will dare to compete against men but not against giants." — *Message from the President of the United States Transmitting Recommendations Relative to the Strengthening and Enforcement of Antitrust Laws,* 75th Cong., 3d Sess. (April 29, 1938). (This letter of President Franklin D. Roosevelt resulted in the setting up of the Temporary National Economic Committee.) Reprinted in T.N.E.C., *Investigation of Concentration of Economic Power,* Part I, *Economic Prologue,* 75th Cong., 3d Sess. (Washington: Government Printing Office, 1940), pp. 185–187.

of the House of Representatives. In 1952 by the Subcommittee of the Senate Select Committee on Small Business.

The attack has continued into 1953. The end is not in sight.

In recent years, big business has looked efficient again. It played a notably, and often spectacularly efficient, role in enabling America to join in the defense of the free world. Along with small business, and with everyone joining in, it produced untold quantities of unheard of weapons with a speed that confounded the enemy. Since the war big business has been profitable. In postwar years, more often than not, big businesses have acted with more restraint than small in the effort to hold prices down. But there are many who still question its social efficacy. They still say that it is monopolistic.

And the fact is — and this is a very important fact, even if it is a fact in the realm of philosophy — the only fully and systematically articulated doctrine of economics, indeed, one which is widely accepted — holds that big business *is* monopolistic. In the realms of theory and ideology, the big corporation is still a deviant from the ideal minute atom of classical doctrine. One of the ironies of our time — and this may come as a shock to many administrators of big business — is that still, at this late date, there does not exist a fully developed logic which reconciles and integrates the big corporation with the very basic, traditional justification of laissez-faire capitalism. Nor, has there been developed a *new* philosophy of laissez-faire capitalism that does provide positively for big business. Men who are practical men of affairs should not underestimate the importance of that fact of the realm of ideas.

Advocates of big business often still try hard to reconcile the large corporation with the traditional, classical doctrine of how and why it is that laissez-faire capitalism leads to the best of all possible worlds. Surveying the world of reality, it looks as though the facts might well justify such a notion. At least as compared to other systems. But those who believe there is a real and important place for big business still don't have the great strength that comes from being supported by a nicely integrated, elegantly elaborated ideology.

This lack shows up in Congressional hearings. It shows up in litigation under the antitrust acts and the Federal Trade Commission Act. It shows up in the public statements of administrators of big business. It shows up in the doubt that many of our friends abroad have concerning America.[2]

So there, in the broadest of strokes, is the history of the economic criticism of big business since the turn of the century. It is a history of the development, and redevelopment, and of the interplay between two problems: Is big business efficient? Critics say no. Is big business monopolistic? Critics say yes.

In the next two chapters we shall review in some detail the contentions on these two counts.

[2] "After all, we agree on some issues with either side: with the Russians, we reject what seems to us the jungle philosophy of big business capitalism . . ." — Tom Driberg (British Labour M.P. and "an influential Christian socialist"); "A British View of U.S. Policy," *Time,* October 12, 1953, p. 23.

CHAPTER 1

"Big Business Is Inefficient"

THE CRITICISM that big business is inefficient has certain distinctions that ought to be noted before we get into it.

First, it is the only one which meets head-on a positive affirmation. No one, so far as I am aware, has propounded a theory to show that big business is less monopolistic or more competitive than small.[1] No one, it appears, has developed a line of reasoning that an economic organization of big businesses leads to a superior social and political order. No one has written poems, sermons, or essays to show that a big-business-industrial society is ethically and morally superior. Perhaps all these things could be done. But they haven't been.

But, on the matter of *efficiency,* the initiative — I think it is fair to say — has been on the side of big business. The tone of the criticism on this score has always been an essentially defensive one: one of *disproof.* On all other counts — I think this is also fair to say — the initiative has rested in the critics.

The second distinction is that critics who are as one on other matters fall out among themselves over the question of the efficiency of big business. Many critics, for example, who have been associated in recent years with the Department of Justice and the Federal Trade Commission appear to believe that big business is both monopolistic *and* inefficient. Such a size-up leads to the policy recommendation that big corporations be broken up into small ones. Such action, they say, would lead to both more competition *and* more efficiency.

1 The late Professor Joseph A. Schumpeter of Harvard, in his own urbane, almost Olympian way produced a number of ideas that, perhaps, *could* be woven into some such theories. See *Capitalism, Socialism, and Democracy* (New York: Harper & Brothers, Third Edition, 1950).

search and of rapid, large-scale assimilation of technological development.[7]

It is against this kind of affirmation that the charge of inefficiency has been directed.

In total, the argument that big business is inefficient goes something like this: (1) Because of complexities of administration and organization, it is impossible to run a large corporation efficiently. (2) Contrary to public belief and the plea of the advocates of big business, the reason underlying the growth of large companies was not really the quest for, and the realization of, operating economies; it was the quest for, and the realization of, the advantages of "monopoly power." Moreover, the argument runs, a principal motivating force behind the growth of large corporations was *really* the opportunities for individual gain, often breath-taking, which they presented for promoters — especially investment bankers. (3) Statistical studies of costs and profits show that large corporations do not really have the advantages claimed for them, certainly not as compared with medium-sized business. (4) Even if big business does *appear* to be efficient, that is only due to antisocial economies which are derived from the exploitation of suppliers and customers and at the expense of the community at large. It is argued that these economies are not "net" from the point of view of the economy as a whole. Furthermore, it is often implied that big business has had little or nothing to do with the increase in the productivity of the American economy.[8] It *is* often

[7] See, for example, the testimony of Crawford H. Greenwalt, *Study of Monopoly Power,* Hearings Before the Subcommittee on Study of Monopoly Power of the Committee on the Judiciary, 81st Cong., 1st Sess., Serial No. 14 (Washington: Government Printing Office, 1950), Part 2-A, pp. 543–591; and testimony of Charles E. Wilson, ibid., Part 2-B, pp. 1158–1248.

[8] See, for example, the testimony of Honorable Stephen J. Spingarn, then a member of the Federal Trade Commission, before A Subcommittee of the Senate Select Committee on Small Business. From none of Mr. Spingarn's remarks could it be inferred that he believes that large-scale research, development, production, and distribution have had anything whatever to do with economic and technological progress in America. See *Monopoly and Cartels,*

argued — as we shall see later on — that productivity and technological progress would be greater if it were *not* for big business.

That's the gist of the argument. Now for a look at some of its particulars and some examples.

"Big Business Can't Be Managed Efficiently"

The idea is not new that it is impossible to administer a large-scale business enterprise efficiently. As every economist knows, one of Adam Smith's pet peeves was the big business of his day — the joint stock companies established by royal charter or by Act of Parliament. In Smith's view, inefficiency was endemic to large companies:

> . . . The directors of such companies . . . being the managers rather of other people's money than of their own, it cannot be well expected, that they should watch over it with the same anxious vigilance with which the partners in a private copartnery frequently watch over their own. Like the stewards of a rich man, they are apt to consider attention to small matters as not for their master's honour, and very easily give themselves a dispensation from having it. Negligence and profusion, *therefore,* must *always* prevail, more or less, in the management of the affairs of such a company.[9]

This view flows logically from the rather dour preconception of "human nature," possibly Calvinistic in its origin, that human beings *naturally* cannot have a sense of responsibility toward property and other interests which are not

---

Hearings before the Subcommittee, 82nd Cong., 2nd Sess. (Washington: Government Printing Office, 1952), Part I, pp. 2–34.

[9] Quoted from the *Additions and Corrections to the First and Second Editions of Dr. Adam Smith's Inquiry into the Nature and Causes of the Wealth of Nations* (London: Printed for W. Straham and T. Cadell, in the Strand, 1784), p. 60. See also "Modern Library" Edition of the *Wealth of Nations* (New York: Random House, Inc., 1937), p. 700. The first edition of Smith's work was published in March, 1776. (Italics added.)

The phrase "other people's money," it will be remembered, was picked up as a book title by one of the leading critics of big business, Louis D. Brandeis, *Other People's Money and How The Bankers Use It* (New York: Frederick A. Stokes, 1914).

their own. Once this premise is granted, it follows inevitably that the large corporation is, *ipso facto,* inefficient. And sure enough, just a few pages further on, we find Smith passing this sort of "ipso facto" judgment on the South Sea Company which did, in fact, have a deplorable history:

> The South Sea Company . . . had an immense capital . . . an immense number of proprietors. It was *naturally to be expected, therefore,* that folly, negligence, and profusion should prevail in the whole management of their affairs.[10]

This same concept of human nature, with its implications for the corporation, led Smith to the particular and often cited conclusion that the only "trades" which could be carried on by corporations without an exclusive privilege are those "of which all the operations are capable of being reduced to what is called a Routine, or to such a uniformity of method as admits of little or no variation."[11] The only trades he could think of which fitted these specifications were banking, insurance, and the operation, not the *construction,* of canals and water companies.

Embedded in these ideas of Smith's is a theorem of administration: the only responsibilities which can be safely delegated to operating executives are those relating to purely routine matters. More complex matters cannot be delegated. Applying this concept to the corporation, it follows (once the premises are granted) that the principal executive, on whom presumably no great reliance is to be placed anyway, since he is dealing primarily with "other people's money," cannot safely delegate major responsibilities down the line. And, it follows further, that since the affairs of a large company are so numerous that *he* cannot himself take care of all these matters, they will not be handled well. It is an inevitable conclusion, given the premises and the deductions, that the large corporation, per se, is inefficient.

[10] *Additions and Corrections,* p. 63; "Modern Library," p. 703. (Italics added.)

[11] Ibid., p. 76; "Modern Library," p. 713.

During the 19th Century, Adam Smith's uncompromising evaluation came to be softened and even reversed in prevailing economic doctrine. John Stuart Mill, one of the most influential of the economists of the Victorian era, shared Adam Smith's misanthropic judgment of those employed by others. "Experience shows," he said,

> how inferior is the quality of hired servants, compared with the ministration of those personally interested in the work, and how indispensable, when hired service must be employed, is the "master's eye" to watch over it. . . .[12]

The "intensity of interest in the subject" that is necessary to the successful conduct of a great business "is seldom to be expected [in a man] conducting a business as the hired servant and for the profit of another." [13]

But Mill saw a saving grace, a way out: the ability of a large concern to hire men whose ability was so great that it more than offset their natural disposition to neglect the interests of others:

> Where the concern is large, and can afford a remuneration sufficient to attract a class of candidates superior to the common average, it is possible to select for the general management, and for all the skilled employments of a subordinate kind, persons of a degree of acquirement and cultivated intelligence which more than compensates for their inferior interest in the result.[14]

Thus it was that 19th Century economics seemed to find a way around the theoretical difficulty posed by Adam Smith. This block having been removed, the way was opened for the triumph of the idea, long put forward, that there were positive economies to be found in mere size. As Mill and others saw them, these economies lay chiefly in the notion

[12] *Principles of Political Economy* (Boston: Charles C. Little & James Brown, First American Edition, 1848), Vol. I, p. 168. (See "Ashley Edition," p. 139; London: Longmans, Green and Co., 1909.)

[13] Loc. cit.

[14] Ibid., p. 170; "Ashley", p. 141.

that the total of certain important categories of costs would not increase proportionately as volume increased. Hence, unit costs would decline with the size of the operation:

> . . . If the business doubled itself, it would probably be necessary to increase, but certainly not to double, the number either of accountants, or of buying and selling agents. Every increase of business would enable the whole to be carried on with a proportionately smaller amount of labour.
>
> *As a general rule,* the expenses of a business do not increase by any means proportionally to the quantity of business.[15]

This simple, mechanistic notion took hold. Many businessmen as well as economists seem to have had what appears now as an almost entertainingly ingenuous faith in the economies to be had mechanically from mere size alone.[16]

A few isolated demurrers can be found among late-Victorian critics of Trusts. Thus, Professor Henry C. Adams of the University of Michigan:

> It is common to say that increase in the size of manufacturing plant permits the production of commodities at less cost than would otherwise be the case. . . . But there is a limit to this rule. Every manufacturing industry, considered from the point of view of production, has at any particular time a size which may be regarded as its normal size of maximum efficiency. . . . While . . . it is true that the concentration of capital and labor under a single direction is followed by economy up to a certain point, it is not true that combination and concentration beyond that point tends to reduce the cost of production. . . .[17]

[15] Ibid., pp. 161–162; "Ashley," pp. 133–134. (Italics added.)

[16] See, for example, the testimony of Samuel Dodd, before the Industrial Commission, *Preliminary Report on Trusts and Industrial Combinations* (Washington: Government Printing Office, 1900), Vol. I, pp. 1049–1062. See, even, Alfred Marshall, the great British economist, who could be cited to the effect that, on balance, "in most of the more delicate branches of manufacturing, where cost of raw material counts for little, and in most of the modern transport industries the law of increasing return acts almost unopposed." *Principles of Economics* (London: Macmillan and Co., Limited, Fourth Edition, 1898), p. 398. (See also Eighth Edition, 1920, p. 319.)

[17] "A Statement of the Trust Problem," address before *Chicago Conference on Trusts* (Chicago: The Civic Federation of Chicago, 1900), pp. 36–37.

But this was a minority view. Professor Charles J. Bullock, then of Williams College, later of Harvard, in questioning the doctrine formulated by John Stuart Mill makes it clear that he was offering ideas contrary to prevailing opinion. His own conclusions were put in the qualified terms befitting an attack on an accepted principle:

> It is certainly unsafe to assume, without much more careful investigation than has been made up to the present time, that in agriculture or mining an increased supply will regularly be produced at a greater marginal cost, and that manufactured commodities can be multiplied at a decreasing cost. . . .
>
> . . . All that can be claimed is that manufactures are subject to a law of decreasing cost more often than agriculture or mining, and that the rate of decrease in this industry is often greater than it is in the others. . . .[18]

Even the Industrial Commission set up to inquire into the Trusts saw fit to question established doctrine and voluminous testimony in rather tentative terms:

> . . . To run a number of plants together is very difficult and requires a high order of intellect. For this reason there may be a limit set to the size and range of work of the combinations.[19]

The general tenor of prevailing economic thinking in the first decade of this century can be inferred from these comments by the influential Professor F. W. Taussig of Harvard. Harking back to Adam Smith, Professor Taussig conceded that "the infirmities of human nature" might impose limita-

[18] "The Variation of Productive Forces," *The Quarterly Journal of Economics,* Vol. XVI, No. 4, August, 1902, pp. 497, 499.

[19] Industrial Commission, *Report of the Industrial Commission on Trusts and Industrial Combinations,* Vol. XIII, "Review of the Evidence," p. xxxiii. For bibliographies of the attack on big business prior to 1900, see ibid., pp. 947–977; A. P. C. Griffin, *A List of Books (with reference to Periodicals) Relating to Trusts* (Washington: Government Printing Office, 1901); C. J. Bullock, "Trust Literature: A Survey and a Criticism," *The Quarterly Journal of Economics,* Vol. 15, No. 2, February, 1901, pp. 167–218.

tions on the size to which efficient large-scale production might be carried:

> . . . The extension of the scale of operations means an ever increasing reliance upon hired labor and an ever-lessening reliance on spontaneous self-interest. If all men worked with as much energy and spirit for an employer as they do for themselves, the spread of large-scale production would be almost without bounds. . . .
>
> The limitations of men's faculties explain why large-scale operations do not make their way, even in manufactures, with unfailing certainty. . . .[20]

But Taussig thought that the then still-new Trusts and "combinations" might have found a way, even so, to get further economies from large-scale, coordinated — "united" — management, despite any limitations to the size of the individual operating unit:

> A new phase of large-scale production has come to be of great and almost ominous importance during the present generation. Perhaps it should be called large-scale management rather than large-scale production; since it involves not so much an increase in the size of the individual establishments as the combination under single management of several establishments. . . .
>
> . . . Though large-scale operation may have reached its limit so far as the mechanical apparatus of production goes, some gain may still be secured from united large-scale administration.[21]

Taussig, though obviously under the influence of Adam Smith, would not condemn the Trusts out of hand:

> . . . Experience, and especially the test of competition, can alone settle with certainty whether the advantages offset the disadvantages.[22]

[20] *Principles of Economics* (New York: The Macmillan Company, First Edition, 1911), Vol. I, pp. 55 and 58.

[21] Ibid., p. 59.

[22] Ibid., p. 60.

It was in this climate of ideas that Louis D. Brandeis, later Associate Justice of the Supreme Court, launched his famous all-out attack on bigness in business. In testimony before a Senate Committee whose work ultimately contributed to the passage of the Clayton Act and the Federal Trade Commission Act, Brandeis made explicit the theorem of administration that was implicit in Smith's *Wealth of Nations,* and applied it to the large corporations of the 20th Century. To this day, critics who believe big business is inefficient show the influence of these ideas.

The affirmation of big business being that it is efficient, it was characteristic of this strong-minded critic that in his testimony which dealt with a number of topics, Brandeis chose to address himself first to rebutting this idea.

> [The] argument in favor of the efficiency of *monopoly* [23] proceeds upon the assumption, in the first place, and mainly upon the assumption, that with increase of size comes increase of efficiency. If any general proposition could be laid down on that subject, it would, in my opinion, be the opposite.
>
> . . . And the reason why increasing the size of a business may tend to inefficiency is perfectly obvious when one stops to consider. Anyone who critically analyzes a business learns this: *That success or failure of an enterprise depends usually upon one man; upon the quality of one man's judgment,* and, above all things, his capacity to see what is needed and his capacity to direct others.
>
> Now, while organization has made it possible for the individual man to accomplish infinitely more than he could before, aided as he is by new methods of communication, by the stenographer, the telephone, and system, still there is a limit to what one man can do well; for judgment must be exercised, and in order that judgment may be exercised wisely, it must be exercised on facts and on a comprehension of the significance of the relevant facts. In other words, judgment

[23] Note the identification of big business with "monopoly." More will be said later on of the common propensity among critics to set up this equation.

> can be sound only if the facts on which it is based are both known and carefully weighed. There must be opportunities for judgment to mature. When, therefore, you increase your business to a very great extent, and the multitude of problems increase with its growth, you will find, in the first place, that the man at the head has a diminishing knowledge of the facts and, in the second place, a diminishing opportunity of exercising a careful judgment upon them. Furthermore – and this is one of the most important grounds of the inefficiency of large institutions – there develops a centrifugal force greater than the centripetal force. Demoralization sets in; a condition of lessened efficiency presents itself. . . .[24]

Just as a theorem of administration was implicit in Smith's thinking about the corporation, so is there one in this passage from Brandeis: The success of an enterprise depends upon judgments, decisions, and actions of *one man.* When an organization becomes large, this one man is unable to be in mastery of facts. And if this one man cannot make the necessary judgments and reach the decisions, the organization will begin to fly to bits. Presumably, also, the quality of the decisions will be inferior; at the very least, the process of reaching decisions will involve a number of people and considerable time.

Given such an authoritarian concept of administration, namely that the ideal organization is that in which only one man (presumably something of a genius) makes decisions and has responsibility, the view naturally follows that as the scale of enterprise grows, administrative inefficiency will be encountered. This authoritarian concept which is only implicit here has been set forth in about so many words on more than one occasion.

An example of how it is brought to bear on the discussion of the efficiency of big business is to be found in the following passage from the British economist, E. A. G. Robinson:

[24] Hearings before the Senate Committee on Interstate Commerce, *Control of Corporations, Persons, and Firms Engaged in Interstate Commerce,* Vol. I, pp. 1147 and 1148. (Italics added.)

> . . . It has been proved by experience that no individual can effectively *control* more than four or five subordinate departmental heads. If he attempts to manage more he must either cause endless delays, or else become no more than a rubber stamp. And so the big firm is a series of wheels within wheels, an elaborate hierarchy, in which every decision requires the consulting of this man, the referring to that man, the permission of a third, the agreement of a fourth, so that decisions become endlessly delayed. Where decisions have to be reached frequently and quickly, such an organization, unless *despotically* controlled, will find itself paralysed, and if it is in fact a *despotism,* much of the gain of specialist control must be lost.[25]

Here, the implicit concept of how efficient organizations are administered is that they are *controlled* and managed by a single administrator who makes the decisions. Especially is this believed to be true, apparently, when the situation is complex and dynamic. Indeed, the concept of "the administrator" is just about equated to the concept of "the despot."

It is sometimes conceded, as by Robinson, that there are some advantages to having more than a one-man administrative machine. Business managements need specialists. Robinson felt that the advantages of specialized management talent gave bigness something of an edge over smallness. Nevertheless, these advantages come to be offset with growing size: ". . . there must come a point at which the machine is too unwieldy to be managed. . . . The managerial optimum sets . . . not only a lower but an upper limit to the scale of operations." [26]

Thus, the line of reasoning which begins, for our purposes here, with Adam Smith leads to a presumption that the administration — which by preconception is equated to "control" and authoritarian, centralized decision-making — of big business *must* be inefficient. Even "decentralized manage-

[25] *The Structure of Competitive Industry* (London: James Nisbet & Co., Ltd., and The Cambridge University Press, 1931), p. 49. (Italics added.)

[26] Ibid., p. 50.

ment schemes," as critics understand administration, apparently will not solve the problem. Control systems and "paper work" are costly. These very schemes themselves "increase the risk of divergent policies and discordant action." [27]

In outline, the logic of this reasoning is this: Administration, in its very essence, is authoritarian. Administration, which is basically authoritarian in its very nature, becomes increasingly more so as the organization increases in size. In large, dynamic, and complex organizations this inherently authoritarian process necessarily becomes *despotic,* if the organization is even to cohere. This is necessary to prevent the large organization, in its various parts, from pursuing divergent policies and doing inconsistent things. Perhaps this despotism can maintain coherence and make decisions, but it cannot make *good* decisions, and it cannot run an *efficient* organization.[28]

[27] George W. Stocking and Myron W. Watkins, *Monopoly and Free Enterprise* (New York: The Twentieth Century Fund, 1951), p. 64.

Professor Edward Chamberlin, of whose work considerably more will be said in the next chapter, has stated that "increased difficulties of co-ordination and management" are the source of costs which cause the average cost per unit to rise after the scale of operation reaches some size. "More elaborate systems of control are made necessary by impersonal relations. They are costly in themselves, and lead, furthermore, to a rigidity of procedure and the stifling of individual initiative." *The Theory of Monopolistic Competition* (Cambridge, Massachusetts: Harvard University Press, Third Edition, 1938), p. 207.

[28] There is no recognition in this notion which is so common among critics that administration in its very essence may *not* necessarily be authoritarian, nor even that very large organizations *may,* in fact, be very democratic with a high degree of decentralization of authority and responsibility. Nor is there any conception that effective administration, in organizations small *or* large, *may* be predicated upon an optimistic and confident set of ideas about "human nature" and concerning the ability and inclination of people to behave competently and conscientiously. In particular, there seems to be no recognition of the possibility that, even if certain major final decisions of policy — those relating to capital investment and major strategy, for instance — may have to be made at the top level of management, there may still remain, nevertheless, wide delegated areas of discretion and decision down through the organization.

In fact, decentralized decision-making may become increasingly useful or necessary in proportion as the operation becomes bigger, more complex, and more critical. Compare:

". . . 'You don't even tell a corps or division commander how to do his

We shall have occasion later on to return to this authoritarian element in the concept which critics commonly have of big business.

"Big Business Does Not Owe Its Growth to Efficiency"

Now for the second particular: The origin and growth of big business were not, and have not been, due to efficiency.

The defenders of bigness in the scale of enterprise have often argued that its growth was inevitable. They have said, first, that bigness was implicit in the new industrial and commercial techniques which were emerging, and that some of the new products could *only* be developed, produced, and distributed on a large scale. Second, that since opportunities for economies in large-scale production, distribution, and organization were inherent in the evolution of technology and the expansion of markets, it was simply a question of which particular companies could realize upon these opportunities first. Third, it was argued that for a very small cost per unit, a large company could afford to engage in developmental work, including research and advertising, and to hire

---

job when you have an army. You assign a mission and it's up to the fellow to carry it out. Of course, if you are in a position to have a look and talk it over with the guy, you may make suggestions, but he doesn't have to take them.' [General Omar] Bradley was so faithful to this principle that, according to a colonel on General Patton's staff, when he was reduced to a 'one-army Army Group' during the Ardennes battle, he declined to interfere with the tactics of that army, the Third. 'It's your Army, George,' Bradley told Patton, according to the colonel. 'You fight it.'" – A. J. Liebling, "Five-Star Schoolmaster," *The New Yorker,* March 10, 1951, p. 48.

I do not wish to engage here in a discussion as to whether or not *any* limits are set for organizations by mechanical factors relating to size. I would, however, be willing to argue against the validity of any line of reasoning which starts with the underlying premises that all administration is *inherently* and *necessarily* an authoritarian process of centralized direction, and that people can work effectively together only under highly centralized authoritarian direction. It is these *a priori* premises, which exclude all other possibilities, that have led the cited critics and others to the conclusion that the limitations of *authoritarian* administration set a *generalized* limit on the scale of *all* organizations. In any case, business, government, military, and educational organizations that far exceed in size anything contemplated not so long ago, have in fact been able to function with at least tolerable, and often astounding, efficiency.

administrative talent which would be too expensive for a small company. This was the nub of the brief offered for bigness by such advocates as Charles R. Flint.

Some of the critics have agreed that there were such real advantages to bigness. But, for the most part, they have tended to minimize them, or — more often — to argue that, beyond some point, they were offset by the dis-economies of excessive size.

Others, as we shall see, have argued that most of the advantages stemming from size are not "net" from a social point of view and only reflect the *relative* advantages of large firms in their dealings with suppliers and customers. But, in any case, there is considerable agreement among critics that a bona fide quest for general economies was not really an important motivating force in the building up of large companies, nor a really significant reason for the growth of large companies after they were organized.

Before we look at what critics have had to say on this score, we might as well note for the record that the promoters and officers of some — not all — of the "Trusts" and "Combinations" gave them plenty to go on. It is perfectly clear in the statements of many of them that there *were* other factors — at least in their thinking and aspirations — besides efficiency as they went about organizing and administering these new entities.

In some cases, the "Whisky Trust" would be as good an example as any, a monopolistic control of an industry *was* an avowedly chief objective in putting the companies together. In some cases, the whole thing gives off the scent of a deal cooked up by promoters to capitalize on a widespread guileless optimism as to what could be achieved automatically by way of gains from real efficiency and/or from "regularizing" the industry. In other cases, the thinking all around seems now to have been very fuzzy. In some cases, happily, there is the ring of strong, imaginative men who conceived of business enterprise, not in terms of monopolistic exploitation of a static, *given* demand by means of static, *given* techniques, but in terms of dynamic and expanding opportunities for growth and development in every direction.

But, over-all, there is no gainsaying that aspirations of a monopolistic nature and fat promoters' fees *were* many times interlarded with more socially acceptable motives. These cases provided critics with lots of material. Much of this material is still being used.

A few examples of the thinking and actions of some men of big businesses of half a century ago will give a sample of the vein which critics were to mine for a long time to come.

First, from the testimony of Samuel M. Rice, President, Distilling Company of America, before the Industrial Commission on November 17, 1899:

> . . . Well, it [the Standard Distilling and Distributing Company] was a part of a general plan to practically control the entire whisky business, as far as control is desired in any business; not a monopoly, but control of the business, so that you may control the production; so that you can stop overproduction.
>
> Q. Overstocking the market?
>
> A. So as to stop overproduction.
>
> Q. Who were the chief promoters of that Standard Distilling and Distributing Company?
>
> A. I cannot tell you.
>
> Q. You do not know?
>
> A. No. Those matters are never known, but the underwriters are generally found among financial men of Wall Street. They do not advertise themselves as a general thing.[29]

Next from the testimony of Daniel G. Reid, President, American Tin Plate Company:

> Q. What was the situation of the tin-plate trade that led to the organization of the American Tin Plate Company?
>
> A. Well, the competition between the old companies had become so strong that business was fast drifting into a con-

[29] *Preliminary Report of the Industrial Commission on Trusts and Industrial Combinations,* Vol. I, Part II, p. 836.

dition where there was little, if any, profit. There were a number of mills losing money and very few of them making any, and it was a matter of the mills getting together. . . .

. . . . .

Q. . . . they claim that a trust or a combination in any business in Europe or here results from three great factors – lower prices, overproduction, and diminished profits. Did all or any of these three influence you to make the combination?

A. Diminished profits certainly did.

Q. Well, did overproduction?

A. Yes – no; overproduction did not.

Q. Would you answer plainly whether your intention was to eliminate or control competition?

A. Neither.

Q. Neither?

A. Neither. It was for the purpose of getting together to do away with foolishness in making prices; and competition, I suppose, would enter into that, although there is competition now in the field against us.

Q. Did you not answer that it was the fierce competition that drove you to make a combination?

A. Didn't I?

Q. Yes.

A. A short time ago I said that competition, perhaps, was one of the factors that entered into it.

Q. Yes, and that you made this combination in order that you might make prices stable and secure more for yourselves than you could with open competition?

A. Certainly; yes.

. . . . .

Q. You would answer that it was not the opportunity to suppress competition that caused your organization?

A. I did not say that.

Q. You do not say that?

A. Well, we never for a moment thought that we should not have competition. In fact, there were mills out, and are now, as competitors; but it was to get a number of mills together that would regulate that very much, and not only in buying and selling tin, but in handling supplies, and handling the business in a very much more satisfactory way.

Q. Do you not practically now, in your great organization, name the prices of tin plate to the consumer?

A. We do; yes.[30]

Finally, a tid-bit from the testimony of John W. ("Bet-You-A-Million") Gates, Chairman of the Board, American Steel and Wire Company. This passage will illustrate how far some of these men were from having a creative, dynamic, socially responsible philosophy of business. It ought to raise the hair, if not the hackles, of modern businessmen:

> Q. So you think that the German Empire does keep control [of Kartels]?
>
> A. I think they keep very close control, and I think they know what the various concerns are making; and are encouraging the German manufacturer, particularly in the export business.
>
> Q. I judge from what you have said that you think that is a wise plan for the German Government to follow.
>
> A. I do; I think if this Government would adopt the same tactics, we should be the only manufacturing concern in iron and steel within the next ten years.
>
> Q. You would favor having necessary Government supervision over every large establishment?
>
> A. Unquestionably; and I should be willing to give up a large percentage of my stock to have it so.[31]

30 Ibid., pp. 866, 885, and 886.

31 Ibid., p. 1018. See also, for further example, testimony of E. R. Chapman, in connection with American Smelting and Refining Company, and of Lyman R. Hopkins, in connection with American Thread Company; *Report of the Industrial Commission on Trusts and Industrial Combinations,* Vol. XIII, pp. 93 and 346 respectively.

The total irresponsibility and disregard for public sensibilities shown in those days by the officers of some of the combinations and trusts is something which today must amaze even the most case-hardened "rugged individualist." This avowal of irresponsibility, not only toward the community at large, but toward employees, and even toward stockholders has to be examined at first-hand to be believed. Wishing not to burden the text with too many lengthy excerpts, I have included, as an Appendix at the end of the book, some extensive excerpts from the testimony before the Industrial Commission of

It is understandable that one of the best informed contemporary students of "Trusts" and "Combinations" should have written:

> . . . In prospectuses and public discussions the savings that may be effected by combinations are often made most prominent; but in private conversation, persons who have entered into [combinations] will usually concede that the chief purpose has been to check competition which they consider excessive. . . .[32]

By the time Brandeis argued before the Senate Committee on Interstate Commerce that the real cause for the tendency "to create large units" was *not* the quest for greater efficiency, his audience had already had a lot of background material supplied by businessmen themselves.

These new large units were created, Brandeis insisted, "because the owner of a business may make a great deal more money if he increases the volume of his business tenfold, even

---

Mr. Henry O. Havemeyer, the then president of American Sugar Refining Company. A perusal of these excerpts should help the reader considerably toward an understanding of why it was that the "Trusts" and "Combinations" became the object of profound resentment and hostility.

[32] Professor Jeremiah W. Jenks, of Cornell, "The Trusts: Facts Established and Problems Unsolved," *The Quarterly Journal of Economics,* Vol. XV, No. 1, November, 1900, p. 47.

In all fairness to some of the early proponents of mergers, consolidations, and trusts it probably should be conceded that some of them, anyway, were genuinely interested in eliminating some of the extremes of competition and in capitalizing on – and *creating* – real, dynamic opportunities and not just in seeking monopoly profits or "plunder."

Some of the industries where consolidation seemed most attractive were ones having highly inelastic demand and high overhead costs. In times of depression, sharp and wide price swings did occur in these industries. There were many episodes of bankruptcy, severe unemployment, and lowered labor standards. Moreover, in some of these same industries technological developments did seem to be making small-scale, isolated plants obsolete.

Not all the protestations by these men that they were in favor of "sound" competition and against the "excesses" of competition, or that they were trying to "bring order" into these industries can be dismissed as completely insincere. Of course, their concepts of what was "sound" and what was "excessive" and what was "orderly" may be open to debate. But if their sincerity and good faith be granted, the motivation of their efforts appears in quite a different light.

if the unit profit is in the process reduced one half." It was, Brandeis said, in the interest of an owner of a business, who could accomplish it, "to forfeit efficiency to a certain degree, because the result to him, in profits, may be greater by reason of the volume of the business."[33]

Many of the critics of big business would certainly have trouble accepting this theory of Brandeis. In the first place, they would contend, large corporations are the products of mergers rather than of internal growth from reinvested earnings. And, far from charging the same or lower prices and taking a smaller profit per unit, the prime motive these critics see behind mergers is the quest for "monopoly power." Here the very objective — they would say — in getting "monopoly power" is to be able, among other things, to charge *higher prices* and to get *bigger margins* of profit. It is this kind of thinking, rather than the particular idea of Brandeis quoted above, that came to be characteristic of this part of the economic attack on big business.

This is how the matter was set forth in a Philippic against big business by Kemper Simpson, a one-time Federal Trade Commission economist:

> It is the popular belief that not only does size lead to efficiency but that efficiency leads to size. If the large profit usually earned by the low-cost plant or low-cost company is reinvested therein, such company or plant can be expected to grow in size. Thus, many believe that the giant corporations in the United States today have been gradually evolved out of the reinvested profits of efficiency. As a matter of fact, most of the mammoth corporations covered in this inquiry[34] were born as giants, conceived by promoters or combiners

[33] Hearings Before the Senate Committee on Interstate Commerce, *Control of Corporations, Persons, and Firms Engaged in Interstate Commerce,* loc. cit. According to this concept of efficiency, a business would be regarded as inefficient, even though it charged customers lower prices and took a smaller margin of profit – so long as costs per unit were higher than they *might* be.

[34] Data are presented relating to the following industries: cement, iron and steel, farm machinery, petroleum, beet sugar, cane sugar, milk and milk products, flour milling, baking, automobiles, chemicals, and rayon.

> who brought together large numbers of smaller corporations, often frankly for the purpose of stifling competition. . . .[35]

In arguing that the formation of "mammoth corporations" was carried on for the purpose of "stifling competition," Simpson was clearly picking up a major conclusion set forth a decade earlier by Professor Frank A. Fetter of Princeton, who for many years was a consultant to the Federal Trade Commission:

> The advantages from mergers appear to lie almost wholly in the field of proprietorship and of private profit, rather than in that of productive efficiency and public benefit. The chief source of expected increased operating profit from mergers is doubtless "control of the market" – monopolistic power.[36]

The quest for monopoly is not the only antisocial force the critics perceive in the *growth* of big business, which by now is pretty much exclusively attributed to mergers. As they see it, the ultimate *raison d'etre* of the big corporation, as a going concern, is to profit at the expense of society generally through the exercise of its "monopoly powers." But, we are told, the *immediate* motive for its creation, through merger, is primarily quest by its promoters for profits at the expense of the investing public.

Thus, Professor Fetter, in the paragraph following the one just quoted, is of the opinion that this drive for profits by promoters may be an even more important force in the creation of mergers than the operating profit from monopoly power that the company is to enjoy after the merger is carried through:

> Next to price control in strength, possibly even greater, as a motive for the formation of mergers, the evidence points to

[35] Kemper Simpson, *Big Business, Efficiency and Fascism* (New York: Harper & Brothers, 1941), pp. 35–36.

[36] Frank A. Fetter, *The Masquerade of Monopoly* (New York: Harcourt, Brace and Company, 1931), pp. 376–377.

speculative profits. These gains come to various insiders in the shape of liberal legal and promotion fees, banking underwriters' commissions, inflated prices for constituent properties sometimes on the verge of bankruptcy, and enhanced prices for the securities of the newly formed merger immediately following the merger.[37]

In 1947 we find the same idea, couched in more colorful journalistic language, put forward by David Cushman Coyle: the creation of mergers was more than just a quest for monopoly, it was a quest for predatory gain by insiders.

The battles of the giants, from Jay Gould to J. P. Morgan, covered far more than mere monopolies of goods or transport. The great game was to get control of a property, water its stock, and sell the watered stock to the public, and by "planned mismanagement" and market manipulation, to run stocks and bonds up and down at will, with the manipulator taking the profits. The methods of the last third of the nineteenth century were crude and spectacular. They made many good stories for muckrakers and investigating committees. The methods are smoother now, but the depression and the Second World War were not without their tall tales, some of which are still waiting to be told.[38]

Still, again, the same charge is made by George W. Stocking and Myron W. Watkins in the recent Twentieth Century Fund publication, *Monopoly and Free Enterprise:*

. . . The prospect of a promoter's fee, limited – because of secrecy of negotiations – only by what the traffic will bear and his modesty in assessing the value of his own services, has been the main incentive behind the merger movement in many an industry. . . .[39]

[37] Ibid., p. 377.

[38] "The Big Cannot Be Free," *The Atlantic Monthly,* June, 1947, p. 72. Mr. Coyle was a consultant to the Celler Subcommittee, on the Study of Monopoly Power, of the House of Representatives in 1949.

[39] Page 77. Dr. Watkins had already, in 1927, taken the view that the prospects of efficiency were not an important consideration in mergers: "If the genuinely economic factor, the promotion of efficiency in the production and distribution of goods, has played some part in the development of the

So, against the widespread idea that bigness in business was the inevitable outcome of new industrial, commercial, and administrative techniques, expanding markets, and economic advantage, the critics launched a two-pronged counter-attack: First, they contended to the contrary that the *growth* of big business rested upon the gains to be had, not from efficiency, but from "monopoly power." Second, they said — and they still say — that the *origin* of large corporations was brought about in the first instance for the purpose of obtaining gains to be had from monopoly power or, simply by promoters who saw opportunities to profit at the expense of investors.

It has been truly said that the iniquities of the fathers shall be visited upon the children unto the third and fourth generation.

Doubtless it was true that some of the largest corporations still operating in the present day, or their ancestors, were — what shall we say? — conceived illicitly. Perhaps for some time still to come their escutcheons must display the bar sinister. So much for their parentage — to generalize without limit for the sake of argument. But what of them, themselves? Once brought into the world, however that may have been, what have they done on their own? *Have* they been efficient? And what of businesses that are big now, whose birth and growth were not tarnished — have *they* been efficient? The critics say no.

They may offer this kind of argument:

> . . . Indeed, if one reflects upon the persistence of small and medium-sized companies in the industries dominated by

---

trust movement, it appears to have been a secondary and an obscure role." *Industrial Combinations and Public Policy* (Boston: Houghton Mifflin Company, 1947), p. 44.

Compare: ". . . Most of the growth of corporate empires during the last fifty or sixty years was not a matter of technological integration of production but rather financial integration of control. . . . There was nothing 'natural' about this growth of business firms into corporate giants. It was merely a matter of shortsighted legislatures and courts, and ingenious lawyers, promoters and businessmen. . . ." Fritz Machlup, *The Political Economy of Monopoly* (Baltimore: The Johns Hopkins Press, 1952), pp. 239–240.

> big businesses, it is apparent that there can be no great advantages to size. If size were a great advantage, the smaller companies would soon lose the unequal race and disappear.[40]

But this line of deduction doesn't really close the case. The smallest unit doing business these days in some branches of industry — say, in automobiles and in certain segments of the steel industry — are huge. In other instances, even though by certain definitions they are in the same "industry," large and small companies do not really compete with one another, the small companies having carved out their own niches of specialization. In other instances, large and small companies are more directly competitive. The question cannot be answered so easily.

The question whether or not big business is efficient is obviously crucial. In the answer to this question there are, clearly, important implications for public thinking and for public policy toward the large corporation. The question is certainly one of fact, and as such cannot be answered definitively by theories. Facts and facts only can supply a truly scientific answer. Considering the importance and nature of the question, it is rather surprising how little effort has been made to obtain the kind of data necessary for its answer. It is to these efforts, and to the use that has been made of the available statistics in the attack on big business, that we shall now turn.

"Statistics Show That Big Business Isn't Efficient"

In taking a look at some of the principal statistical analyses which have been made relating to the efficiency of large-scale enterprise, our interest will not be primarily in what they show as to whether big business is or is not efficient and genuinely profitable. We will not, it should be emphasized, try to reach here any final judgment as to whether the data show

40 Professor George J. Stigler of Columbia, "The Case Against Big Business," *Fortune,* May, 1952, p. 162.

that large corporations *in general* are or are not more efficient or more profitable than smaller companies. We *can,* however, learn a good bit about the nature of the attack on big business through a study of some of these analyses, of the claims made for them, and the way some of these analyses have been used in argument. And that is our purpose.

Nor shall we engage in a probing examination nor repetitious summary of these statistical analyses. That would be much too tedious and would take us far afield. And, in any case, that sort of thing has already been done elsewhere, by others, and anyone with further interests in the matter can pursue them in company with these other authors. But we cannot escape entirely scot-free from detailed examination of these studies. Some amount of it will be especially helpful in increasing our understanding of the nature of the criticism.

One of the earliest analyses of the efficiency of big business was the study of the profitability of certain "consolidations" published in 1921 by Dr. A. S. Dewing of Harvard.[41] In this analysis, Dr. Dewing studied the earnings of thirty-five corporations which were the results of the merger of five or more "separate, independent, and competing plants." He made several comparisons between the earnings of each new consolidated corporation with the earnings of the individual component companies prior to the consolidation. His comparisons included the following: the ratio of the earnings of the component companies (before the consolidation) to the earnings of the consolidation in its first year, in its tenth year, and to the average earnings of its first ten years. He also compared the earnings which the consolidation's bankers and promoters estimated for it, with the actual earnings in the first year, the tenth year, and to the average of the first ten years.

[41] "A Statistical Test of the Success of Consolidations," *The Quarterly Journal of Economics,* Vol. 36, November, 1921, pp. 84–101.

Dewing found that the earnings of the component individual companies' *previous*[42] *earnings* were typically *greater* than (1) the earnings of the consolidations in their first year; (2) than the earnings in their tenth year; and (3) than their average earnings per year over the first ten years.[43] The earnings of the consolidations in their first year, in their tenth year, and for the average of the first ten years were, on the average, only about 55%–60% of what had been estimated in each case. In 5 of the 35 cases, the average earnings of the ten years following consolidation were greater than previous earnings.

This study of Dr. Dewing's has been cited again and again by the critics of big business.[44] This study, it is fair to say, has been one of the main props in the statistical case which the critics have endeavored to build up for the thesis that big business is inefficient.

Other investigations have come to the conclusion that Dewing's study resulted in an essential misevaluation of the profitability of mergers and consolidations. They have pointed out that his sample was a restricted one, and very small, hence not fully representative. It has been argued that the time period, ten years, was too short to permit a final assessment.[45] These later studies throw at least some doubt

[42] "Previous" covers different periods for different companies.

[43] The median ratios of previous earnings to earnings in the first year after consolidation, to earnings in the tenth year, and to the average earnings of the ten years following consolidation, were 1.18, 1.01, and 1.16 respectively. (Ibid., p. 100.)

[44] For example, by Frank A. Fetter, *The Masquerade of Monopoly*, p. 369; by Morris Ernst, *Too Big*, pp. 210–211; T.N.E.C., *Relative Efficiency of Large, Medium-sized, and Small Business*, Monograph No. 13 (Washington: Government Printing Office, 1941); John M. Blair, a Federal Trade Commission economist, in his paper "Does Large-Scale Enterprise Result in Lower Costs? Technology and Size," *American Economic Review*, Vol. 38, No. 2, May, 1948.

[45] For other remarks on this study, and for further references to other commentators, see Richard C. Osborn, *Effects of Corporate Size on Efficiency and Profitability* (Urbana, Illinois: University of Illinois, Bureau of Economic and Business Research, Bulletin No. 72, Vol. 48, No. 7, August, 1950). This publication is also a good reference to the various studies which have been made of the efficiency and profitability of big corporations.

on the validity of the general notion to the effect that mergers and consolidations were not successful.[46] Perhaps the most thorough, certainly the most extensive, study is that of Dr. Shaw Livermore.[47]

Dr. Livermore found that of over 150 mergers formed during 1888–1905, which "could rightfully claim . . . power enough to influence markedly conditions in their industry," 63 were "failures," sooner or later; 17 formed a "limping" group — they were not failures but hardly "successes"; 76 were judged as "successes," ten of them after reorganizations which affected the interests of equity owners but not of creditors. In other words, not counting the "limping" group, slightly less than half were adjudged successful. In an examination of an additional 172 smaller mergers of the same period, which "did not bulk large in the world of business when they were formed," Livermore found a very similar pattern.[48]

Dr. Livermore also suggested that among those mergers which did fail, there were a number of reasons which were more important as explanations of failure than "difficulties of management or control." He listed, as these more important reasons, "original poor judgment of promoters and organizers in the selection of units," "the presence of outright dishonesty," and the decline of particular industries. (This latter category would include, presumably, such companies as American Bicycle and American Saddlery and Harness.) Dr. Livermore reached other conclusions which were indeed quite favorable to the large corporations which were "successful," but they need not concern us here. For we are

[46] See, e.g., National Industrial Conference Board, *Mergers in Industry* (New York, 1929), pp. 36–41; and Edward S. Mead, *Corporation Finance*, pp. 473–478. Neither of these analyses is really top quality but they do show that some of the consolidations were very successful indeed. Mead's data suggest that a number of Dewing's companies attained considerable success in the decade following the earlier study.

[47] "The Success of Industrial Mergers," *The Quarterly Journal of Economics*, Vol. 50, No. 1, November, 1935, pp. 68–96.

[48] Ibid., p. 72.

not trying to settle the question here whether, in fact, big business is efficient or not.[49]

Having described something of two studies which bear on the question of the profitability of mergers, it will now be illuminating to see something of how they have been used by the critics. We shall take a particular case and look at it in some detail. The purpose here is not to argue that mergers in general were or were not efficient, or even that Livermore's statistics are to be preferred to Dewing's. The purpose is to further our understanding of the nature of the criticism of big business.

In a paper delivered at the annual meeting of the American Economic Association in December, 1947, Mr. John M. Blair, long-time economist with the Federal Trade Commission, mentioned both the Dewing and Livermore studies.[50] He cited Dr. Dewing's study as his first point of evidence in his statistical case that big corporations aren't efficient. Mr. Blair quotes Dewing's statement as summarizing his own point: "In brief, the earnings of the separate plants before consolidation were greater than the earnings of the same plants after consolidation." [51] He dismisses Livermore's study in a footnote. The reasoning in this footnote casts an illuminating light on the economic attack on big business.

A good many people ordinarily pay little attention to footnotes. But in this instance the reasoning is worth picking up for close scrutiny. The first criticism Blair makes of Livermore is that he did not compare "the profitability of identical enterprises before and after consolidation, and therefore his study provides no direct evidence on the ques-

49 It is interesting to note that later studies which question the general validity of Dr. Dewing's conclusions are most often disregarded by the critics of big business. For example, Livermore's study is not referred to by either Morris Ernst in his book *Too Big,* or in the T.N.E.C. Monograph, *Relative Efficiency of Large, Medium-sized, and Small Business,* although both of them cite Dewing in proof that mergers and consolidations have been unprofitable — hence inefficient.

50 "Does Large-Scale Enterprise Result in Lower Costs?"

51 Ibid., p. 145.

tion of whether or not the act of consolidation promotes efficiency." [52]

Mr. Blair is in effect saying that Livermore should have compared the profitability in the period 1925–1932 of such companies as Eastman Kodak, General Electric, and United States Rubber against the profitability of their component parts for years prior to 1904 and even as far back as 1888. This, despite the technological revolution in photography, electricity, and transportation. Actually, if any such statistical comparison were to be undertaken along these lines, it should be — in rigorous logic — to compare the actual earnings of the consolidations against the earnings (hypothetical, necessarily) that the component companies *would have had* if they hadn't been consolidated. This would be *some* job.

Mr. Blair seems to be overlooking the enormous changes which have been experienced in products, techniques, wants, and so on over the last fifty years. The tendency of critics to think in static terms and to neglect the dynamic aspects of reality is a point to which we shall return.

But Blair offers another criticism of Livermore which is even more significant from the point of view of understanding the economic attack. Livermore had found that the profitability of a sample of successful mergers compared very favorably with that of the average of successful companies. He attributed this fact to good management. Maybe so; maybe not. But Blair says "it might just as well be attributed to monopoly power." [53] In this rejoinder is revealed the "uncommitted division," or, to change the metaphor, the "Ace-in-the-hole," kind of argument which often appears in the thinking of enthusiastic critics.

With this argument in reserve, critics can, and have made analyses of this order: "Statistics show that big business is unprofitable. That's because it's inefficient. Inefficiency is socially undesirable. If figures should show that big business *is* profitable, why that's because of its monopoly power.

[52] Ibid., p. 146, n. 50. [53] Loc. cit.

Monopoly power is socially undesirable. Ergo, big business is socially undesirable." [54]

We shall see further examples of this kind of reasoning.

The other line of factual inquiry into the relative efficiency of big business has been through the analysis of costs. Here again, the facts all told don't yet add up to much. But a few of these studies have been heavily relied upon by the critics, even long after serious question has been raised concerning the validity of the data. Critics have used these data to reach generalizations about big business.

The study of costs of different-scale businesses which is probably the most often cited is that entitled *Relative Efficiency of Large, Medium-sized, and Small Business,* Temporary National Economic Committee Monograph No. 13. This monograph was prepared by members of the staff of the Federal Trade Commission, and submitted by the Commission to the T.N.E.C. Within two years of its appearance,

[54] This is a painful thing to say. But it is a significant fact just the same. Even in what are ostensibly objective, scientific discussions by inveterate critics of big business, there is often revealed a deep, persistent emotional hostility. Their discussions are often marked — as I think Mr. Blair's is here — by pettifoggery and efforts, not to analyze facts, but to handle data in such a way as to "make a case" against big business. Even argument *ad hominem* and the technique of "finding guilt by association" are resorted to.

For example, Professor Fetter dismissed a study of mergers made by the National Industrial Conference Board by referring to the Board as ". . . a group of businessmen all connected either by financial ties with consolidated industries or by close personal ties with those who are." — *The Masquerade of Monopoly,* pp. 461–462. Actually, a major conclusion of the Board study of the merger as a business technique was that, "It has not provided an instrument for profit-making so effective simply from its own structural characteristics as to emancipate business executives from the necessity of cultivating those traditional requisites of success in industry: prudent investment, sagacious management, and technical ingenuity." (*Mergers in Industry,* p. 41.)

It seems — alas — to be true that many of the economic attacks on big business appear to have the earmarks of being primarily rationalizations of preconceived hostility. Some substantial portion of the economic attack gives the impression that it consists of rationalizations of feelings of hostility that have their origins elsewhere, for instance on social and political, or on the ethical and moral levels. (Compare Professor Schumpeter's comments of the attack on "bourgeois capitalism" by "intellectuals," *Capitalism, Socialism, and Democracy,* Chapter XIII, *et passim.*)

it was torn to tatters by its critics.[55] Mr. Blair, whom we were discussing a moment ago, was among those who attacked it.[56] There is no point here in offering further criticisms of the study itself. The cup already runneth over. But a look at it should give a further "feel" for the nature of much of the economic attack on big business.

The Federal Trade Commission, in presenting this study, said that it felt that "the efficiency tests adopted in this inquiry are the best available scientific tests. They had the endorsement of experts who were consulted on this problem and are used by businessmen themselves. . . . The commission was unable to find that these basic data were at any time seriously challenged. . . ." The results of these tests, said the Commission, "reveal that the largest companies made, on the whole, a very poor showing." The Commission went on:

> The Commission in submitting the results of these tests to the Temporary National Economic Committee offers no definite opinion as to whether they conclusively disprove the claim frequently made that large size in American business is more efficient than medium size or small size. . . .
>
> . . . Whether the results of the tests conducted by the Commission cast serious doubt on the superior efficiency of large size in American business must be left to the judgment of the Committee.[57]

The Commission presented this summary of its findings:

> In but 1 of the 59 individual company-cost tests did the largest company have the lowest cost.

[55] See, e.g., R. N. Anthony, "Effect of Size on Efficiency," *Harvard Business Review,* Vol. 20, No. 3, Spring, 1942, pp. 290–306; and John Scoville and Noel Sargent, *Fact and Fancy in the T.N.E.C. Monographs* (New York: National Association of Manufacturers, 1942), pp. 190–200.

[56] "The Relation between Size and Efficiency of Business," *Review of Economic Statistics,* Vol. 24, No. 3 (August, 1942) pp. 125–135.

[57] Monograph No. 13, pp. 10–11. The experts who endorsed the techniques of the study are not identified. Mr. Blair says that he, as economist for the Commission, challenged "the statistical procedure." (See "The Relation between Size and Efficiency of Business," p. 125.)

> In 21 of these 59 tests, a company classified as medium-sized had the lowest cost.
>
> In 37 of these 59 tests, a company classified as small had the lowest cost.
>
> Of particular significance is the fact that in these 59 tests, on the average, over one-third of the companies in every array had costs lower than that of the largest company.[58]

Others, especially Professor R. N. Anthony of the Harvard Business School, have made trenchant criticisms of the study on substantive grounds as to adequacy of definitions, concepts, measurements, comparability of the data, and so on. We here will ignore such considerations and merely ask, Do the data, *on their face value,* fairly suggest the impressions the FTC tried to convey? What do the data look like which were offered in evidence?

Let's take just one example, "Table 3," which purported to measure the costs of producing cement in mills of different size in the Lehigh valley. This table is reproduced on the next page. The Commission's "Comments on Table 3" were as follows:

> (a) In Lehigh Valley, [the] lowest-cost mill of the 20 covered was seventh largest mill; next to lowest-cost mill was sixth largest mill.
>
> (b) None of the lowest-cost mills belonged to the largest company.
>
> (c) Large companies had some low-cost, some average-cost, and some high-cost mills.
>
> (d) Best net mill prices [were] realized by mills of small companies, suggesting that the costs of distributing their cement were smaller than the costs of distributing the cement of the larger companies.[59]

[58] Ibid., p. 12. Maybe it is superfluous to point out that the unstated obverse of the last comment is: "In these 59 tests, on the average, about two-thirds of the companies in every array had costs *higher* than that of the largest company." This is scarcely an obvious "very poor showing."

[59] Ibid., p. 24.

TABLE 3. COSTS OF CEMENT PLANTS IN LEHIGH VALLEY IN 1929, ARRANGED IN ORDER OF ASCENDING COST PER BARREL

Big Five or independent	*Rank* [1]	*Percent of capacity utilized*	*Cost per barrel*	*Net mill price received per barrel*	*Margin per barrel* [2]
Big Five	7	87	$0.88	$1.32	$0.44
Do	6	86	.90	1.28	.38
Independent	(3)	87	.91	1.46	.55
Big Five	8	97	.92	1.31	.39
Do	15	79	.95	1.31	.36
Do	12	81	1.00	1.31	.31
Independent	10	64	1.02	1.43	.41
Big Five	(3)	61	1.07	1.34	.27
Do	18	81	1.11	1.32	.21
Do	(3)	73	1.13	1.31	.18
Independent	(3)	63	1.13	1.49	.36
Do	(3)	94	1.15	1.47	.32
Do	13	75	1.19	1.39	.20
Do	14	83	1.20	1.51	.31
Do	19	67	1.24	1.31	.07
Big Five	16	98	1.30	1.31	.01
Independent	11	63	1.31	1.32	.01
Do	17	86	1.33	1.63	.30
Do	20	53	1.37	1.31	−.06
Do	9	60	1.50	1.36	−.14

[1] Rank in size indicated by number. For example, 1 was the plant with the largest production in barrels.

[2] Not profit, since costs include imputed interest but no selling expense.

[3] Disclosure of rank of this plant might disclose its identity.

Source: Files of the United States Tariff Commission. (T.N.E.C. Monograph 13, p. 24.)

The implication of these comments is reasonably clear.

For our purposes, we may disregard such questions as whether the costs, products, locations are strictly comparable. We may disregard, also, the fact that for these plants, the figures of "per cent of capacity" varies — however that figure is arrived at. The mills were not, apparently, operating at the same rate of capacity. Waiving these matters, we shall look at the data presented to see what they suggest on their face. One easy way to do this is to see what the data look like when they are shown in graphic form. A graphic picture of the data presented by the Commission is shown on the next page.

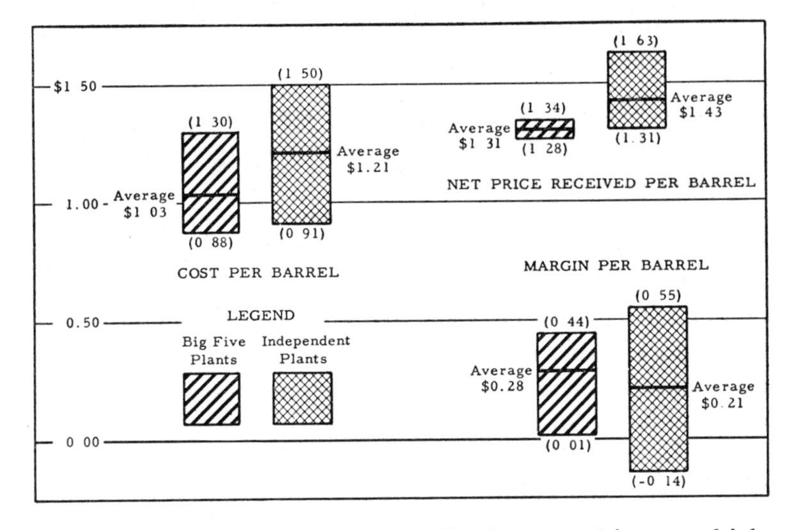

Pretty clearly, if the figures really show anything — which is open to grave doubt — it would be that, on the average, the plants of the "Big Five" companies had *lower costs,* charged *lower prices* at the mill, and obtained *wider margins* than the plants of the "Independent" companies, as a group.

The Commission's own data, on their very face, do not support the impression which the Commission tried to convey.

Actually, however, so far as the Federal Trade Commission's way of thinking was concerned, it looks as though "the case" *for* big business would not have been established even if the data had shown with the most compelling clarity that large-scale enterprise had lower costs and higher rates of return. For, the Commission said, in presenting this Monograph:

> If the abundance of cost and financial data in the files of Government agencies had shown that the largest companies had invariably had the lowest costs and the best rates of return on invested capital, the use of the tests of business efficiency which the Commission adopted might have been exposed to the criticism that such tests might not have eliminated certain savings obtained by large-size business

> and certain sources of revenue obtained by such business which were realized through predatory business practices.[60]

In other words, "If you have high costs and poor profits, you're inefficient. If you have low costs and good profits, it's because you're predatory."

It's a toss-up whether, from a semantic point of view, it's worse to be *inefficient* or *predatory*.

To make a long story short, the data presented in the Monograph seem actually to show that large plants generally tend to be more, rather than less, efficient than medium-sized and small plants; but the monograph itself arrives at conclusions different from those indicated by its own figures.[61]

Despite its manifest inadequacies, and despite the articles which have been published criticizing it, the Monograph has continued, nevertheless, to be cited years later as a factual authority on the inefficiency of big business. The continuing citation of the Monograph, despite all this, is the kind of thing which suggests that much of the attack stems from deep-lying hostility which overpowers the capacity for objective thought.[62]

One more example of how statistical analysis of efficiency has been used in the attack on big business. In his paper

[60] Ibid., p. 6.

[61] So agrees Mr. Blair ("The Relation between Size and Efficiency of Business," pp. 125 and 135).

[62] This Monograph was cited as an authority in May, 1952, by George J. Stigler in his article in *Fortune,* "The Case Against Big Business." It was cited by Mr. Justice Douglas in 1948 in his dissent in the "Columbia Steel Case." Richard C. Osborn, in the University of Illinois pamphlet, *Effects of Corporate Size on Efficiency and Profitability,* lists a number of works which cite this study. In 1951, in their volume *Monopoly and Free Enterprise,* George W. Stocking and Myron W. Watkins, recognizing that the Monograph had been attacked, tried, nevertheless, to turn it into part of "the case" against big business by suggesting that it might be taken as *disproof* that size *is* an important factor leading to efficiency: "The Commission's study has been severely criticized; and, if the imperfect data it assembled would support any inference at all, it would probably be that other factors are at least as important as size (beyond a certain minimum) in determining productive efficiency." Op. cit., p. 67. The fact is that the data are such a hodge-podge that no objective, hard-headed analyst would take them as supporting any inference of any kind.

in the *American Economic Review,* Mr. Blair offered some cost data compiled by the Federal Trade Commission. These were cost figures for wholesale bread bakeries in the months of March and September of 1945. Here are the figures for the month of March (the September figures are much the same):

UNIT COSTS IN CENTS PER POUND [63]

	Materials	*Labor*	*Selling and Delivery*	*General and Adminis-trative*	*Total Cost*
Big Four	3.66	1.83	1.83	0.23	7.55
10 medium-large	3.87	1.50	1.63	0.39	7.39
Medium-sized	3.87	1.56	1.67	0.49	7.56
Small	3.92	1.64	1.67	0.65	7.88
Smallest	4.62	2.11	1.83	0.78	9.34

Mr. Blair's reader is left to assume that for all these bakery companies the materials used, the wage rates per hour, the products and their packaging, the methods and channels of distribution, processes, the manufacturing locations — geographical region, "Big City," "Small City," etc., — cost accounting definitions and systems, are identical or so close to being identical that they are strictly comparable. In short, that there are no significant variables affecting the data other than size of company. Assuming all this, however, the figures would appear to show that, among these groups of companies, only the "10 medium-large" companies had average unit costs lower than the "Big Four" group.

Is that a pretty fair record? No.

Says Mr. Blair:

> What is perhaps most significant, however, is the fact that in both months the Big Four had the lowest costs of materials, which is more of a reflection of buying power than of any operating efficiency. Given equal costs of materials, not only the ten medium-large but also the next group, the medium-sized companies, would have had much lower costs than

63 "Does Large-scale Enterprise Result in Lower Cost?" p. 147.

> the Big Four. Similarly, the Big Four had the lowest overhead costs, which are influenced by the volume of production; according to the commission, the Big Four's volume of production is secured in large part not by lowering prices generally but by the use of practices which only the financially powerful concerns can inaugurate and use, such as consignment selling, furnishing retailers with free bread racks, giving premiums, allowing special discounts, distributing free bread, etc.
>
> In other words, it was only through the use of two forms of economic power – the power to buy materials cheaply and the power to force their products on the market through questionable competitive practices – that the Big Four were able to rank as well as they did.[64]

To the extent that big business makes a poor statistical showing, that is due to its inefficiency. To the extent that big business makes a good showing, that is due to "economic power."

Again, perhaps it should be emphasized that the point in taking up and commenting on these analyses by critics was not to "prove" that big business, conceived as a generality, *is* efficient after all. The point is to convey some of the *flavor* of the criticism, especially of its deeply underlying bias and hostility against big business.

"The Economies of Big Business Are Not Net for Society"

We will now move to the argument which holds that any advantages big business may have as to costs and profits are antisocial in their nature and are not "net" from the point of view of the economy as a whole. This argument has been prominent in its own right in the attack on big business.

[64] Ibid., p. 148.

This same kind of reasoning is used by Stocking and Watkins in their handling of the findings of Professor W. L. Crum's *Corporate Size and Earning Power* (Cambridge: Harvard University Press, 1939). Crum found that there was a "surprising consistency" in the tendency of the net rate of return on investment to increase with the size of corporation. But of this, Stocking and Watkins say "High earning rates may reflect monopoly power rather than productive efficiency." (*Monopoly and Free Enterprise,* p. 67.)

And we have seen how it is sometimes used to interpret statistics that do not seem to prove the inefficiency of big business in the first instance.

Louis D. Brandeis, as we saw in the testimony already quoted, took this line on the efficiency and profitability of big business: The big corporation is naturally and intrinsically inefficient and unprofitable. Where, in fact, large corporations have been profitable, Brandeis argued, it is because "They have succeeded through their monopolistic position. They dominated the trade and were able to fix the prices at which articles should be sold. To this monopolistic power, in the main, and not to efficiency in management, are their great profits to be ascribed." [65]

So, we are told, *if* a large corporation *is* profitable, it is because (a) the corporation is able to exact monopoly gains, and/or (b) it is able to lower its own costs in a way that is of no advantage to society at large since it is simply a matter of shifting costs on to other elements in the economy.

In this testimony, Brandeis laid down a line of reasoning which has had its followers ever since.

We can see, in the following paragraph by Professor Fetter, the long-time adviser to the Federal Trade Commission, the influence of Brandeis' idea that the profitability of large corporations is to be traced to antisocial causes. It is worth noting that there are also implicit in this one paragraph two other common charges against the large corporation: (a) The idea that big business can't be administered efficiently—a notion which stems back to the premised authoritarian "one-master" concept of administration; and (b) that the origin of the large corporation is not to be found in the quest for efficiency:

> . . . In truth, as single factories grow larger and the founders pass off the scene, and separate concerns are merged into

[65] Hearings before the Senate Committee on Interstate Commerce, *Control of Corporations, Persons, and Firms Engaged in Interstate Commerce*, p. 1148.

great combinations, one master ceases to know all and one master's eye to see all, responsibility becomes subdivided, the motives of personal financial gain of the management are weakened, red tape multiplies, office overhead costs mount, and often nepotism and favoritism begin to honeycomb and undermine the morale of the whole organization. . . . Then is when its management is tempted to misuse its greater financial powers to assert and maintain by restraint of commerce a domination in the industry to which its technical efficiency in no manner entitles it. The highly lauded "industrial statesmanship" of its president, for which, besides his salary, he receives in a single year a bonus of $1,600,000, consists in what? Not in making better steel to be sold cheaper to the public, but rather in acquiring one after another all of the company's competitors in a great industrial region, a process not justified by increasing technical efficiency, but only by the added control it gives over price policies, by the dominating power it gives to a single enterprise, and perhaps by the speculative gains it makes possible in the stock market.[66]

In his famous memorandum giving some of his ideas as to what the T.N.E.C. should be concerned with, A. A. Berle, Jr., suggested that one of the things the Committee should look into was antisocial advantages in bigness:

. . . It may well be that so-called "efficiency" [of a "large unit"] is not a real saving, but consists of shoving the cost item of production from the back of the buyer to the back of the seller or by him onto the back of labor. It would be interesting, for instance, to know whether the real profits of a chain store corporation came from actual saving of waste or whether they come from the fact that, in place of many small shopkeepers, there are now a highly exploited group of so-called "store managers," on the distribution side and a highly exploited group of small suppliers on the production side.[67]

[66] *The Masquerade of Monopoly*, pp. 374–375.

[67] *Berle Memorandum* (Suggestions to the Temporary National Economic Committee). Text as published by The Kiplinger Washington Agency, August 23, 1938, p. 13.

Clearly the ability of a large corporation to shift systematically a part of its real costs on to others would make for "efficiency" so far as the individual corporation is concerned — its own costs could be lower. And, of course, its own profits would appear larger on that account. But from the point of view of society considered as a whole, this would bring no advantage: the costs are still there, only they are now borne by some other party. From the point of view of accounting for the product of the national economy as a whole, no product is added and there is no saving of resources used.

Most often, the idea that apparent efficiency of large corporations is traceable really to the shifting of costs on to others — especially small suppliers — appears only in fragmentary terms. Only occasionally is this idea set forth so explicitly as by Mr. Blair in his interpretation of the bakery statistics. An example of this argument, from the *Fortune* article by Professor Stigler, is especially interesting because it acts simultaneously as an argument, in its own right, against big business and as a way of estopping any counter argument by appeal — if possible — to fact:

> . . . Big businesses may be efficient in the social sense, and usually they also possess, because of their monopoly position, private advantages. But the ability of a company to employ its dominant position to coerce unusually low prices from suppliers is not of any social advantage.
>
> It follows that even if big companies had larger profit rates or smaller costs per unit of output than other companies, this would not prove they were more efficient in socially desirable ways. Actually big businesses are generally no more and no less efficient than medium sized businesses even when the gains wrung by monopoly power are included in efficiency. . . .[68]

If it were true that big business has no lower real costs and no higher real profits than small business, even taking

[68] Op. cit., p. 162.

into account gains "wrung by monopoly power" and from the ability to shift part of its costs on to the back of others, then it would follow that, from the point of view of the national economy as a whole, its *real* costs must be higher. From this it would immediately follow that big business operates to depress the level of the national product. With the same input of resources a larger output of product would be obtained if business were organized on the basis of small units — if big business were broken up. And, of course, some critics advocate just that.

"Big Business Holds Back Invention"

There remains yet one further count in the indictment against the efficiency of big business. From a social point of view, I take it, efficiency is not just efficiency of the moment. In the Western World we generally assume and take for granted the possibility of improvement, of progress. If there is not improvement, there is inefficiency in an important dimension, whatever may be the current costs of output. The capstone of the critics' brief that big business is inefficient is the argument that it holds back technological progress.

Adam Smith had so little confidence in the ability of corporations to handle nonroutine matters that he thought they could be entrusted, for instance, only with the *operation* of canals — not with their construction. Now, nothing is less routine than invention: the searching out beyond what is known and beyond what has been done. Given the set of mind that men in groups, working together as an economic organization, are incapable of handling anything but the routine, the expectation would naturally follow that big business would be incapable of organizing and carrying through developmental activity.

When there is added to this idea the concept that one of the fundamental purposes of organizing large corporations is to obtain a monopoly, another reason may be brought forth for supposing that no innovation or development can be looked for from big business: Since the large corporation is — by the definition of its critics — a monopoly, it has little to fear, so they say, from competition. There is no stimulus to big business for improvement. Indeed, since it has a vested interest in the *status quo* which it has brought about, the large corporation will be expected to exert positive effort to maintain the given state of affairs.[69]

With this set of mind, the large corporation is visualized as having no interest in innovation. And even if it did, nothing could be expected to come of this interest. If, in the large corporation, as Professor Fetter says, "the motives of personal financial gain of the management are weakened" — it being *assumed* those are the principal human motives — the management cannot be expected to take much interest in enhancing "other people's money" through innovation. And, in any case, the corporation could not be expected to administer such complex activity as innovation. Much of this kind of activity, of necessity, would have to take place beyond the purview of the top responsible administrator — beyond the range of "one master's eye." And since there is no incentive and no feeling of responsibility for the interests of others, this work cannot be expected to be of good quality. In brief, big business is said to stifle invention, ingenuity, and improvement. As a corollary, for many critics, invention and the introduction of new techniques flow from *small* business.

For over 40 years this has been a major contention of the critics of big business. Mr. Brandeis attacked the "Steel Trust" on these very grounds:

> . . . Efficiency is ordinarily manifested in two ways: One is in respect to quality – whether there has been an advance in the art as to the quality of the products – and the other

[69] For an example of the idea that big business – and big *labor,* too (at least, it would seem, the United Mine Workers) – views technological change with some horror, see the paper by Evsey D. Domar, "Investment, Losses, and Monopolies," in *Income, Employment, and Public Policy: Essays in Honor of Alvin H. Hansen* (New York: W. W. Norton & Company, Inc.), 1948, especially pp. 51–52.

is whether there has been an advance in the art lessening the cost of the article.

Now, what is the situation in regard to the Steel Trust? There are two steel products in common use in the United States in which the American people are particularly interested. One is steel rails; the other is fence wire. The Steel Trust has failed in respect of both of those important articles of production to keep up with the demand of the community – not in quantity, but in quality.[70]

The same point was advanced by Woodrow Wilson in the presidential campaign of 1912: "Do you know," he asked in a question which does appear a bit pessimistic when viewed from the perspective of 1953, "Do you know, have you had occasion to learn, that there is no hospitality for invention nowadays?" He continues with this explanation of why there is "no hospitality for invention nowadays":

. . . Wherever there is monopoly, not only is there no incentive to improve, but improvement being costly in that it "scraps" old machinery and destroys the value of old products, there is a positive motive against improvement. . . . Of course, I am not saying that all invention has been stopped by the growth of trusts, but I think it is perfectly clear that invention in many fields has been discouraged, that inventors have been prevented from reaping the full fruits of their ingenuity and industry, that mankind has been deprived of many comforts and conveniences, as well as the opportunity of buying at lower prices.[71]

During the T.N.E.C. hearings, just before World War II, much was again made of the alleged technological backwardness of big business, and of the suppression of patents by large corporations. Since the war, in 1949, during the "Celler Committee" Hearings, a number of persons again put forward the contention that big business inherently suf-

[70] Hearings before the Senate Committee on Interstate Commerce, *Control of Corporations, Persons, and Firms Engaged in Interstate Commerce*, p. 1149.

[71] *The New Freedom* (New York and Garden City: Doubleday, Page and Company, 1913), pp. 266–267.

fers from an incapacity for invention and — more generally — for innovation. This contention was generally linked with the counterpart argument that only small business can be looked to for technological and economic progress. Sometimes this notion is only implicit in the idea actually expressed. Sometimes it is stated categorically. A few examples will be interesting.

The Honorable Tom C. Clark, then Attorney General of the United States and now Associate Justice of the Supreme Court of the United States:

> . . . It is usually the small-business man who is willing to take a chance, who dares to try something new, and thereby provides us with the development and advances which have characterized this country.[72]

Dr. John D. Clark, a member of the Council of Economic Advisers:

> By and large, however, bigness results in power being used in the market place instead of ingenuity. . . .[73]

Mr. Fred I. Raymond, author of a book entitled *The Limitist*[74] in answer to a question put by Representative Emanuel Celler, Chairman of the Subcommittee:

> [Mr. Celler] We are told that large-scale operation is necessary for important research and development of new patents. What do you think of that idea? Do you think that is a fallacy or is that sound?
>
> *Mr. Raymond.* I think it is an absolute fallacy and I would state from my own personal experience and knowledge that the large companies which have claimed to introduce, which have introduced new products as a result of their research, have not produced the products.
>
> They have waited until the products were already produced, and in a lot of cases marketed, and then they have gone out and bought the patent. They do not develop the thing.

72 *Study of Monopoly Power,* Part 1, p. 92.
73 Ibid., p. 130.
74 *The Limitist* (New York: W. W. Norton & Company, Inc., 1947).

The General Electric Co. did not develop the radio. It has done research with it afterward, and even if we admit that they take an embryo idea and develop it somewhat, I maintain that throughout history we will find that the real generic developments do not come from those people who are supposed to know about these fields.

It takes somebody who does not know enough about the field to think that a problem can be solved. Just as fools rush in where angels fear to tread, and once in a while the fool makes it.

I am very much satisfied myself that we would have a great deal more research if we had smaller units.[75]

Mr. David M. Kasson, businessman and one-time member (1945–1947) of the Small Business Advisory Committee of the Department of Commerce, in an interchange with Representative Celler:

[Mr. Celler] . . . We often hear that big concerns are more efficient. Are you prepared to say that we could get better lamps for less money if they were made by smaller companies, rather than the manufacture thereof being more or less monopolized by one company?

Mr. Kasson. Definitely; yes.

The Chairman. [Mr. Celler] Would you like to expatiate just a little bit more on that?

Mr. Kasson. Well, I believe I did, Mr. Celler, in this lamp situation.

In the first place, if the company has patent protection, it ceases to do much development work because it does not have to do development work. There is no competition to force it to do development work.

The Chairman. You mean after it reaches more or less a pinnacle of power the initiative is gone, and lethargy sets in, and they feel that having stifled competition there is no need for new patents, new processes, that the sheer power of their vast outlets are sufficient to carry them along from success to success without paying very much attention to improving their product?

[75] *Study of Monopoly Power,* Serial No. 14, Part 2-A, p. 319.

Mr. Kasson. That is correct, sir. That has proven historically many times to be so . . .

The Chairman. Now there have been many men thinking about that subject, and who have come to your conclusion, and I would like at this point to quote President Wilson, who gave a great deal of thought to this very interesting proposition that you have expressed. President Wilson said the following:

> I am not saying that all invention has been stopped by the growth of trusts, but I think it is perfectly clear that invention in many fields has been discouraged, that inventors have been prevented from reaping the full fruits of their ingenuity and industry, that mankind has been deprived of many comforts and conveniences, as well as the opportunity of buying at lower prices.

I take it you subscribe to that statement by President Wilson?

Mr. Kasson. Yes, sir; I read that.[76]

Mr. Thomas K. Quinn, a one-time vice president of General Electric, in answer to a question put by Mr. C. Murray Bernhardt, Counsel for the House Committee on the Judiciary and in interchange with Mr. David Cushman Coyle, Consultant to the Subcommittee:

Mr. Bernhardt. Did General Electric develop all of its improvements, or did it buy some of them?

Mr. Quinn. Oh, no. The principal development, the principal research work they have done is in what I have cited to you in the incandescent lamp case. They bought into the vacuum cleaner — they bought a vacuum cleaner company; they bought an electric-range manufacturer et cetera, scores of companies. They bought a heating-device manufacturer; electric-clock manufacturer. No one laboratory could begin to develop all the things that General Electric has, a thousand items.

Mr. Coyle. A good many of these new additions to the art came from comparatively small sources, did they not?

Mr. Quinn. I think, as a rule, they all came from small sources.

[76] Ibid., p. 349.

Mr. Coyle. What do you think of this: We keep being told that, unless you have the big companies with their laboratories, technological progress would stop.

Mr. Quinn. I think just the opposite of that. Inventions are accidents, major ones, for the most part; and what you want is the maximum number of people in their little workshops working on them, not a few large research laboratories whose attention is directed in some one way.

Mr. Coyle. You mean you want a maximum number of people in independent laboratories, with no one directing their attention?

Mr. Quinn. Oh, yes; surely.[77]

Many people have supposed, and some have argued, that there must be some causal relationship between the great changes which the American economy and industry have undergone and the great increase in production which has taken place in the last fifty years or so, on the one hand, and the rise of big business on the other. This relationship is minimized or denied by the critics, as in the passage from the recent work of Doctors Stocking and Watkins which is quoted below. These economists appear to be attributing technological change and increase in output primarily to *other* factors — "The progress of science," "the discovery of new resources," "invention," for example. In this kind of appraisal, such factors are conceived of as high-level abstrac-

[77] Ibid., p. 397. In all fairness to the General Electric Company which is here specifically mentioned it should be noted that Mr. Charles E. Wilson, president, and Dr. C. G. Suits, vice president and director of the company's research laboratory, in testifying at length before the Subcommittee described some of the company's research activity – for example, on the steam turbine ("$20,000,000"), on the gunfire control system of the "B-29", and on X-ray equipment. The company also submitted a statement addressed to particular points made by Mr. Quinn among others. (See *Study of Monopoly Power,* Serial No. 14, Part 2-B, pp. 1158–1248.)

In his article in *The Atlantic Monthly* (June, 1947) from which a quotation has already been drawn, Mr. Coyle had previously had this to say about innovation by large corporations: ". . . The record of big business in general is that when several concerns are merged their production costs go up, as their ability to use new techniques is stifled by lawyers, bankers, and red tape." ("The Big Cannot Be Free," p. 75.)

tions and impersonal "forces," not as the concrete accomplishments of particular people and groups. (We shall return to this kind of mechanistic interpretation of the world which is found so often in the criticism of big business.) And these "forces" are thought of as being entirely unassociated with the rise of big business.

> The productivity of American industry as a whole has steadily increased and now vastly surpasses that of other countries. Considering this fact in the light of the transformation of the American industrial structure, one might be led to infer that the primary cause of the rise of big business was a quest for industrial efficiency. But this interpretation ignores other factors no less important.
>
> Many forces have contributed to the increase in productivity. The progress of science, the discovery of new resources, the accumulation of capital, the increase and refinement of special skills, the improvement in transport and communication, invention, the gradual adjustment of diversities in law, custom, language, and education – these and similar influences have played important roles in promoting productive efficiency. *Undoubtedly the per capita output of American industry would have increased greatly during the past half century had business units remained much smaller and more numerous.*[78]

Conclusion

That last sentence, in half the words of a night-letter, summarizes one whole wing of the economic attack on big business: We *could* have had an efficient, prosperous, dynamic economy *without* big business; perhaps — or probably — even more efficient and prosperous, and more dynamic.

This brings us to the end of the first point of critics' economic attack on big business: "It is inefficient." We will now take up the second point: "It is monopolistic."

[78] *Monopoly and Free Enterprise,* p. 53. (Italics added.)

CHAPTER 2

"Big Business Is Monopolistic"

THE CHARGE that big business is monopolistic is far more sweeping, and presents a challenge on a wider front than the charge that it's inefficient. For, as we shall see, a well-nigh unlimited armoury of specific counts streams from the basic proposition that big business represents a departure from the norm of competition. Indeed, the total effect of this proposition and all its implications is to deny the validity of claims by big business to share the traditional justification which endorses laissez-faire capitalism as the best of all possible economic systems.

Putting it more positively, the charge of monopoly can be — and has been — developed in detail to argue that monopolistic big business leads to an economic state of affairs which is *inferior* in every particular to the ideal blue-printed for individualistic — "atomistic" — capitalism. The charge can even be extended — if only certain political, social, and moral assumptions be granted — and developed into a *rationale* for ideological convictions that monopolistic big business leads to a state of affairs which is inferior, even, to a system of government control — "public interference" — or to a system of government ownership.

The history of this particular attack on big business is an account of rise, fall, and revival. It reached one "high-water" mark in the years prior to World War I — perhaps around 1914, when a federal district court ordered International Harvester Company to be broken up. That early surge, however, was held off. In fact, for more than a decade after World War I, what with prevailing legal and economic doctrines rallying to the defense of big business, it looked as though the attack had been turned back. But in the years of the Great

Depression the attack was renewed with greater power and mass than before. It is still too early to discern the outcome of this engagement.

History of the Monopoly Charge

To pick up the matter as of the turn of the century: the burden of what the economic critics were saying about big business and monopoly in those days can be reduced to crystalline form something like this: The intensity and efficiency of competition depends upon the competitors being small and numerous. As the size of business organizations in an industry increases and their number decreases, by the same token the forces of competition are enfeebled. The remaining large organizations — or remaining one large organization, if the process of consolidation is carried that far — then can, and will, increase prices and profits.

It was just about as simple as that. This basic idea was put forth, in effect, as a self-evident proposition. But therein lay a major weakness of the critics' case.

The starting point of this line of attack in those days was the automatic identification of the large corporation with "monopoly." This sort of identification runs through and through the speeches and articles of the critics of fifty years ago:

> . . . The essential feature of the trust . . . is its monopoly character. While legally it is only a large corporation . . . yet . . . there is all the difference in the world between . . . [a] group of competing corporations [and a] giant consolidation which is possessed of monopoly features *by virtue* of its enormous size and of the large proportion of the business of the country in its hands along the special line of its work.[1]

* * *

[1] Professor Edward W. Bemis, "Trust Evils and Suggested Remedies: A Problem for a Generation to Settle," *Chicago Conference on Trusts,* p. 395. (Italics added.)

> . . . If the tendency towards combination means anything, it means the substitution of centralized and consolidated management for the rivalry of independent concerns; and this may fairly be termed monopoly.[2]

It was taken for granted by the critics — as self-evident — that these large organizations had the power to establish prices at levels which would suit themselves and that having that power, they would naturally raise prices above the level which would prevail if only there were competition. They would, by this means, also increase their margins of profit over the competitive level.

There was a certain appeal to the line of reasoning that took it as self-evident that bigness confers monopolistic power. It corresponded to widely held popular belief. It gained no little acceptance in professional economic circles

[2] Professor C. J. Bullock, "Trust Literature. . . ," p. 187.

There are lots of suggestions, here and there, that behind the hostility which some critics expressed toward "monopolies," "trusts," "combinations," and "big business," there was a much deeper hostility toward *any* sort of *corporate* business enterprise and even toward business enterprise itself. Sample:

". . . We believe that there are some things more valuable, more to be desired and more worthy to be contended for by a free people than mere industrial activity, commercial progress or the accumulation of worldly wealth. . . . We love to recall that Washington warned his countrymen against the dangerous seductions of commercial power and the corrupting influence of consuming wealth. . . . We recollect . . . that Webster declared that 'the deadliest canker that can attack the heart of the nation is the corroding disease of commercial avarice.' . . .

"Remembering and revering these ancient and approved principles and precepts, we must be allowed to believe that the modern trust and its more modern successor – the consolidated corporate monopoly – are the practical realization of the commercial spirit in its most despotic form. . . .

"Corporations for private profit are in themselves essentially vicious and inconsistent with that equality of right and absence of special privilege guaranteed by the institutions of a free republic, but if they must exist, then they should be limited to as few purposes as possible, and their capital stock should never be beyond that which a fair and reasonable conduct of private business requires." – "Principles and Sources of the Trust Evil as Texas Sees Them," speech by Dudley G. Wooten, then a member of the Texas legislature and later a member of Congress, at the *Chicago Conference on Trusts,* pp. 43, 45, 50. See also, for further example, the speeches at the Conference by William Jennings Bryan and Hon. Hazen S. Pingree, then governor of Michigan. Ideas along these lines are treated in Parts II and III, below.

and among the judiciary.[3] But it wasn't rigorous enough to hang the charge of monopoly on big business and make it stick. The argument wasn't strong enough, as matters turned out, to enable the critics to make the charge stick even on the "trusts" and "combinations."

Against this reasoning, men of big business held that "trusts," "combinations," "consolidations," and big corporations generally, were *not* inherently monopolistic, no matter how big they were and no matter how large a fraction of the business in their respective lines they might account for. If nothing else, the threat, the likelihood, the certainty, that *potential* competition might enter the field against them would always hang over them, would ever be in the offing. If a large company, even a "combination" doing practically all the business in an entire industry, should raise prices too high, make more than averagely attractive profits, or fail to give as good service or to employ as productive techniques as possible, these potential competitors would stream into the field. If the mere *threat* of such entry of potential competitors into the field was not a sufficient force to ensure competitive results from the large corporations, ultimately *actual* entry would be.[4]

In this counter-argument, the businessmen were sustained

[3] An interesting example, from a later period, is to be seen in the dissenting opinion of Mr. Justice Day in the "Steel" case (*United States* v. *United States Steel Corporation et al.*, 1920, 251 U.S. 417, 418). He noted, among other things, that the company's total assets, in 1913, amounted to $1,800,000,-000; that its "cash on hand," $75,000,000, exceeded the total "capitalization" of any of its competitors and even the total capital and surplus of any of them save one. He went on, "That such an organization thus fortified and equipped could if it saw fit dominate the trade and control competition would seem to be a business proposition too plain to require extended argument to support it." (Page 464.)

[4] ". . . The testimony of substantially all of the combination men is to the same effect — that unless a combination has either some natural monopoly of raw material, or is protected by a patent, or possibly has succeeded in developing some very popular style or trade-marks or brands, any attempt to put prices at above competitive rates will result in failure, although it may be temporarily successful" — *Report of the Industrial Commission on Trusts and Industrial Combinations,* "Review of the Evidence," Vol. XIII, p. xxi.

by at least a few economists of some prestige. The distinguished and influential Professor John Bates Clark of Columbia, for instance, combined this defense of big business against the charge of monopoly with the positive affirmation of its greater efficiency. The result was quite a brief for bigness:

> . . . Monopoly is evil, almost wholly so; and if the massing of productive wealth necessarily means monopoly, farewell to centralization. . . . The fact is [however] that massed capital does not need to bring with it a regime of true monopoly. . . . [The "natural and centralizing tendency"] means the survival of the most productive forms of business. It is first and chiefly because they can give more for a dollar than little establishments can give that the great establishments supplant them. . . .
>
> To keep the new mills from coming into existence a wise policy keeps prices at a moderate level. Within limits it is safe to raise them, but beyond such limits it is not safe. The competitor who is not now in the field, but who will enter it at once if prices are unduly raised, is the protector of the purchasing public against extortion. He is also the protector of the workmen, for the fact that he will begin his operations if too many of the old mills are closed, prevents the closing of them. In technical phrase it is potential competition that is the power that holds trusts in check. The competition that is now latent but is ready to spring into activity if very high prices are exacted, is even now efficient in preventing high prices. It is to be the permanent policy of wise and successful peoples to utilize this natural economic force for all that it is worth.[5]

[5] "The Necessity of Restraining Monopolies While Retaining Trusts," *Chicago Conference on Trusts,* pp. 405 and 407.

Compare: ". . . a great mass of idle capital exists in the hands of enterprising men ready to enter any specific field of production, whenever the profits of that industry offer sufficient inducement. So that to avoid this new competition, prices must be lowered or profits shared with the consumer." — Professor James R. Weaver, of De Pauw University, "Efficacy of Economic Checks in Regulating Competitive Trusts," ibid., p. 297.

A similar position was taken by the great Professor F. W. Taussig of Har-

Some of the academic defenders, to be sure, agreed that big companies sometimes did, in fact, engage in monopolistic practices and unfair competition to enhance their own position and to handicap competitors. Big companies might, for instance, deliberately undersell small competitors in certain localities, while maintaining high prices elsewhere, in order to drive them out of business. They might, so it was agreed, engage in commercial espionage and bribery of competitors' personnel. Force customers into tying-contracts to the detriment of other competitors. All that sort of thing. But, these people continued, such practices did not *inhere* in size as such. Such practices were aberrations. Where such practices occurred, size was merely adventitious — such practices might be engaged in by business of any size. Most importantly, it was concluded, practices of this sort could be prohibited by law, if Congress willed, and prevented. If this were done, competition and potential competition would take care of everything else.

This is how John Bates Clark put it:

> . . . There are abnormal difficulties and dangers [as of now, in the way of the potential competitor], and the consequence of this is that he is often reluctant and tardy in his action; and the fear of him is a far less potent influence with the managers of the trusts than it easily might be made to be. . . . we should prevent patents from being instruments of extortion or oppression. . . . The ability to make discriminating prices puts a terrible power into the hands of a

---

vard — competition, actual and potential, would hold the prices and profits even of combinations and trusts down to competitive levels: "Whether or no . . . combinations and trusts will prove to hold their own permanently, it seems certain that in the ordinary manufacturing industries, even in those where large-scale operations prevail, nothing but a precarious and limited monopoly can result. The trust must always be on its mettle, always on the watch against interlopers. These may be browbeaten or bought up; but new ones will constantly appear if the profits are very high. The trust may become a dominant form of organization, and by good management, may maintain itself permanently without bringing about true monopoly prices or extraordinary profits." (*Principles of Economics,* Vol. II, pp. 432–433.)

> trust. If in my small field it can sell goods at prices that are below the cost of making them, while it sustains itself by charging high prices in a score of other fields, it can crush me without itself sustaining any injury. . .
>
> Predatory competition that is evil and that crushes producers who have a right to survive rests mainly in . . . methods of discriminating and unfair treatment of customers. That power must be destroyed. With a fair field and no favor the independent producer is the protector of the public and of the wage-earner; but with an unfair field and much favor he is the first and most unfortunate victim. . . .[6]

Thus, between attack and defense, the lines were drawn and issue joined. There were occasions — the 1914 decision of the District Court in the case of *United States* v. *International Harvester Co.*, for instance — when things didn't look too good for the "combinations."[7] But in time the theory came to prevail that trusts and combinations — corporations, generally, which did a large fraction of the total business of their industries — were *not* monopolies necessarily by their very nature and standing.

This view became legal doctrine in the "Steel" case. The Supreme Court through the opinion written by Mr. Justice McKenna, conceded that "the corporation is undoubtedly of impressive size, and it takes an effort of resolution not to be affected by it or to exaggerate its influence."[8] But the Court, in rejecting the government's contentions and accepting the defendant's, voiced such ideas as these:

[6] Ibid., pp. 407–409. The connection is obvious between these ideas and the philosophy embodied in the Clayton Act (directed at discriminatory pricing) and the Federal Trade Commission Act (directed at unfair competition.)

[7] The attack on International Harvester was, perhaps, as close to a clear-cut case of an attack on bigness as such as there was. This case differed from the earlier "Standard Oil" and "American Tobacco" cases to the extent that even a concurring opinion to break up the company went out of its way to emphasize that the business conduct of the company toward its competitors and the public had been "honorable, clean, and fair." (See concurring opinion of Circuit Judge Hook, 214 F. 1002.)

[8] *United States* v. *United States Steel Corporation, et al.*, 251 U.S. 417, 451.

We have seen that the judges of the District Court unanimously concurred in the view that the corporation did not achieve monopoly, and such is our deduction. . . .

. . . . .

. . . its power over prices was not and is not commensurate with its power to produce.

. . . . .

. . . the law [the Sherman Act] does not make mere size an offense. . . .

. . . . .

. . . Whatever there was of wrong intent [in the formation of the Corporation in the first instance] could not be executed. . . .[9]

Even International Harvester, thirteen years after the adverse decision of 1914, ultimately received something of a vindication at the hands of the Supreme Court in its decision of 1927:

The law, however, does not make the mere size of a corporation, however impressive, or the unexerted power on its part, an offense, when unaccompanied by unlawful conduct in the exercise of its power.[10]

The arguments of the defenders of bigness in business in time achieved a status akin to accepted doctrine in the field of economics also. In 1932 a typical, widely used text book in economics — that of Professors Fairchild, Furniss, and Buck, of Yale — still followed the reasoning outlined by people like John Bates Clark: If conspiracy and contracts in restraint of trade are prevented by the Sherman Act, price discrimination by the Clayton Act, and unfair competition by the Federal Trade Commission Act, the beneficent effects of competition will be achieved. These effects will be achieved no matter how big companies grow, either in absolute size or in relation to their respective industries.

[9] Ibid., pp. 444, 445, 451, 452.

[10] *United States* v. *International Harvester Co., et al.* (1927), 274 U.S. 693, 708.

. . . Frequently [the position of the one leading producer] is maintained only because his price policy is reasonable. Let him begin charging excessive prices, and some of his small and hitherto negligible competitors may be induced to enlarge their operations and challenge his supremacy. And even when there are no competitors in the field, this is often not because competition is impossible but because the inducements are not sufficient to lead a new producer to embark on the long uphill fight against the well-entrenched monopoly. However if the price of the product is high enough and the monopoly gains great enough, someone is likely sooner or later to make a bid for a share, and so competition starts.[11]

. . . . .

. . . [the reader] will not confuse mere size with monopoly power. Some of the very largest industrial concerns are in active competition with rivals, perhaps equally large. Nor must combinations be confused with monopoly. . . .[12]

. . . . .

[The desire "to secure monopoly profits" is "deeply ingrained"] but there is reason to believe that here the power of organized society, acting through legislation and administration, is strong enough to cope with the situation . . . progress has been made toward check-mating the attacks of those enterprises who are not willing to "play the game" according to the rules. With such influences eliminated, there is good reason for the conclusion that, throughout the greater part of the industrial field, fundamental economic forces are working, not to bring about monopoly, but rather to preserve a state of active competition, none the less intense because it may be often carried on by a relatively small number of powerful rivals.[13]

Despite isolated voices here and there,[14] that is pretty much how matters stood up until the early Thirties. Widely ac-

[11] F. R. Fairchild, E. S. Furniss, and N. S. Buck, *Elementary Economics* (New York: The Macmillan Company, Revised Edition, 1932), Vol. I, p. 359.

[12] Ibid., Vol. II, p. 55.

[13] Ibid., Vol. II, p. 72.

[14] Perhaps the outstanding one, surely one of the most strident, was that of Thorstein Veblen. See Chapters 3 and 4 below.

cepted doctrines favored the defenders, not the critics of big business. On the charge of monopoly, big business as such seemed to have been acquitted.

How this came to pass is a vitally important, even though it is a rather philosophical, point: The basic concepts of the economics of the times worked against the critics. They lacked the necessary, generally recognized analytical tools with which to conceive of, and to think theoretically about, the real world as it appeared to them. They lacked accepted concepts with which to form hypotheses for research, for use in elaborating their ideas, with which to communicate with their fellows at the theoretical level, with which to build up a "case."

The basic categories into which market situations were classified worked against them. Economic theory identified and provided for only two possibilities — a simple dichotomy — into which all market situations were to be categorized: "monopoly" or "competition."[15] And "monopoly"

[15] For instance, the outstanding theoretical work in Anglo-Saxon economics during the first quarter of the Twentieth Century, Alfred Marshall's *Principles of Economics,* provided theoretical analyses for only two categories of firms: "representative" (i.e., competitive) firms and "monopolists." This latter category he illustrated by references to "a gas company that has a monopoly of the supply of gas to a town" and to railways. Marshall himself did feel that "giant businesses" could not fairly be described as "representative" firms. (Appendix H.) (He was inclined to regard a "trust" as a *"prima facie"* monopoly; however, he went on to concede that even in such a case competition has a much greater force than seemed probable *"a priori."*) But he developed no parallel, systematic theory to describe the behavior of "giant businesses" as distinct from that of "representative" firms.

As early as 1838, Augustin Cournot, a Frenchman, had published a theoretical study of the working out of a somewhat different category, corresponding approximately to what is now conceived of as "oligopoly" — the market situation where sellers, especially of identical products, are few in number. For many years this study attracted little attention. Later, the topic was the subject of a rather esoteric discussion by a small group of mathematically inclined economists (see, e.g., F. Y. Edgeworth, *Mathematical Psychics, An Essay on the Application of Mathematics to the Moral Sciences,* London: C. Kegan Paul & Co., 1881 (Reprinted, 1937, by the London School of Economics and Political Science); and "Theory of Monopoly," in *Papers Relating to Political Economy,* London: Macmillan and Co., Ltd., 1925, Vol. I.) But it was generally of little interest to the main body of economists. It is fair to say that they regarded this kind of situation as little more than a curiosity of pure logic — certainly of no practical significance.

as an *economic* concept was such a narrow one, as it was generally understood, that text-book writers were hard put to it to find examples. About all they could come up with to fit this definition were historical trading and commodity monopolies created and protected by government franchise or patent, and — the perennial "monopoly" — the local water company. All other situations, including big business, fell — perforce — into the one remaining category, "competition." The critics were stymied.

In the second place — and this was a consequence of the state of the basic theoretical concepts of economics — the generalizations derived by economics from assumptions, concepts, and deductions current before the Depression, were pretty well lined up against the critics of big business.[16] The defense had seemingly been able to make provision for these new big business entities within the time-hallowed doctrines handed down from the time of Adam Smith — a system of thought which was highly developed and widely understood. Big business, in these lights, was not a novel and congenital departure from the norm of competition. Competition did not cease to exist merely because some businesses were large. Big business needed only to be restrained, as government had been restrained earlier, from interfering with the naturally beneficent process of free enterprise and free competition. In particular, big business needed to be restrained from seeking and obtaining artificial advantage by means of col-

[16] It is probably fair to say, also, that from the beginning many of the critics were unclear in their own minds as to what it was, precisely, that they were opposed to. Thus we find Professor Bullock who, apparently, was opposed to "combinations" which did as much as 65 per cent of the business in their industries, nevertheless affirming at the same time that he was in favor of "large independent companies." ("Trust Literature . . .", p. 192, *et passim.*) But he did not spell out what he meant by "large independent companies." By this reasoning, "large" companies which did x per cent of the business were all right. But companies — "combinations" — which did 65 per cent were not. Where was the line to be drawn? No criterion was given, either in theory or in practical judgment. Such a vague position was necessarily weak. This imprecision of thought in the case pressed by the critics persisted until the advent of the theory of "monopolistic competition."

lusion, price discrimination, and "unfair competition." That done, classical doctrine — with only a little face-lifting — seemed as winsome as ever. Up-dated, the central proposition now ran: The greatest wealth of the nation will be assured if business enterprise, including *big* business enterprise, is truly free to act under the incentive of profit and to pursue its own best interest — free from hampering restrictions imposed by government *or* by big business.

Big business could be covered by the same mantle which economics threw — and still throws — about the wheat farmer. If aberrant behavior on the part of big business could be prevented — and people believed it could — then competition would, as ever, lead to the best of all possible worlds. Competition working on big business in the form of actual and potential entry of rivals would keep prices and profits down and output and quality up.

Critics, despite their intuitions and emotional impulsions, simply didn't have a rigorously and fully developed intellectual brief. The defenders did.

In the early 1930's all this was changed.

After that, the shoe was on the other foot.

The Theory of Monopolistic Competition

In 1933 there were published *The Theory of Monopolistic Competition*[17] by Professor Edward H. Chamberlin of Harvard, and *The Economics of Imperfect Competition*[18] by Mrs. Joan Robinson of Cambridge University. From these works came new concepts for economic thought and new deductive generalizations which rapidly achieved wide currency — generalizations which seemed to confirm the charges that the critics of big business had been advancing for decades. More. Now, at last, the critics were to have access to a widely esteemed and accepted theoretical apparatus — an apparatus

[17] Cambridge: Harvard University Press.
[18] London: Macmillan and Company, Ltd.

which itself was broadly and specifically sympathetic to their point of view.

In particular, these new works, and the scores of others they inspired, provided a systematically worked out theoretical basis for the contention that big business *was* monopolistic, after all. Monopolistic in its very nature. Monopolistic to the point that, though the entry of rivals might or might not compete profits *away* — this is the nub — *prices* would *still* be higher and output smaller than under "competition." [19] Moreover, so generally as to be almost universal, the quality of the goods produced would be inferior, dollar for dollar, as compared to what true — "pure" — competition would provide.

The new theories were snapped up at an "unprecedented pace." [20] Within three years of their appearance, one economist pointed out quite frankly their significance for the critics, not only of *big* business, but of private enterprise generally:

> In the sphere of ethico-economic thought . . . the prospect of widespread recognition of the new theoretical developments is certain, for in them the groping of social welfare advocates for a rationale of public interference in private capitalistic enterprise effectively to combat that of laissez-faire finds glorious realization.[21]

At last the critics could press the charge of monopoly not only with great verve but with seeming intellectual power. In short order, the social and ethical critics attacking for so long on the flanks were joined in the center by a fresh new corps of economic critics. Now they could advance the argument in force not only that big business was undesirable from a social and political and moral point of view — which they

[19] Now, strictly speaking, *"pure"* competition.

[20] Robert Triffin, *Monopolistic Competition and General Equilibrium Theory* (Cambridge: Harvard University Press, 1940), p. 17.

[21] Horace G. White, Jr., "A Review of Monopolistic and Imperfect Competition Theories," *American Economic Review,* Vol. XXVI, No. 4, December, 1936, p. 649.

had long contended — but that it could no longer be condoned even as an efficient expedient toward material welfare.

Especially far-reaching, so far as thought in the United States was concerned, was the contribution of Professor Chamberlin: the theory of "monopolistic competition." By providing a highly developed basis for identifying big business with a new, latter-day version of "monopoly," this work re-opened an avenue of attack that had been blocked for over a decade. By providing a set of generalizations relating to the shortcomings of this new version of "monopoly," it supplied — ready-made — a number of specific charges which the critics were immediately to cast at big business.

We cannot here go into the details and intricacies of Professor Chamberlin's assumptions and line of reasoning.[22] There is space and time merely to note the major points and conclusions of his theory. This done, we shall go on to review the attack as it has been elaborated and worked out over the past twenty years.

To go back for a moment before taking up the theory of "monopolistic competition" to pick up the thread: The theoretical defense of the "combinations" and, later, of big business generally, had rested its case on two major propositions. First, it was said, true monopoly was scarcely to be found in real life. At most, there was concentration of business in some industries in the hands of a small number of firms. Under the motivation of self-interest and profit-seeking these

22 For a popularized version of the main outline of the theory see H. S. Dennison and J. K. Galbraith, *Modern Competition and Business Policy*, (New York: Oxford University Press, 1938). For textbook versions, see Paul A. Samuelson, *Economics, An Introductory Analysis* (New York: McGraw-Hill Book Company, Inc., First Edition, 1948), Chapter 21; and Albert L. Meyers, *Elements of Modern Economics* (New York: Prentice-Hall, Inc., Revised Edition, 1941), various chapters. Professor Richard S. Meriam, in his article "Bigness and the Economic Analysis of Competition," *Harvard Business Review*, Vol. XXVIII, No. 2, March, 1950, makes a number of comments which throw light on the relationship between the theory and the criticism of big business. A recent comprehensive exposition of theoretical models of various kinds of competitive situations is Fritz Machlup's, *The Economics of Sellers' Competition* (Baltimore: The Johns Hopkins Press, 1952).

firms would compete with one another. That is, they would, if prevented from entering into collusive agreements and understandings. This competition among the few relatively large firms would give buyers and the public at large at least as good results as competition among a larger number of smaller ones. Probably better.

Second, it was said that potential competitors — "interlopers" — were always lurking about on the sidelines of every situation, ready to enter any field where more than normal profits were being made. The pressure of this competition — even of merely potential competition — would operate to keep prices down and output and quality up.

The theory of monopolistic competition struck directly and heavily at these two points.

In opposition, the theory of monopolistic competition built up an argument to show that where the number of competitors is small — the case of "oligopoly" — the results in terms of price and total output of the group will necessarily tend to approximate those which are characteristic of what might be called true monopoly. These results would come to pass quite apart from, and quite independently of any collusion. The monopolistic results of "oligopoly," it was said, involve "no combination — not even a tacit agreement among the sellers." [23] Monopolistic results, by this theory, are inherent in small numbers and intelligent self-interest.

Compressed and simplified, the reasoning runs thus: Where the number of sellers is small, aggressive behavior on the part of any one competitor has immediate and perceptible impact on all the others. In self-defense, they would have to respond to such behavior by retaliation. The originator of this chain-reaction might then have to retaliate in turn. This would give rise to further reaction, and so on. Such aggression, retaliation, and counter-retaliation — stopping goodness knows where — would leave the entire group, including the initiator

[23] See *The Theory of Monopolistic Competition,* Sixth Edition, 1950, Chapter III, especially pp. 46–54 and pp. 100–106.

of the whole thing, in a position far inferior to what they could all enjoy if he had only refrained from starting the whole business in the first place.

But since each competitor is intelligent and has foresight, each is perfectly aware in advance of what the consequences of aggressive behavior would be. And, since each is interested in maximizing his profit, each, in fact holds back from aggressive action. Since they all refrain from aggressive behavior, the net result is the same that would come about if they actually had a noncompetitive compact among themselves or if the whole group were consolidated into one monopolistic firm. Thus, if each of the "oligopolists"

> . . . seeks his maximum profit rationally and intelligently, he will realize that when there are only two or a few sellers his own move has a considerable effect upon his competitors, and that this makes it idle to suppose that they will accept without retaliation the losses he forces upon them. Since the result of a cut by any one is inevitably to decrease his own profits, no one will cut, and, although the sellers are entirely independent, the equilibrium result is the same as though there were a monopolistic agreement between them. . . . No one would cut from the monopoly figure because he would force others to follow him, and thereby work his own undoing. . . .
>
> If sellers have regard to their *total* influence upon price, the price will be the monopoly one. Independence of the producers and the pursuit of their self-interest are not sufficient to lower it.[24]

[24] Ibid., pp. 48–54. (Italics in original.) The passage refers, necessarily, to what might be termed a *perfectly* operating oligopoly. The argument, as set forth here specifically relates to the situation where the sellers offer identical products. But this case illustrates the "nature of the problem and the chief forces at work" even when they are offering somewhat different — "differentiated" — products, say different makes of automobiles. (See ibid., pp. 100 and following.) Compare: ". . . each firm is taught the lesson that other firms will not stand idly by while it cuts its prices; rather, they too will cut their prices so that everyone will end up worse off. Therefore, tacitly or explicitly, the firms try to agree on a price that maximizes the profit of all. . . ." — Paul A. Samuelson, *Economics, An Introductory Analysis,* p. 513.

That is, depending on particular circumstances, when sellers are few, prices may attain, and *remain* at any level up to the point where each seller realizes a sort of true monopoly profit, without anyone being prompted to undercut. And no collusion whatever is needed to bring this about.[25]

In brief, this was the spearhead of the attack on the defenders' traditional first point — that big businesses would give perfectly satisfactory results by competing among themselves.

As to the defenders' second point — concerning the influence of the *entry* or the *potential entry* of new competitors — Chamberlin's theory seemed to provide the means for battering down that one also. The theory built up the argument that, in the first place, the entry of newcomers might *not* eliminate all monopoly profits. In the second place, even if it did — so the theory ran — prices would still be higher, and utilization of capacity and quality of product would be lower than under "pure competition."

Tactically, one of the most important of Chamberlin's

[25] The idea that "oligopoly" — especially *big* "oligopoly" — necessarily leads to monopolistic results even in the absence of collusion has some potentially important implications for the interpretation of the Sherman Act. Such a view would lead, first, to the idea that Section 1 of the Act, directed at *willful* conspiracy and contracts in restraint of trade, does not really strike at the heart of the matter, since such knowing collusion of this sort is essentially superfluous or, in any event, of secondary importance.

Second, if "oligopoly" *inherently* and *per se* leads to monopolistic results, perhaps it could be argued that "oligopoly" itself is *inherently* and *per se* a violation of Section 2 of the Act, which holds that "Every person who shall monopolize . . . shall be held guilty of a misdemeanor." This line of reasoning would open up the possibility of using the Act to attack big business corporations, not on the grounds that they are *big* — as in the "Steel" and "Harvester" cases — but on the grounds they are *few*.

This possibility of a new line of attack to get around the doctrines of the "Steel" and "Harvester" decisions, has apparently appealed to some who, within the past few years, have held key positions in the Department of Justice. See, for example, the testimony of Mr. Herbert Bergson, then Assistant Attorney General in charge of the Anti-trust Division, before the Celler Committee, *Study of Monopoly Power,* Part 1, pp. 365–366; and *A Study of the Development of the Anti-trust Laws and Current Problems of Anti-trust Enforcement,* Report of the Department of Justice to the Subcommittee on Monopoly of the Select Committee on Small Business, 82nd Cong., 2nd Sess. (Washington: Government Printing Office, 1952).

arguments as to the results of "monopolistic competition" was that monopolistic prices, monopolistic output, and monopolistic quality — inferior, that is, dollar for dollar — are entirely consistent with profits no greater than purely competitive profits. For this conclusion meant that the absence of monopolistic profits in an industry, or on the part of any one company, could *not* be taken as demonstrating that price, output, and quality were the equivalents of those of competition. In other words, the absence of monopoly profits, by these lights, was no proof that the equivalent results of pure competition were being obtained.

In the first place, where there is "product differentiation" — where sellers are able to differentiate themselves, or their products, from one another in consequence of patents, trademarks, brand names, exclusive designs, and so on — strictly speaking there cannot *be* freedom of entry.[26] Others cannot come into an industry where the profits of the field as a whole are greater than the general competitive level, and compete directly with the sellers of differentiated products by producing and selling items identical with those already being offered. They can only produce and offer *alternative* items. These may be more or less satisfactory substitutes. The more satisfactory they are as alternatives, from the buyer's point of view, the more likely they are to cut away some of the original sellers' markets and their profits. But the less satisfactory, the less can they make a dent. In any given industry, newcomers will find it easier to take away sales — and profits — from some of the competitors than from others. As a result of these varying degrees of imperviousness on the part of the several sellers to the competition of new substitute articles, monopoly profits will be left "scattered through the group — and throughout the price system." [27]

Moreover, "oligopoly" — fewness of sellers — may be combined with "product differentiation" to produce a situation

[26] Edward Chamberlin, op. cit., pp. 200–204.
[27] Ibid., p. 113.

where an industry is composed, for instance, of a "Big 3" or a "Big 4" who offer products which, while they are alternatives, are not identical. These "oligopolists," for reasons we have seen, are not likely to pursue an aggressive price policy. And the cost of their differentiated products will be greater than would be the cost of generically similar but undifferentiated products produced under "pure" competition. Thus, prices in this kind of industry are necessarily at least one stage higher than under pure competition, and may go considerably higher even than that.

> . . . Certainly, over a wide range of economic activity, the price not only *must,* on account of a differentiated product, be higher than the purely competitive level . . .; it *may* rest at any higher point up to a figure which would maximize the joint profits of those whose markets are related.[28]

Thus, potential competition and even actual entry, the theory holds, cannot necessarily eliminate all monopoly profits nor will it bring about the price of "pure" competition where there are reasons for buyers to distinguish among sellers, and/or the number of sellers is small.

In the second place, the theory went on to contend that even if monopoly profits *are* eliminated, prices will nevertheless be higher, utilization of capacity will be lower, and quality of product will be inferior when the number of competitors is small and/or products are differentiated.

The chain of deduction by which these conclusions are reached is an extended one, and the assumptions involved are numerous. We won't go into them here. The chain of reasoning relates to firms which are producing — so to speak — varieties of a *given* species of product (say, the automobiles of 1953) by means of *given* productive techniques and which are selling in a *given* market.[29] It describes in highly abstract

[28] Ibid., p. 104. (Italics in original.)

[29] In the course of reaching its final, static equilibrium position, a firm in "monopolistic competition" may experiment with and produce different "varieties" of the given "species" of the product. The firm may add or change

terms how these firms work their way — by competitive action, reaction, and interaction — to a final, static equilibrium position. This is the ultimate state of things when all the original given data and forces have thoroughly worked themselves out and have run down to a halt. The theory also describes how firms under "pure" competition — where the sellers are many and their products identical — work *their* way to a final, static equilibrium position. The conclusions of the theory are then derived by comparing the ultimate

---

various gimmicks. But the "species" itself is *given*. It is not originated. It does not evolve. It does not become extinct.

In the static world of this theory little, if any, account is taken of the competition for survival and growth between different species of products within their genus – for example, of the competition among the various kinds of edible vegetable oils: corn oil, olive oil, cottonseed oil, peanut oil, soybean oil, etc. No account is taken of the competition which may exist between one genus of products and another – say, between vegetable oils and animal fats; or among the different kinds of fuels: various kinds of coal versus each other, and all versus various petroleum distillates and natural gas. Nor, of course, is account taken of the competition which may exist among even larger orders and classes of products. No account, for instance, is taken of the fact that a maker of television sets has to compete for the buyer's dollar, not only against other makers of television sets, but against makers of broadloom rugs, winter resorts in Florida, and, even, savings banks and life insurance companies.

The essentially static world that the theory is concerned with is highlighted by the concept that the "oligopolist" maximizes his profit by refraining from aggressive behavior. Such passive behavior as is visualized for the "oligopolist" is consistent with the concept that he and his competitors are concerned with the exploitation of *given* opportunities and markets for a *given* species of product, using *given* techniques. For there, the problem would be, How can they best – from the point of view of *all* of them – divide up a *given* "pie"? The answer is, By static, forbearing behavior.

In contrast, the maximum exploitation of *dynamic* opportunities, in which products, markets, and techniques are all *in flux,* would seem to call for dynamic and aggressive – in any event, adaptive – rather than static and passive behavior. It is dynamic behavior, of course, that is associated with the appearance of new species of products, and their evolution, and the extinction of others.

The fact is, the theory of monopolistic competition was not concerned with the processes whereby a new species, genus, or family of products originates – for example, the development of various kinds of synthetic fibres. Nor is any account taken of the processes involved in the adaptation and descent of species – how, for example, it came to pass that the automobiles of 1953 are different from the automobiles of 1933. Nor is account taken of the processes whereby species become extinct – like some of the early sulfa drugs, lisle stockings, and the Marcel wave.

Nor is account taken that productive processes undergo more or less con-

static equilibrium position which is deduced for firms in "monopolistic" competition against the ultimate static equilibrium position which is deduced for firms in "pure" competition.

These are the conclusions as stated by Professor Chamberlin, himself:

> . . . Competition, in so far as it consists of a movement of resources into the industry, reduces profits to the competitive level, but leaves prices higher to a degree dependent upon the strength of the monopoly elements. Competitive profits, then, never mean competitive prices under monopolistic competition. . . .
>
> In the second place, the price is inevitably higher and the scale of production inevitably smaller under monopolistic competition than under pure competition. . . .[30]
>
> . . . . .
>
> The conclusion seems warranted that just as, for a given "product," price is inevitably higher under monopolistic than under pure competition, so, for a given price, "product" is inevitably somewhat inferior. After all, these two propositions are but two aspects of a single one. If a seller could, by the larger scale of production which is characteristic of pure as compared with monopolistic competition, give

---

stant change — that industries, for example, develop new, specialized tools, and methods for training personnel and handling materials. Productive techniques — the "physiology" of production — are *given* to begin with and are assumed to remain unchanged.

No account is taken that markets — demand — may be created, fundamentally altered, or closed, not only for individual varieties of goods but for whole species, genera, and families; not just by impersonal forces, but in consequence of deliberate efforts by particular firms.

In technical phrase, the theory does not conceive of, nor provide for dynamic, evolutionary, ecological processes.

As a philosophical aside, one can speculate that this is because the theory is descended from a mechanistic, deterministic philosophy rather than from an organic, evolutionary one. But to pursue that idea would take us far afield indeed.

[30] Ibid., p. 88. See, also, pp. 77–78. There are points — this is one — at which Chamberlin, himself, seems to set up implicitly the dichotomy: "monopolistic competition" and "pure competition."

> the same "product" for less money, he could, similarly, give a better "product" for the same money. . . .[31]

In sum, when the number of sellers is small, and/or products are differentiated, the optimum results of "pure competition" cannot be equalled, even if new competitors — "interlopers" — stream into the field, and even if monopoly profits are all eliminated.

Thus it was that the new theory seemed to set at naught the two principal forces which economic doctrine previously believed would hold monopoly power in check: competition among the firms already in the field, and the competition of newcomers. As the efficacy of these two checks were denied, the two major propositions of the defense against the charge of monopoly also apparently went by the board.

The theory having been carried up to this point, it was but a matter of simple logical extension to develop ideas as to the adverse effects which "monopolistic competition" has on the operation of the economy as a whole. Since ideas of this sort have been so very important in the economic attack on big business, we shall sample a few.

Renewal of the Monopoly Charge

Many economists hold that "pure competition" — the competition among large numbers of sellers of undifferentiated products — combined with perfectly working processes of adjustment, leads to an "ideal" national product. Item by item, supply is adjusted perfectly to demand. Product by product, the price mechanism functions perfectly to call forth additional supplies when desired and to curtail production when less is wanted. Labor and capital are distributed among all various possible uses in such a way as to command their highest possible compensation while at the same time turning out a national product of ideal composition. In no case could the "mix" of this national product be improved

[31] Ibid., p. 99.

by curtailing the production of any one product in order to produce more of another. It sometimes appears that some theorists believe there would be no booms and depressions under "pure" and "perfect" competition — all costs, prices, wages, and the like being so nicely and quickly adjusted as to keep the economy going along at full capacity at all times. All products, as we have seen would, of course, be produced at minimum cost. Any improvements in efficiency would circulate, if not instantly, at least quickly, among all producers in such a way that only the most efficient methods would ever be used.[32]

But under "monopolistic competition" these benign results are not achieved. In particular, because of oligopolistic "jurisdiction over price," the business world is said to lack "the self-regulating character which is present when competition involves no such jurisdiction." [33] Because of this, the national product suffers. As to the quantity of each of the various goods which is produced, it is only an accident if the amount desired by society coincides with the amount which gives the greatest profit to the producer.[34] The price charged by the monopolistic firm, of course, is higher. In consequence, the national product is not made up of what people *really* want.

[32] See, for example, the description by H. S. Dennison and J. K. Galbraith, *Modern Competition and Business Policy*, pp. 13–18.

Actually, however, there is no general theory as to how technological change and product and market development can take place under "pure competition." For "pure competition" – like "monopolistic competition" – is an essentially static concept. Indeed, some economic critics have been among those who have advocated – perhaps quite soundly, so far as that goes – that government research agencies should be set up to aid *small* business in research and developmental work in much the same way that state and national research agencies assist agriculture. The reason given in both cases is that small scale undertakings cannot engage in development of their own to the significant degree that is socially desirable because of their small size and the probability that others who had borne no part of the cost would share fully in all benefits.

[33] Ibid., p. 31. This is an expression of the vision which equates the "ideal" state of things to a "self-regulating," deterministic mechanism. We shall see more of this concept later on.

[34] Ibid., p. 33.

> . . . Consumers who would be willing to purchase larger quantities of [the firm's] product at lower prices are forced instead, to buy goods that are wanted less. Capital and labor are thus diverted from those things which the community prefers to those which are, at best, a second choice.[35]

This, of course, is bad enough. But this diversion of capital and labor has another unfortunate result. The economy loses the benefit of their fullest productivity:

> The resources that are excluded from the superior occupation compete with others for employment in inferior ones and their productivity declines.[36]

And "the consumer" is "plundered":

> . . . wherever there is ability to control price and supply there is a potential danger of exploitation and, indeed, of "plunder" of the consumer. . . . In fact, which form the "plunder" of the consumer may take can only be surmised.[37]

Not only are prices likely to be too high and too rigid because of "oligopoly" but, oddly enough perhaps, "oligopoly" may also lead to price wars, and prices may become too low. This will give rise to economic waste and impaired wage standards.[38]

"Monopolistic competition" leads to other kinds of waste. Individual plants operate short of the capacity point where they would have lowest average costs. This means, because of "monopolistic competition," that the economy's investment in plant is inefficiently used.

And then, there is the waste of advertising and other selling efforts. Since — it is assumed — the wants of society are given, and since — it is assumed — the national income is

[35] Clair Wilcox, *Competition and Monopoly in American Industry,* T.N.E.C. Monograph No. 21; Senate Committee Print, 76th Cong., 3rd Sess. (Washington: Government Printing Office, 1940), p. 16.

[36] Ibid.

[37] K. William Kapp, *The Social Costs of Private Enterprise* (Cambridge: Harvard University Press, 1950), p. 177.

[38] See *Modern Competition and Business Policy,* pp. 38–44.

fixed, the only result of expenditures on advertising and selling is to divert business from one seller to another. As a result of advertising outlays, for example, ". . . demand for the advertised product is increased, that for other products is correspondingly diminished." [39] This is fine for the successful individual seller. But there is no social advantage. The national "pie" is no bigger; it is just cut and distributed differently. Accordingly, all the resources which go into selling and promotion are necessarily just so much waste from a social point of view.

Indeed, there is scarcely any end, in theory, to the social waste of "monopolistic competition." It may take subtle forms. Even the efforts of large corporations to improve their efficiency is likely to be a social waste. For instance:

> If the efficiency of the large unit is improved so that it yields normal profits upon a capital which does not include promotion profits, the large unit has been rendered economical, but no more so than the formerly existing small ones. Unless the changes introduced can be applied to smaller firms or to firms in other industries these activities of the management have resulted in the application of part of the aggregate social fund of skill and knowledge available for increasing the efficiency of production to no more economically valuable an end than increasing the range of the size of the most economical firm in the industry. . . .[40]

We need go no further. More examples would simply add more detail. The purport of these ideas is clear: "monopolistic competition" is inimical to society's economic welfare.[41]

[39] *The Theory of Monopolistic Competition,* Sixth Edition, p. 120. See, also, *Modern Competition and Business Policy,* op. cit., pp. 44–48. This, of course, assumes that advertising and selling efforts have no dynamic effect on the *size* or composition of the national "pie," only its allocation and its distribution.

[40] Arthur Robert Burns, *The Decline of Competition* (New York: McGraw-Hill Book Company, Inc., 1936), pp. 9–10, footnote 2.

[41] Professor Chamberlin has stated that he does not regard *"pure competition"* as *"in any sense an 'ideal' for purposes of welfare economics."* (Italics in original.) (Op. cit., p. 214.) But others building on his theory, however,

This, then, is the theory of "monopolistic competition." It concludes with some profoundly serious charges against competition which is not "pure."

Once the theory was formulated, it was only necessary to equate "big business" with "monopolistic competition," in order to mobilize the concepts of the theory and its generalizations on the side of the attack. Once this was done, all that could be said about "monopolistic competition" could then, automatically, be said about "big business." The equation was easy to make, and the theory was quickly brought to bear. How this equation was made, and how the theory has been used in the attack will be our next subjects.

Expansion of the Monopoly Charge

In the theory of "monopolistic competition" as enunciated by Chamberlin, himself, *size* as such does not figure as a monopolistic factor. For Chamberlin, the monopolistic elements were small *numbers* and product differentiation. Strictly speaking, Chamberlin's theory applies just as much to *small* business as to large. A small number of *small* competitors, by this theory, is just as monopolistic as a small number of large competitors. Strictly speaking, Chamberlin's theory of monopolistic competition was not, in and of itself, a part of the attack on *big* business. But it provided critics with a *rationale* for their attack.

An immediate effect of the theory was to displace the old categories of "competition" and "monopoly" from economic thinking. It is true that Professor Chamberlin, himself, thought he was describing an intermediate category — "monopolistic competition" — a "blend of competition and monopoly" which, apparently, shaded off in one direction into

---

very explicitly *do* hold up "pure competition" as the ideal. For example, see Dennison and Galbraith, *Monopolistic Competition and Public Policy.* For some further views, see e.g., Joe S. Bain, *Price Theory* (New York: Henry Holt and Company, 1952), especially pp. 339–376; and George J. Cady, *Economics of Business Enterprise* (New York: The Ronald Press Company, 1950), especially Part V.

"pure" competition, and in the other direction into "pure" monopoly.[42] So conceived, the new category would have been the intermediate band in a continuous spectrum of situations ranging from one extreme limit to its opposite. But, in fact, the theory led, at the hands of others, to the setting up of a new pair of mutually exclusive, opposing categories — a new dichotomy: "pure competition" and "monopolistic competition." All market situations, in this view, were still to be classified "either, or." Only now, the two categories available for the classification of economic phenomena had been changed. Now, all producers were to be divided as between "pure" or "perfect" *competitors* and *monopolists* — thus:

> A monopolist is not a fat, greedy man with a big moustache and cigar who goes around violating the law. . . . *He is anyone important enough to affect the prices of the things that he sells and buys.* To some degree that means almost every businessman, except possibly the millions of farmers who individually produce a negligible fraction of the total crop. . . .
>
> The ["ordinary businessman"] is not a perfect competitor in the economist's sense . . . he is not like a perfectly competitive farm producer.[43]

Explicitly or tacitly — as above — the new dichotomy came to underlie, and so to color, much of the economic thought of the past twenty years.

[42] See *The Theory of Monopolistic Competition,* pp. 4–5, 63–64, 195, 205, 208, *et passim.* Actually, there are some difficulties attaching to the idea of "pure" – in the sense of *absolute* – monopoly. Absolute monopoly could be attained only if it were a monopoly of *all* substitutes. But since all products, even if only to a negligible extent, are substitutes for all others, no *absolute* monopoly could be attained short of a monopoly of *all* products. (See *The Theory of Monopolistic Competition,* p. 63.) No such difficulty attaches to the idea of "pure competition." All that is required is that the number of competitors be sufficiently large that they all behave with absolute disregard for the impact of their actions on others and upon the market generally. This lack of symmetry may have contributed to the setting up of the new dichotomy described just below.

[43] Paul A. Samuelson, *Economics, An Introductory Analysis,* p. 39. (Italics in original.)

This new dichotomy worked powerfully to the advantage of the critics of big business and against the defenders. On the one hand, there was the concept of *pure* competition. And into this category, so strait was the gate and so narrow was the way that few other than farmers could enter. On the other hand, there was *monopolistic* competition. And into this bracket, perforce, fell everything else, including big business.

Now it was the defenders who were stymied. They were "boxed in" by the available and prevailing concepts of economics. Now, business — especially *big* business — was set apart from truly, "purely" competitive enterprise. The new concepts, in themselves, made a variety of *prima facie* case against big business.

That was one thing that the theory did for the critics.

Another was the fact that the theory, by means of the generalizations it cast up as to the results of monopolistic competition, put a whole new series of charges within easy reach of the critics of big business. The critics needed only to identify big business with "monopolistic competition," and immediately all the conclusions of the theory could be brought to bear in their attack.

This identification was easy to make. *Big* business necessarily entails *small numbers.* And big business quite generally produces "differentiated" products — articles which are sold under brand names and which have special, unique features. Thus, it embodies both of the two elements which the theory holds are the bases of "monopolistic competition." These things being so, all the conclusions relating to the category of "monopolistic competition" seemed necessarily to apply to big business.

The identification being made, the critics could turn the full battery of the conclusions of the theory onto big business at will.[44] Not only could they apply the general con-

[44] "Big business" is a term which is not much used nowadays by economists. They are more likely to use the term "oligopoly," or some less for-

clusions, but they could use its many parts in casting up a variety of particular criticisms.

One of the earliest, and certainly one of the most influential, works to identify big business with "oligopoly" was the book *The Decline of Competition* by Professor Arthur R. Burns of Columbia University. His line of reasoning set the pattern which many have followed since: Big business is "oligopolistic" because the large firm cannot act without regard to the consequences of its own actions:

> . . . It is a commonplace that the number of firms in many industries has been falling. In many markets, e.g., those for steel, automobiles, rubber tires, sugar, corn products, electrical products, air transportation, agricultural implements, the number is already too small for sellers to ignore the effect of changes in their output upon the price of the commodity and, therefore, upon their revenue. . . .
>
> The characteristic of industrial organization during the present century is the growth of firms large enough in relation to their industries as a whole for it to be irrational for them to disregard the effect of changes in their output, or

---

bidding counterpart, such as "corporate concentration." Or they may speak of "concentration of economic power," or "substantial control of the market." Or, departing from the restricted meaning of traditional and legal usage, they may even speak simply of "monopoly" and "monopolists."

For practical purposes, and in the niceties of theory, the terms have wide interchangeability. They all refer to the departures from "pure" competition which economists associate with market situations where the number of firms is less than "many," and where, by the same token but speaking less strictly, their size is greater than "small."

For example, Professor B. S. Keirstead, in the space of just a few paragraphs, uses the terms "trusts," "great size," "conditions of monopolistic competition," "oligopoly," "monopoly," "large-scale organization," "monopolistic industry," and "monopolists" as substantially synonymous terms. (*The Theory of Economic Change*, pp. 361–364.) He puts in one and the same category such companies as Bell Telephone, Canadian Industries, Ltd., and the "newsprint firms." According to the theory as it is commonly understood, this is quite acceptable usage and practice, since these various terms imply no *qualitative* differences. At most, and if anything, they imply only vague differences in degree. This, of course, is a consequence of the idea that there are only the two categories, "pure competition" and "monopolistic competition."

> their price policy, upon the market as a whole; they must take account of the effect of a reduction in price not only upon the volume of their sales but also upon the total revenue from these sales. They find themselves in the position of a monopolist in that, in pursuit of the maximum of income, they must choose the best combination of price and sales, having regard for the effect of changes in output upon costs. . . .[45]

This is the same line of thinking followed by Corwin D. Edwards in his book *Maintaining Competition.* (Dr. Edwards until recently was Chief Economist and Director of the Bureau of Industrial Economics of the Federal Trade Commission) —

> . . . If activity is concentrated under the control of two or three *large* business units, if sales are not greatly reduced by high prices, and if no one of the *large* sellers has a strong incentive to seek additional business as a means of reducing unit costs, each *large* enterprise, acting separately, may prefer a policy of high prices and reduced sales. Each *large* seller is likely to believe that aggressive competition will evoke aggressive retaliation by the other *large* concern and that to live and let live is more profitable. Where each has a similar incentive for a policy of high prices, each is encouraged to adopt it by belief that the other is more likely than not to follow suit. Thus there is a tendency for the number of effective competitive alternatives to be reduced still further by adoption of similar selling policies. Moreover, collusion, explicit or tacit, becomes easier with each reduction in the number of competitors. As business units become few and *large,* the vigor of competition tends to be reduced and business policies tend to become monopolistic in character.[46]

[45] Pp. 8 and 40–41.

[46] Corwin D. Edwards, *Maintaining Competition* (New York: McGraw-Hill Book Company, Inc., 1949), pp. 93–94. (Italics added.) Compare: ". . . where three or four firms control more than two-thirds of the industry . . . each manager of a major firm knows that each of the others is similarly concerned to maintain a satisfactory market price and will rate his production to that end. The industry has an historical pattern of the share of the business to be enjoyed by each of the leaders, and each manager keeps within that pat-

So much for the kind of behavior which is automatically to be attributed to individual large corporations in consequence of their having been identified with "monopolistic competition" and "oligopoly." The argument having reached this stage, it is but a short step to extend the line of thought to develop ideas as to what must be the consequences of bigness in business for the economy as a whole.[47]

A whole body of ideas has come into being which holds that with the rise of big business, the American economy has departed from the ideal system of pure competition. Competition, it is said, formerly assured the production of maximum economic welfare and the optimum national product, and protected the economic interests of all. In the opinion of many economists, big business, because it is "oligopolistic" leads the economy away from these benign results. To this way of thinking, the rise and spread of big business has made for an economy which departs from the ideal in every particular. Such, for example, is the burden of the following excerpt from a postwar report of the Federal Trade Commission to Congress:

> Consumers, smaller producers, workers, farmers — all are assumed to be protected by this invisible force [pure compe-

tern while adjusting his production to changes in demand. Each is confident that the one thing his nominal competitor will not do is to cut price in order to maintain production and sales." — The Council of Economic Advisers, *Third Annual Report to the President* (Washington: Government Printing Office, 1948), p. 17. See, also, the statement of Dr. John D. Clark, of the Council of Economic Advisers, *Study of Monopoly Power*, Part 1, pp. 109–110. For a still further example of the identification of oligopoly with *big* business, see the testimony of Dr. Walter Adams, ibid., p. 338.

[47] Not only has big business been identified with "oligopoly" and "monopolistic competition," but the equation has been reversed by some, so that — at their hands — "oligopoly" and "monopolistic competition" became identified with *big* business only, rather than with business of *any* size where numbers are few and/or products are differentiated. Some critics simply set up this reverse equation and proceed from there. Dr. Edwards reverses the equation after arguing that so long as the power of firms that are smaller than big can be "neither pyramid nor consolidated, its existence may be regarded as consistent with competition." (*Maintaining Competition*, pp. 107–108.)

tition]. It keeps open the opportunities for improvement and advancement and yet prevents the abuses of size and power. It absorbs revolutionary technological and economic changes and yet requires no revolution in our system of government. It is no exaggeration to say that the theory of competition has been the heart of the American philosophical and political system.

So much for the theory; but what of the actuality? In practice, competition has proved to be a somewhat crudely working but, on the whole, highly effective theory and system. Yet, it would be blindness not to recognize the obvious fact that the effectiveness of competition, as the protector of the public interest, has been seriously weakened during the last several decades. In industry after industry, prices, production, employment and, in fact, all forms of economic activity have come under the domination of the Big Four, the Big Six, or in some cases, the leader.[48]

The general purport and the inevitable implication of ideas like this, I take it, are that the American economy would have progressed and prospered far beyond where it is, had it not been for big business.

In this vein, perhaps the most important single charge against big business is that, because of monopolistic price policies and practices, it has made the American economy unstable from a cyclical point of view. Less has been heard on this score of late than during the years before the war. And many economists do not hold with such an idea.[49] But

[48] *Report on the Merger Movement* (Washington: Government Printing Office, 1948), p. 68. This, of course, is also an expression of the idea that production in the American economy is more concentrated now than at some former time. This is a widely held view among the critics of big business. I shall take up this idea again, and at some greater length, in Chapter 5 below.

[49] See, for example, Alfred C. Neal, *Industrial Concentration and Price Inflexibility* (Washington: American Council on Public Affairs, 1942); E. M. Doblin, "Some Aspects of Price Flexibility," *Review of Economic Statistics*, Vol. 22, 1940; D. H. Wallace, "Industrial Markets and Public Policy" in *Public Policy*, C. J. Friedrich and E. S. Mason, editors (Cambridge: Harvard University Press, 1940); Jules Backman, "Price Flexibility and Changes in Production," *Conference Board Bulletin*, Vol. XIII, No. 5, 1939.

it still has its partisans among the more thorough-going critics. For instance:

> . . . the free-wheeling bandwagon of big business came to an abrupt and painful halt late in 1929. Critics of the era and its developments, looking back on the course of events, point out that the rampant and unchecked growth of "bigness" during the 1920's brought with it a short-sighted and muscle-bound private control over the economy that produced a rigidity in the price system primarily responsible for the extreme severity and depth of the 1929–32 depression.
>
> . . . . .
>
> Once trouble appeared on the economic horizon, production and output were reduced to hold up prices and profits. Labor was laid off and payrolls and purchasing power fell off, thus necessitating still further cuts in production, shrinking purchasing power still more, and on and on in a vicious downward spiral.[50]

Beyond such general pictures of the harm that big business inflicts on the American economy, the particular undesirable results which various writers have described are legion. Here, from a well-known textbook, is a sort of compendium

[50] Report of the Department of Justice to the Subcommittee on Monopoly of the Select Committee on Small Business, *A Study of the Development of the Anti-trust Laws and Current Problems of Anti-trust Enforcement,* p. 8. See, also, the colloquy between Mr. H. Graham Morrison, Assistant Attorney General, Anti-trust Division, Department of Justice, and Senator Russell B. Long in *Hearings before a Subcommittee of the Select Committee on Small Business,* 82nd Cong., 2nd Sess. (Washington: Government Printing Office, 1952), Part I, p. 62.

For a further recent expression of this thought, see statement of Everett M. Kassalow, Associate Director of Research of the CIO, in the "Panel Discussion of the Economics and Legality of Bigness," *Current Business Studies,* No. 5, February, 1950, pp. 39–41, 57–58.

For earlier expressions of the same idea, see, for example, National Resources Committee, *The Structure of the American Economy,* Part I (Washington: Government Printing Office, 1939); and T.N.E.C., *Investigation of Concentration of Economic Power,* Part 1, *Economic Prologue,* especially p. 187.

of the most important particular failings which economic critics have seen in big business (equals "substantial control of the market" equals "corporate concentration" equals "faulty control of production" equals "the large corporation" equals "monopoly"):

> Monopoly seems to offer no production gains to offset its essential fault. A certain amount of the labor and other productive resources of the country are kept out of the monopolized field and are forced into other employments. And they produce a smaller value product than they otherwise would. This loss does not seem to be offset by any marketing or production advantages of monopoly.
>
> Many related evils grow out of the faulty control of production. In a number of instances substantial control of the market has brought injury to the consumer in the form of high prices; and it always leaves the consumer with inadequate defenses against deterioration in the quality of goods. Labor may be forced to sell its services without the presence of the competitive bidding needed to protect wages and conditions of employment. The small enterpriser is robbed of an opportunity or is placed in a vulnerable position if he pits his little strength against the power of the monopolist. By pouring large incomes into a few hands monopoly generally decreases the economic satisfactions derived from the national income. The concentration of ownership present in the large corporation means that monopoly profits increase an already excessive inequality in the distribution of income.
>
> In addition to creating a continuing economic waste in the restriction of production, the single firm adds seriously to the instability of industrial production. When economic conditions change in various phases of the business cycle the prices of monopolized goods remain much more stable than other prices. The rigidity not only increases the impact of depression and prosperity changes in the monopoly industries, but distorts the connection between monopolistic and competitive fields. Particularly in recession periods may such maladjustments create serious injury. An unnecessary amount of unemployment is created in the monopolized fields and an

injurious rigidity of costs is laid on any industry using the monopolized products.[51]

So.

Conclusion

The charge that big business is monopolistic has become highly systematized. The bill of particulars has been extended. From its modest beginnings of more than half a century ago, it has come a long way. But it still rests on the same basic proposition that it did then — on the belief that there is an ideal economic mechanism, and that it is made up of myriads of small, individually negligible producing units.

This basic proposition is supplemented and rounded out by the idea, which we saw earlier, that small units are also, in themselves, the most efficient component parts for that ideal mechanism. Together, and reinforcing each other, these two ideas give rise to a body of thought inevitably and implacably hostile toward big business.

It wasn't so very long ago that big business had a *rationale* that seemed entirely secure. But the economic attack overwhelmed this system of thought and left it a shambles. As of now, there simply does not exist an integrated, rigorous, systematic theory which justifies big business as a means for organizing economic life. More than that. In the opinion of many, the economic attack has succeeded in placing big business beyond the pale of the traditional justification of free enterprise.[52]

Perhaps this ideological situation may change in the course of the next decade. For the economic criticism of big business rests upon a theoretical apparatus that may be displaced

[51] Reprinted by permission from H. L. Purdy, N. L. Lindahl, and W. A. Carter, *Corporate Concentration and Public Policy,* Second Edition (Copyright 1942, 1950, by Prentice-Hall, Inc., New York), pp. 299–300. See, also, *Competition and Monopoly in American Industry,* T.N.E.C. Monograph No. 21, pp. 16–18, which this passage follows closely.

[52] Some critics even use the term "free enterprise" as a label for the very antithesis of "big business."

in its turn. This body of theory is essentially static in its concepts. It seeks to explain how stereotyped business firms exploit "given" techniques and work toward static equilibrium positions in "given" market situations, under the assumed single motive — to maximize profits. It is a body of theory, also, which deduces principles by means of an analysis which proceeds at very high levels of abstraction.

There are signs that a number of economists are becoming more interested in the dynamic processes of growth, change, and decline of firms and industries, processes, products, and markets. More economists, also, may come to be much more interested than they have been in the past in firsthand clinical *observation* of business behavior and motivation. They may come to be more interested in the vast range of human diversity to be observed in concrete organizations, and less interested in deducing, from *a priori* assumptions, the attributes of idealized theoretical models. If this happens, big business might once again come to be supported by a powerful intellectual justification. New concepts, new research methods, and so on, *could* lead to new conclusions. Conceivably, that could happen. Perhaps this *may* come to pass. Perhaps not.

But even if it does, the criticism of big business nevertheless will not be stilled.

For much of the hostility toward big business has little or nothing to do with *economic* considerations. It wells up from entirely different planes — from political and social ideas, and from ethical and moral convictions. In the past, social and moral critics have not been unwilling to have their positions buttressed by economic arguments. But, the hostility which has its origin in such other sources would not be turned back by even the most incontestable showing — if such could be made — that big business was, after all, a useful form of organization from a material point of view.

The critical ideas of these other planes are more than just *independent* of the economic attack. They take priority of place. Even for some of the all-out economic critics themselves, it is not the economic argument that is decisive. Thus, for example, we find one of them saying quite explicitly that it is *not* the *economic* charges that he puts in first place even in his own feelings toward big business, but *social* and *political* ideas:

> The evils of the trust, the dangers of ownership concentration cannot be exaggerated. They consist in part of conspiracy against the public, of price-rigging, of misallocation of resources, of interference with the free flow of trade, of the waste of excess capacity, of excessive profits, and of consequent economic instability, indeed of all these economic evils which economists since Adam Smith have recited. But I doubt if these are, even in sum, the chief part of the indictment to be made against them. The gravamen of the charge to be preferred is the awful social and political effects of the concentration of economic power.[53]

As we shall see, there are those who would insist on giving prior place to *ethical* and *moral* judgments. We shall come to them in due course. Now we turn to the social and political criticism of big business.

[53] B. S. Keirstead, *The Theory of Economic Change,* p. 364.

PART II

The Political and Social Criticism of Big Business

Introduction

> . . . I believe that the Declaration of Independence was the grandest document ever penned by human hands. The truths of that declaration are condensed into four great propositions: That all men are created equal; that they are endowed with inalienable rights; that governments are instituted among men to preserve those rights; and that governments derive their just powers from the consent of the governed. Such a government is impossible under an industrial aristocracy.
>
> – William Jennings Bryan [1]

OLDER, and more widespread, than the idea that big business is a socially inefficient means for organizing economic activity, is the deeper and more powerful fear that big business is incompatible with political and social democracy. It is to the criticism of big business which expresses that fear that we now turn.

The lineage of contemporary political and social criticism of big business can be traced back to the earliest reaction against the industrialization of the Western world and to the even earlier protests against privilege and economic, political, and social inequality in the Old Order. In the United States, a family resemblance to misgivings expressed in the 1950's can be seen in the mixed reception given in the 1790's to Alexander Hamilton's *Report on Manufactures* — in Jefferson's often-expressed insistence upon the need to safeguard small-scale independent agriculture as a cardinal foundation of democracy — in Andrew Jackson's attack on the Second

[1] An address at the Chicago Conference on Trusts, 1899 (*Proceedings of the Chicago Conference on Trusts,* p. 512). ["Twice after he had finally pushed his way through the crowd which rushed forward to congratulate him, did Mr. Bryan have to rise and bow his acknowledgments of the applause which ensued after he had finished speaking." (Ibid., p. 514.)]

Bank of the United States — in the agrarian reaction led by John C. Calhoun.

In the generations since the Civil War, both the Republican and Democratic parties, at one time or another, have adopted platforms more or less explicitly embodying political and social criticisms of big business. At least two political parties — the Populist, in 1892, and the Progressive, in 1912 — came into existence primarily as expressions of hostility toward big business. They were able, on this stand, to win the support of large numbers of voters. Each of the last three Democratic Presidents has voiced criticism of big business on political and social grounds, as distinguished from economic. In the dicta of the Supreme Court of the United States, and in the opinions of individual justices, political and social criticism of big business has been expressed on numerous occasions.

At about the turn of the present century there was added to this lineage of thought which, at least in the United States, goes back to the materialism of the Enlightenment of the 18th century, another stream which traces back to the dialectical materialism and economic determinism of Karl Marx. Some of the criticism in this tradition rather "welcomes industrial concentration as a step away from the economic anarchy of the nineteenth century toward a more perfect integration" which is to be operated or controlled by the state until "inequality" finally disappears in a "classless community." [2] Some of the criticism in this vein seems to bear a Communist rather than a Socialist watermark. But the distinction is not always clear, turning, as it often does, on very fine, subtle points of materialist ideology.

A little later, somewhat more so in Europe than in the United States, there was further added the criticism, represented by writings of the Englishmen Hilaire Belloc and G. K. Chesterton, which has been described as an attempt "to

[2] M. H. Dobb, *Capitalist Enterprise and Social Progress* (London: George Routledge & Sons, Ltd., 1925), p. 394.

recreate the ideal Catholic peasant proprietorship in a world of railways and factories." [3] Other strains of criticism have appeared. And in a number of recent critics various of these streams seem to have been merged in all sorts of proportions, permutations, and combinations.

Accordingly, by mid-Twentieth Century, the political and social criticism of big business manifests great diversity — not so much in the pattern of the criticisms advanced, perhaps, but in the historical processes which are seen at work and in the programs of political action proposed by the various "Schools." The criticism ranges from the reaction of the extreme Right to the reaction of the extreme Left.

To trace the development of these ideas would involve a review of the history of the major political and social ideas of the world over the course of the past hundred and fifty years. And that is not our present purpose. It is sufficient for us to note here that these ideas do have venerable ancestries and that the criticism of big business on political and social grounds represents a wide range of viewpoints.

In these introductory comments there are two other points to be taken up. First, there is the question as to whether it does violence to theory and to reality to take up political and social criticism of big business as a thing apart from economic criticism. Ultimately, this goes back to the question as to whether matters political are, or are not, a universe apart from matters economic. And *that* is a knotty and ancient question indeed.

There *are* critics for whom political and economic phenomena are inextricably interrelated parts of an organic whole. There are others for whom matters political and matters economic are essentially one and the same. This category of critics includes broadly those for whom the essential problem of politics is *power* and for whom the key to *political* power is *economic* power.

[3] Graham Wallas, *The Great Society* (New York: The Macmillan Company, 1921), p. 351.

It is true that the criticisms of people of this persuasion cannot be neatly pigeon-holed as to whether they are *political* or *economic* in nature. There *is* an organic unity in their ideas. Pulling these ideas apart, or even cataloguing them, *is* something of an arbitrary job at best.

But there *are* critics, also, who in their own works do separate political and social matters from economic. There are those, for instance, who specifically confine their attacks or concentrate their bulk to the one plane, ignoring or treating the other only sparingly. And there are those who not only explicitly separate the one plane from the other, but who push on to reach separate judgments on each of the two.

For example, critics in this last category include those who are prepared to concede that big business *is,* or *may* be, efficient from an economic view, but who deplore the social and political consequences which they attribute to it. Indeed, some of these critics see the ultimate cause of the lamentable political and social effects they lay at the door of big business in its very economic and technological superiority. This is the terribly effective driving force, as they see it, which makes it inevitable that big business will remake society along political and social patterns they do not approve of, unless it is somehow turned back or checked.

The essential ambivalence of this particular judgment is characteristic of the feelings many people have toward big business.

Anyway, without trying to resolve the basic philosophical question, we shall proceed in the next three chapters *as if* political and social criticism is a thing more or less distinguishable from economic criticism. In numerous instances we shall, in this, simply be following the critics themselves. In others, we must be prepared to find the distinction fuzzy or even nonexistent. All things considered, this seems to be about the most convenient, and for present purposes, therefore, the best thing to do.

This brings us to the next point — the way in which the

American people, as measured statistically, feel about big business. Apparently, their judgment also is an ambivalent one, and they appear to reach a substantially different judgment when they are considering big business from a political and social viewpoint than they do when judging it by an economic yardstick.

The body of firm factual knowledge as to what the American public at large thinks and feels about big business is limited. But what *is* known suggests a definite pattern, for studies by two leading professional polling organizations reveal much the same pattern, and thus corroborate one another.[4] Briefly, what these organizations have both found is that the American public has a distinctly ambivalent attitude toward big business: On *economic* grounds, the attitude is positive; on *political* and *social* grounds, the attitude is negative.

Depending on the particular question, sample, and research technique used, it looks as though about two-thirds to three-quarters of the American people apparently reach favorable judgments about big business when they are considering *economic* questions. For example, giving some of the highlights from a series of studies over a period of years, Elmo Roper reported that his organization had found that

> between 65% and 70% of the people have told us on numerous occasions that a big corporation will develop inventions much better and much faster than a smaller corporation. Majorities ranging from 62% to 69% say that they are sure a big company will give them the best radio set for their money. And between 60% and 67% say big companies will give them the best gasoline for the money.[5]

Asking different kinds of questions, as part of a major research effort directed specifically toward discovering public

[4] The two organizations are that of Elmo Roper, located in New York City, and The Survey Research Center of the Institute for Social Research, at the University of Michigan.

[5] "The Public Looks at Big Business," *Harvard Business Review*, Vol. XXVII, No. 2, March, 1949, p. 170.

attitudes toward big business as such, a survey research group of the Institute for Social Research at the University of Michigan found a similar pattern: People reach favorable appraisals on the basis of economic considerations but have negative feelings on other grounds. Even so, the poll asked people to reach an over-all, *on balance,* judgment. The results of this over-all question were as follows: [6]

Over-All Evaluation of Effect of Big Business

The good things outweigh the bad things	76%
They seem about equal	2
The bad things outweigh the good things	10
Don't know	5
Confused; evaluation not ascertainable	7
	100%

The Michigan group asked persons, independently of their over-all assessment, to state both the "beneficial" as well as the "adverse" effects of big business as they saw them. Of respondents who said the "*good* things" about big business outweigh the bad, 61% mentioned factors relating to big business in its "employer role" ("creates jobs . . . Pays high wages . . . Improves working conditions . . ."); 36% mentioned factors relating to big business in its "producer role" ("Mass production and mass distribution develops and improves products . . ."). Even among those who believed that the "*bad* things" about big business outweigh the good, 39% of the respondents believed that big business does have "beneficial effects" in its role as employer, and 29% saw the effects of big business in its "producer role" as beneficial. About a quarter of the people in both categories also mentioned as beneficial such economic effects as "Keeps prices down, makes things cheaper . . . Helps raise standard of living." [7]

[6] Burton R. Fisher and Stephen B. Withey, *Big Business As The People See It* (Ann Arbor: The Survey Research Center, Institute for Social Research, University of Michigan, December, 1951), p. 20.

[7] About 20% of the people on both sides mentioned other "beneficial

So much for the people's judgment of big business in its *economic* role. On the political and social side the verdict is quite different. On this count Elmo Roper reported:

> Many people believe "big business" violates Thomas Jefferson's concept of over 100 years ago that every individual should aspire to his own plot of land, on which he will live his private economic and social life.[8]

The findings of the Roper organization also suggest that the public, on political and social grounds — *not* on economic — mistrusts big business, inasmuch as "a large part of the public wants someone to keep an eye on business — and the people's candidate for that 'someone' is government . . . [most people believe] that business should have a strong counterbalancing factor in government."[9]

A similar pattern of mistrust of big business on political and social grounds was revealed by the Michigan study. Given an opportunity to mention "adverse effects" of big business, 37% even of the people who, on balance, thought the *good* things outweighed the bad, mentioned factors reflecting the idea that big business had too much power: "Too much power . . . squeezing out the little man . . . [has too much power] over other institutions — government, newspapers, schools, etc. . . ." Among those who thought the *bad* things outweigh the good, 60% mentioned as "adverse effects," political and social factors such as these.[10]

---

effects," including "Supports non-industrial research, philanthropic endeavors," etc. (The percentages add up to more than 100 in each case since numbers of people mentioned "beneficial effects" in more than one category.) Ibid., Table 8, p. 24.

This apparent favorable judgment on economic grounds *may* be merely a product of the times – of postwar prosperity and full employment. In the presence of widespread unemployment this judgment might be profoundly different. I should guess it *was* different in the period of the great depression. Certainly the interest which some unions show in the guaranteed annual wage suggests, even now, the existence of a concern over the *stability* of the economic performance of big business.

8 Elmo Roper, op. cit., p. 170.

9 Ibid., pp. 166 and 173.

10 A significant number of people here were also critical of the "manage-

Among even those who believed that the *good* things about big business outweigh the bad *on balance* — the principal misgivings were of a political and social nature. And among those who believed the *bad* overbalances, the factors they chiefly had in mind are things of this order — not the economic performance of big business. This fits in directly with these findings of Roper's:

> . . . a great many people believe that too much of business is at best amoral and at worst greedy. . . . There is *pride* over the *achievement* of big business but some *apprehension* over the possible *abuses* of power inherent in big business.[11]

This summary of the public's general attitude points up the essence of the political-social attack made upon big business. The criticism boils down to this: Whatever may be said — good *or* bad — of its efficiency as a means of organizing economic activity, big business is a threat to political and social democracy.

By and large, the attack of the *economic* critics apparently does not reflect the feelings of the general public. At least to date, *their* criticisms seem not to have received general public acceptance. The general proposition advanced by political and social critics, on the contrary, *does* correspond closely to feelings held by large fractions of the public at large. To what extent this is because these critics are simply voicing in a more articulate way the attitudes already present in the public, and to what extent the public's attitude is moulded by what these critics say, is hard to tell. But, because of this correspondence — whatever its cause — the ideas of the critics we are now going to survey must take on

---

ment-worker relations" of big business: "Cause or contribute to strikes or labor unrest . . . Lack of consideration for rights of workers . . . Kills craftsmanship — stultifying effects on worker. . . ." Of those believing the *bad* things of big business are dominant, 27% mentioned such things as these. And among those who believe the effects of big business are *good* on balance, 12% did believe there were "adverse effects of this nature." Burton R. Fisher and Stephen B. Withey, op. cit., Table 9, p. 25.

[11] Elmo Roper, op. cit., pp. 166 and 170. (Italics in original.)

especial importance for the responsible administrators of big business.

The general criticism of the political and social critics of big business can be summarized into three principal arguments:

First, that big business is the foundation of a plutocracy which runs the country — an oligarchy which rules our business and economic life. This would be bad enough, and undemocratic enough, all by itself. But to make it even worse, the big business plutocracy — the oligarchy — does not use its power to further the *general* welfare, but its own.

Second, that big business — the large corporation — in its very nature, and entirely apart from anything which it consciously does, is incompatible with the basic economic premises and conditions of liberal democracy.

Third, apart from anything it intends, the effects and consequences of the operations of big business are such as to undermine the social bases of liberal democracy and to bring about structural changes in our society and system of government which lead to totalitarianism.

These are the headings under which we shall now review that part of the attack on big business which rests upon political and social grounds.

CHAPTER 3

"Big Business Runs the Country"

A MAJOR POINT which repeatedly occurs in the political and social criticism of big business is that big business is the force in the nation which *really* controls our political, economic, and social institutions. The control of these institutions by any *minority* group is undemocratic, by generally accepted definition. Under democracy, no one fraction of the community — whether it be a racial or ethnic group, an economic group or class, a geographical group, or whatever — should have anything like a monopoly of the control of these institutions. Even an "undue" control by any one fraction or minority of the community is incompatible with the strict ideals of democracy.

Under a rigorous concept of democracy, it makes no difference if the policies and programs of a dominant minority are "enlightened," public spirited, and — in some sense — objectively attuned to the general welfare. A benign and competent paternalism is not democracy.

A fundamental point in the philosophy of democracy is that all individuals and all groups should participate in the control of our institutions. A democracy cannot remain a democracy if this general franchise for participation is usurped, even by a majority, let alone by any minority. A nation cannot remain democratic even if this franchise is delegated voluntarily to one group or class. In its very nature, minority control, or even predominance, is undemocratic. It is undemocratic per se. The operations of our institutions should *directly* represent the composite general will.

Again and again, critics say that big business, which is obviously a minority by any definition, has achieved a position of control in our society, and thus violates these ideals and principles of democracy.

That, all by itself, would be bad enough, even *if* it were accepted that big business is well-intentioned. But, very commonly, the critics go on to say that big business is far from being well-intentioned. They say it is predatory and rapacious. They say that big business exercises this control to further its own interests to the disadvantage of the rest of the community. This being so — they say — government and other instruments of power and influence do not, in fact, act as agencies for the expression of the will, and for the furtherance of the welfare of the nation as a whole. National policies, we are told, are designed to further the interests of big business, of property — especially of *big* property. National policies — it is said — are unresponsive to human needs; they are unmindful of the general welfare and of social justice.

Thus, in the eyes of the critics, an inherent evil is compounded to an intolerable degree in the specific instance.

In later chapters we shall hear arguments with more or less elaborate philosophical and theoretical bases to the effect that big business inherently is at odds with democracy. The present point simply holds that big business, *in its actions,* is bad. This point is to the effect that big business has *in fact* undermined democratic control of our institutions; that it has *in fact* taken over control; that it has *in fact* subverted the workings of our institutions so that they no longer serve the general will, democratically expressed, but serve rather, the narrow, material, selfish interests of big business.

The argument that big business runs the country breaks down into three principal counts: First, that a big business oligarchy or plutocracy controls the business community and, through it, the national economy. Second, that big business has reached out beyond this to control other societal institutions — principally the press and our educational system. Third, that a big business plutocracy has captured the instruments of government itself — legislative, executive, judiciary — from local up through national levels. And, then, there is the further count sometimes made: Big business is not content merely to control and subvert the workings of existing democratic institutions, it works positively to recast our system into an authoritarian, a Fascist pattern.

"A Big Business Oligarchy Controls American Business"

First, the matter of the big business oligarchy.

The point before us now is not merely that big business exercises some sort of undue influence upon the workings of the economy because of its disproportionate or monopolistic power in the market place. The point here is that big business has developed an organization structure — a power structure — at its very pinnacle which enables a small group of men to exercise direct and deliberate, even if obscure, control over the largest corporations in the country. Through its influence on this group of companies — this large and key fraction of American business — this oligarchy reaches out to control the whole economy.

The charge has been made for at least sixty years that a big business oligarchy controls the business community and, through it, the national economy. At first, it was said that this control was achieved through the money-power of large financial institutions and banking houses. Some critics still perceive this pattern of control. But since the 1930's, there has been a tendency to emphasize that the source of this control is primarily the organizational structure of large corporations, and to explain its nature in terms of the legal and operating relationships among stockholders, directors, and corporate executives. The older explanation has by no means disappeared from critical writings and is still often to be found.

In the accounts of the history of the United States between the Civil War and the First World War as given in contemporary textbooks, it is still almost standard to find this sort of picture: With the rise of large fortunes and big business, financial control achieved ascendancy and became centralized. At the very center of things a small group of men came to control the large banking institutions. These institutions — especially the "House of Morgan" — exercised a most thoroughgoing control over the large corporations. These big businesses directly controlled a large fraction of our national economic activity, and indirectly exercised great influence over smaller businesses through the power they were able to exercise. Thus, even if several stages removed from actual day-to-day business, a small financial oligarchy actually came to have ultimate control of our business world and national economy.

This is the picture drawn by the late historian Charles A. Beard and his wife, Mary R. Beard, in their profoundly influential text, *The Rise of American Civilization:*

> With financial control, managerial sovereignty was transferred from the operators of industries and railways to the directors of capital accumulations – a fact illustrated in a striking fashion when Morgan brought about the union of fifteen great railway organizations and created a steamship trust, a harvester trust, the United States Steel Corporation, and numerous other combinations less pretentious in scope. . . . On the whole, the high command in the empire of business was now in the hands of great banking corporations, and captains of industry were as a rule no longer evolved by natural selection; they were chosen by the dominant bankers who served as financial guardians. . . .
>
> . . . About the same time, the authority on trusts, John Moody, recorded that two mammoth financial complexes – the Morgan and Rockefeller interests – had gathered under their suzerainty a network of enterprises which constituted "the heart of the business and commercial life of the nation."
>
> Of course there was always warfare on the borders of this new Roman empire; novel industries were continually springing up with the progress of invention; and minor princelings and earls, as long as they restrained their pretensions, enjoyed

a high degree of local autonomy. But new enterprises of any moment found it hard, if not almost impossible, to obtain a foothold without paying tribute to the grand seigneurs; certainly no large issue of stocks and bonds could be floated in defiance of their orders.[1]

This picture of the centralized control of business, including colorful, pamphleteering figures of speech which describe the big business oligarchy in terms of the political power-structures of earlier times, has found its way not only into textbooks, but also into more popular literature — such as Ferdinand Lundberg's *America's 60 Families,* a best seller of fifteen years ago:

> The United States is owned and dominated today by a hierarchy of its sixty richest families, buttressed by no more than ninety families of lesser wealth. Outside this plutocratic circle there are perhaps three hundred and fifty other families, less defined in development and in wealth, but accounting for most of the incomes of $100,000 or more that do not accrue to members of the inner circle.
>
> . . . . .
>
> The uprush of the American fortunes, led by the monolithic Rockefeller accumulation, emphasizes that although the United States was once a great political democracy it has not remained one. Citizens may still be equals at the polls, where little is decided; but they are not equals at the bank tellers' wickets, where much is decided.[2] The United States has produced, in the Standard Oil Company, the Aluminum Company of America, E. I. du Pont de Nemours and Company, the Ford Motor Company, and other industrial enterprises, what are essentially feudal, dictatorially ruled, dynastic fiefs that make the old crown properties of Romanovs,

[1] New York: The Macmillan Company, 1927, 2 vols. (Also New York: The Macmillan Company, 1930, one volume edition.) The quoted passage appears on pp. 196–197 of Vol. II, *The Industrial Era.* (Quoted with the permission of The Macmillan Company.)

[2] Note the implication that the *political* power of the individual is of little consequence and that *economic* power is what counts. We shall take up this idea in the next chapter.

Hohenzollerns, Hapsburgs, and Hanovers seem, by comparison, like will-o'-the-wisps, unsure and insubstantial.[3]

Following the appearance, in 1932, of *The Modern Corporation and Private Property* by A. A. Berle, Jr., and Gardiner C. Means,[4] interest was revived in the idea that since ownership and control are separated in large corporations, control of them rests in self-perpetuating groups of — presumably — irresponsible managers.[5] On the basis of this idea, a different theory as to the nature of the big business oligarchy came to be more generally accepted than the older one.

First, Berle and Means started with the theory that a large and increasing fraction of all economic activity was being taken over by big business — especially by the largest corporations. This idea also, of course, was not new.[6] But Berle and Means did present data in an effort to show just how important a part was played in the economy by the 200 largest nonbanking corporations in the United States. They pointed out that in many fields — for example, in steel, auto-

[3] Copyright by The Vanguard Press, 1937 and 1938, pp. 3 and 7.

[4] New York: The Macmillan Company, 1932.

[5] See Adam Smith's ideas as quoted in Chapter 1, above, as well as in footnote 11 on page [119] below.

The late Professor F. W. Taussig, some twenty years or more earlier, had argued that the separation of ownership and control was an essential and distinguishing characteristic of the large corporation. See, for example, *Principles of Economics,* Vol. I, pp. 88–89.

Compare: "The administration of a joint stock association is, in the main, administration by hired servants. Even the committee, or board of directors who are supposed to superintend the management . . . have no pecuniary interest in the good working of the concern beyond the shares they individually hold, which are always a very small part of the capital of the association . . . [the management of the business is] the principal concern of no one except those who are hired to carry it out . . ." – John Stuart Mill, *Principles of Political Economy,* Vol. I, pp., 167–168; "Ashley" edition, pp. 138–139.

[6] Ideas of this sort had been put forth for some time. For example: ". . . We observe in almost every form of business that industrial power is concentrating itself, that organizations are growing in size, that individual industry and small enterprises are being crowded to the wall, and that the sphere of competition is constantly being narrowed . . ." – Professor Henry C. Adams, "A Statement of the Trust Problem," *The Chicago Conference on Trusts,* p. 35.

mobiles, tires, plumbing and heating equipment — the large corporations accounted for the bulk of the total output.

But such data were only part of the story, a picture only of the *direct* consequences of big business. For, as they truly said, "Even where the individual does not come in direct contact [with these largest corporations] he cannot escape indirect contact with these companies, so ubiquitous have they become. There are few articles of consumption to whose production one of the big companies has not to some extent contributed." They showed, for example, that in 1929 these corporations held at least 49.2% of all the assets of nonbanking corporations and received at least 43.2% of the net income of such companies.[7]

Moreover, they contended, the influence of these companies extended far beyond their own operations and own property: "Smaller companies which sell to or buy from the larger companies are likely to be influenced by them to a vastly greater extent than by other smaller companies with which they might deal." [8]

Such concentration of direct and indirect power and influence over economic and business life, they said, would be significant enough all by itself. But that is not all: "This concentration is made even more significant when it is recalled that as a result of it, approximately 2,800 individuals out of a population of one hundred and twenty-five million are in a position to control and direct half of industry." [9]

Thus, they said, there is a tight little oligarchy that sits at the apex of the corporate power-system. But this is not the oligarchy of financial moguls of previous decades, or even of the Sixty Families. For it includes a large number of salaried executives who control corporations without having any significant financial interest in them. In fact, out of the 200 largest nonbanking corporations, 65 of them, holding almost

[7] A. A. Berle, Jr., and Gardiner C. Means, op. cit., pp. 25–26, 28–29.
[8] Ibid., p. 32.
[9] Ibid., p. 33.

half of all the assets of the very largest firms, were described as being controlled by managements which had but little financial investment in them and, in particular, held no appreciable fraction of their stock.[10]

This control is made possible, Berle and Means said, because of the widely diffused ownership of the companies. Where even the twenty largest stockholders altogether own only a small fraction of the voting stock — as in the case of the Pennsylvania Railroad, United States Steel, and American Telephone and Telegraph — the managements take over control. They control the proxy machinery, and the board of directors. They become self-perpetuating.[11]

This proposition became a turning point in the thinking regarding the corporate power-structure. In the next few years it was widely taken up and much made of — as in *The Managerial Revolution* by James Burnham.[12]

10 See, also, R. A. Gordon, "Ownership by Management and Control Groups in the Large Corporation," *The Quarterly Journal of Economics*, Vol. 52, 1938, p. 371.

11 In the *Wealth of Nations,* Adam Smith saw a similar separation of "ownership" and "control" in the joint stock companies of the 18th Century: "The trade of a joint stock company is always managed by a court of directors. The court, indeed, is frequently subject, in many respects, to the controul of a general court of proprietors. But the greater part of those proprietors seldom pretend to understand anything of the business of the company; and when the spirit of faction happens not to prevail among them, give themselves no trouble about it, but receive contentedly such half yearly or yearly dividend, as the directors think proper to make to them."

In Smith's view, indeed, this very freedom from administrative problems and burdens encourages investment in corporations by people who might not otherwise invest in business enterprise at all, for he goes on to say, "This total exemption from trouble and from risk, beyond a limited sum, encourages many people to become adventurers in joint stock companies, who would upon no account, hazard their fortunes in any private copartnery. Such companies, therefore, commonly draw to themselves much greater stocks than any private copartnery can boast of." *Additions and Corrections . . .*, p. 50; "Modern Library" edition, pp. 699–700.

12 Compare: "Through size, corporations, once merely an efficient tool employed by individuals in the conduct of private business have become an institution which has brought such concentration of economic power that so-called private corporations are sometimes able to dominate the state. The typical business corporation of the last century, owned by a small group of individuals, managed by their owners and limited in size by their personal wealth, is being supplanted by huge concerns in which the lives often of hun-

Since the publication of Berle's and Means' work, the critics of big business have gone on to say that the concentration of corporate control in the hands of hired company managements does not stop there. There are, they argue, further relationships which further concentrate real control. The most influential of subsequent works on this topic was one which Dr. Means himself directed, *The Structure of the American Economy* (*Part I*), which was published in 1939 by the National Resources Committee. This report put forth the view that there are a variety of relationships which serve to mould the largest companies into a "corporate community":

> If each corporate management were quite independent of every other corporate management and subject only to market controls in its development of policy, the structure of non-market controls might be of only secondary importance. In fact, however, there is a great deal of interrelationship between corporate managements. Partly through interlocking directorates, partly through the activities of the major financial institutions, partly through particular interest groupings, partly through firms rendering legal, accounting, and similar services to the larger corporations, and partly through intercorporate stockholdings, the managements of most of the larger corporations are loosely brought together in what might be called the corporate community.
>
> . . . . .

---

dreds of thousands of employees and the property of tens or hundreds of thousands of investors are subjected, through the corporate mechanism, to the control of a few men. Ownership has been separated from control; and this separation has removed many of the checks which formerly operated to curb the abuse of wealth and power. And, as ownership of the shares is becoming increasingly dispersed, the power which formerly accompanied ownership is becoming increasingly concentrated in the hands of a few. The changes thereby wrought in the lives of the workers, of the owners and of the general public, are so fundamental and far-reaching as to lead . . . scholars to compare the evolving 'corporate system' with the feudal system, and to lead other men of insight and experience to assert that this 'master institution of civilized life' is committing it to the rule of plutocracy." — Mr. Justice Brandeis, dissenting, in *Louis K. Liggett Co.* v. *Lee* (1933), 288 U.S. 517, 565.

In the same way, the leading legal firms, advertising firms, engineering firms, public relations counsellors, and espionage firms are apt to have a score or more of the larger corporations as their clients and come into intimate contact with one or another phase of their major policy problems.

All of these firms rendering special services to the big corporations necessarily deal with some important phase of corporate policy for each of the corporations which they serve. Almost inevitably they contribute in conferences and individual discussions to that climate of opinion within which corporate policies are formed, carrying from one corporation to another some degree of common background and temper of thought which adds a measure of unity to the corporate community.[13]

Moreover, the concept of centralized *financial* control reappears in a new, modern form. The central figure, however, is no longer the imperious, dominating, heavily moustached individual. But inside the "corporate community," there is the financial "common interest group." Such an informal system of relationships is said to be revealed when there are interlocking directorates, when all the security issues of a company are handled by one investment banking firm, and "when other evidence of a less precise nature points to a close association between the companies." [14]

In the study directed by Dr. Means, eight such "common interest groups" are listed, the principal one being the "Morgan-First National [Bank of New York] interest group." In this group, aside from the two financial institutions themselves, were listed 39 of the largest 250 corporations. The list includes the American Telephone and Telegraph Company, the General Electric Company, the Guaranty Trust Company, and the United States Steel Corporation.[15]

This report does say that, while this group of very large

13 Washington: Government Printing Office, 1939, pp. 158 and 159.

14 Ibid., p. 161.

15 Ibid., Chart II, facing p. 162.

companies, for example, was "in no sense subject to a simple centralized control," it does go on to argue that:

> . . . it is equally certain that the separate corporations are not completely independent of each other. The climate of opinion within which their separate policies are developed is much the same, many of the same people participate in the formulation and review of the policies of the separate corporations, financing is carried on for the most part through the same channels, and in many other ways this group of corporations constitutes an interrelated interest group.[16]

From the works of Berle and Means in the Thirties, there emerged a new popular picture of a somewhat less personal but none the less powerful institutional oligarchy which controls American business.

It is to these works, and others that were inspired by them, that critics still turn for support in their contention that our democratic — atomized — political structure is a thing gone by. Thus, Professor Theodore J. Kreps of Stanford eleven years after Dr. Means' study, and in the postwar period, was still taking over these ideas and data intact:

> . . . there have appeared in recent decades even larger colossi commanding in addition to the undoubted economies of large scale production and the alleged economies of holding company management the bludgeon of unlimited financial power. By stock ownership, interlocking directorates, common affiliations with investment banks, and by intangible personal and family ties, there have emerged a few financial groups, eight of which in the United States control 106 of the 250 largest corporations and nearly two-thirds of their combined assets. These are the Morgan-First National, Kuhn-Loeb, Rockefeller, Chicago, Mellon, Dupont, Boston and Cleveland groups.
>
> The Morgan group, for example, cements together in

[16] Ibid., p. 162.

friendly, cooperative relationships no less than 41 of these 250 largest corporations.[17]

"Big Business Controls the Schools, the Press, etc."

Many critics, including petulant men in a serious frame of mind and serious men in a petulant frame of mind, have charged that big business controls the press, among other institutions. A few have said that it controls our educational institutions — presumably those that are not controlled by "Reds" or "Fifth Amendment Communists." The purpose, of course, of this control is to extend the control of big business still further throughout the society, ultimately to government itself. There is a wide range in the views of the people who make points of this order.

Since it is important to get on to the next major point, four samples of this sort of charge will simply be listed, without further comment, to show its tenor:

> . . . Courtesy as well as expediency inclines . . . schools to cultivate such appearances and such opinions as may be expected to find favor with men of wealth. . . .
>
> . . . Nothing should go in a popular magazine which would cast a sinister shadow over any form of business venture that advertises or might be induced to advertise.[18]

* * *

> . . . the rise of the great corporations and the concentration of economic power within these agencies has facilitated the mobilization of financial resources and of the instruments for controlling public opinion, with the result that pressures may be put upon the elected representatives to obtain legislation favoring those who control the corporations. So well organized are the methods of "reaching" the legislature and

[17] Theodore J. Kreps, "Preserving Free, Competitive Enterprise," *Twentieth Century Economic Thought,* edited by Glenn Hoover (New York: Philosophical Library, 1950), p. 529.

[18] Thorstein Veblen, *The Theory of Business Enterprise* (New York: Charles Scribner's Sons, 1904), Edition of 1923, pp. 384 and 387–388.

so easily are the desired responses obtained that business men often look upon this method as the normal, legitimate, and expected mode of government performance. Without comprehending that they do so, frequently they look upon the legislature as their legislature whose function it is to serve their interest. . . .[19]

* * *

The press is controlled by big business. Look at the advertising pages if you don't believe it. It's always been against President Roosevelt. It has always been against me, and if it was for me, I'd know I was wrong.[20]

* * *

. . . The profession [of journalism] . . . is, in the material sense, the private property of a few rich and soulless corporations, and is editorially cunning rather than brave.[21]

* * *

. . . The instruments which shape the minds of citizens are not freely at the disposal of anyone who wishes to operate them. They are controlled, for the most part, by men or bodies who can afford either to create or to employ them . . . for the most part they are controlled by the vested interests. . . .

. . . Broadly speaking, just because each of these three media [press, cinema, radio] is a branch of Big Business, its object is not the communication of truth, but the making of profit; and the truth it can afford is rarely the whole truth. . . .[22]

[19] David Lynch, *The Concentration of Economic Power* (New York: Columbia University Press, 1946), p. 293.

[20] Harry S. Truman, Address at the Democratic National Convention at Chicago, July, 1952. Reported in *United States News & World Report,* August 1, 1952, p. 93.

[21] Westbrook Pegler in *The Cincinnati Inquirer,* Tuesday, June 9, 1953, p. 4.

[22] Harold Laski, *The American Democracy* (New York: The Viking Press, 1948); p. 617. In this book, Mr. Laski devoted a whole chapter to this topic. See Chapter XIII.

The spreading, pervasive control of America by big business, emanating from the inner core of the top managements of the very largest corporations, does not stop here. It reaches into the government itself.

"Big Business Runs the Government"

The contention that a big business plutocracy has captured control of the government has a long lineage. At one time or another, all kinds of people have argued in this vein. They have given a variety of explanations for this development. Sometimes they have said that this has come about through outright corruption of the most venal sort. The late Senator George W. Norris of Nebraska, I think, suggested this control was achieved by "boring from within." Others have attributed the success of big business in capturing government to its inherent power. Others, inclined toward a materialist interpretation of history, have a more complex explanation: Big business is in control, they allege, because this *is* a capitalistic society and big business is the epitome of capitalism. Government officials, including the judges of the country, are naturally led by their ideological predilections to favor big business quite independently of any corrupt practices. Most of them are members of the capitalistic class. And, in any case, big business and the plutocracy which is based upon it represent the apex of the economic power system, which, after all — they say — is the foundation of the *real* power system.

In 1892 the Populist Party was brought into being chiefly for the purpose of throwing off the control which big business was visualized as having fastened, by means of corruption, upon both major political parties as well as state and federal government. Seldom has big business been condemned in stronger terms:

> . . . Corruption dominates the ballot-box, the legislatures, the Congress, and touches even the ermine of the bench. The people are demoralized; most of the states have been com-

pelled to isolate the voters at the polling places to prevent universal intimidation or bribery. The newspapers are largely subsidized or muzzled, public opinion silenced, business prostrated, our homes covered with mortgages, labor impoverished, and the land concentrating in the hands of the capitalists. . . . The fruits of the toil of millions are boldly stolen to build up colossal fortunes for a few, unprecedented in the history of mankind; and the possessors of these, in turn, despise the republic and endanger liberty. From the same prolific womb of governmental injustice we breed the two great classes — tramps and millionaires. . . .

. . . . .

We have witnessed for more than a quarter of a century the struggles of the two great political parties for power and plunder, while grievous wrongs have been inflicted upon the suffering people. We charge that the controlling influences dominating both these parties have permitted the existing dreadful conditions to develop without serious effort to prevent or restrain them. Neither do they now promise us any substantial reform. . . . They propose to drown the outcries of a plundered people with the uproar of a sham battle over the tariff, so that capitalists, corporations, national banks, rings, trusts, watered stock, the demonetization of silver, and the oppressions of the usurers may all be lost sight of. They propose to sacrifice our homes, lives, and children on the altar of Mammon; to destroy the multitude in order to secure corruption funds from the millionaires.

. . . we seek to restore the government of the republic to the hands of "the plain people." . . .[23]

Twenty years later, in the presidential campaign of 1912, Woodrow Wilson, as the Democratic candidate, was telling the people:

Suppose you go to Washington and try to get at your government. You will always find that while you are politely

[23] From the platform of the National People's (Populist) Convention of 1892, as given in Thomas H. McKee, *The National Conventions and Platforms of All Political Parties — 1789 to 1904* (Baltimore: The Friedenwald Company, 1904), pp. 280–282.

> listened to, the men really consulted are the men who have the biggest stake, — the big bankers, the big manufacturers, the big masters of commerce, the heads of railroad corporations and of steamship corporations. . . . The government of the United States at present is a foster-child of the special interests. . . . The government of the United States in recent years has not been administered by the common people of the United States. . . .[24]

These strictures, of course, were directed at the Republican Party, which had been in power since 1897.

In the same year, Theodore Roosevelt, who had been the Republican President from 1901 to 1909 — presumably in frequent consultation with men of big business — was campaigning as the candidate of the Progressive, "Bull Moose" Party. Interestingly enough, one of his chief pleas as to why voters should vote the Progressive ticket was that the two major parties, including the Democratic Party of Woodrow Wilson, were merely the tools of big business:

> [A "boss"] is a go-between between the money power and the politicians; that he is the man responsible for the alliance between crooked politics and crooked business which has produced nine-tenths of the corruption in American political life.
>
> . . . In their essence the Democratic and the Republican machines are alike. Both are controlled by the like powerful beneficiaries of political and financial privilege. The differences between the men who really dominate the two parties are merely the differences between great corporation attorneys who for the moment represent different corporations but who come together instantly against any movement which is meant to establish the people as masters over both. . . .[25]

Wilson, of course, was elected. And some critics say that big business took over *his* Democratic administration. Pro-

24 *The New Freedom,* pp. 57–59.
25 Theodore Roosevelt, *Progressive Principles* (New York: Progressive National Service, 1913), pp. 191–192.

fessor Robert A. Brady of the University of California in his book *Business as a System of Power* — a work which linked big business and Fascism — saw big business in control of our wartime economy during the First World War, and portrayed that control as part of an international phenomenon.

> . . . As in all belligerent countries, war control in the United States was exercised primarily through the intermediation of businessmen and business organization. Businessmen held the principal control offices and made the key administrative decisions in economic affairs. And in all their activities they naturally and habitually turned to their own organizations for the instrumentation of policies – policies which combined, so happily, patriotic performance of a critical "public duty" with lucrative gains to the trades and industries which the businessmen represented and which must now supply the necessary goods and services.[26]

Professor Brady points out that the Food Administration was presided over by Herbert Hoover, "a mining industrialist"; the Fuel Administration, by Harry A. Garfield, a director of the Cleveland Trust Company; the War Industries Board by Bernard Baruch, "a Wall Street financier and stock market operator"; the War Trade Board, by Vance McCormick, "of the family associated with the International Harvester Co." Through the decisions and actions of businessmen such as these, "their concerns achieved large, and in a few cases, colossal earnings." [27]

Many people take it for granted that big business controlled the government during the Republican administrations of 1920–1932. But some critics have said that big business wormed its way into a controlling position even during the Democratic administrations of Franklin D. Roosevelt and Harry S. Truman. Thus, it has been said, among other things, that big business captured the National Recovery Administration and the Agricultural Adjustment Ad-

26 New York: Columbia University Press, 1943, pp. 194–195.
27 Ibid., p. 195, footnote 18.

ministration — two of the principal agencies of the New Deal. For outstanding instances, a review committee appointed by President Roosevelt and headed by the nationally famous attorney, Clarence Darrow, reported of the NRA that:

> . . . In industry after industry the larger units [through trade associations] . . . have for their own advantage written the codes, and then, in effect and for their own advantage, assumed the administration of the code they have framed. Thus, privilege has exerted itself to gather more privilege. . . .[28]

An editorial in *The Christian Century* stated that:

> [Both the NRA and AAA] represent recovery programs . . . controlled by the big corporations involved, giving a subsidiary attention to the interests of the labor movement, and hoping that the consumers will be satisfied with a few kind words and a seat out in the alley.[29]

Nor was it only during the New Deal era of the Roosevelt administration that the critics say that big business had its sway and its way. Professor Robert S. Lynd, co-author of the famous *Middletown* and *Middletown in Transition,* has suggested that big business penetrated Roosevelt's wartime administration; that, in the prosecution of World War II, the government deliberately adopted policies favorable to big business:

> . . . the management of the present war has been taken over by representatives of big business. And this time they may be in Washington for keeps. . . .
>
> . . . effective organization and the crisis nature of the present, requiring quick decisions and encouraging decisions in terms of blunt short-run objectives, favor those who seek

[28] National Recovery Review Board, "Third Report to the President." Quoted by Eric F. Goldman, *Rendezvous with Destiny* (New York: Alfred A. Knopf, 1952), p. 347.

[29] March 6, 1935, Vol. LII, p. 294. Quoted in *Rendezvous with Destiny*, p. 350.

> to exploit the war to make the United States safe for big business. The *de facto* power of big business is reflected in the fact that the Government itself is, for the most part, timid and afraid of what big business will do if the war is not made "worth its while." [30]

Recently Blair Bolles, in his best-selling *How to Get Rich in Washington,* has suggested that big business profited handsomely at the hands of both the Roosevelt and the Truman administrations. For example, he says that not only during World War II, but afterwards, the policies of the government with respect to war contracts and later with respect to its policies on reconversion (policies drafted by Bernard Baruch, "a millionaire," and John M. Hancock, "an industrial banker") worked greatly to the benefit of big business — in considerable measure at the expense of small business.[31]

In more general terms, Mr. Bolles charges that under the presidency of Harry S. Truman:

> . . . the welfare state has been undergoing a subtle change into the rich man's welfare state, aiding those who don't need help or who don't deserve it at public expense. The agencies created to end privilege have become bulwarks of privilege. . . .
>
> . . . . .
>
> . . . easy money comes in the form of protection which the government gives to vested interests. . . . The Interstate Commerce Commission, created to defend the public from abuses by the railroads, keeps the public treasury open to the railroads. . . . A government organization that President Franklin Roosevelt developed in order to restrain those whom he called "economic royalists" is now making it possible for the "royalists" to regain their paramountcy in the national economy. The Sugar Section of the Department of Agriculture went out of its way in 1948 to protect sugar refiners in the United States by drafting and pushing through Congress

[30] Robert A. Brady, *Business as a System of Power,* Foreword by Robert S. Lynd, pp. xvi and xvii.

[31] New York: W. W. Norton & Company, Inc., 1952, Chapters 3 and 11.

a bill which restricted the refinement of sugar in Puerto Rico.[32]

Actually, if we are to believe Mr. Bolles, the solicitude and beneficence of the executive branch of the government toward big business is nothing new.

> . . . For more than sixty years the Capitol has been whaling away at bigness in business with the energy and moral enthusiasm of parsons denouncing sin. The effort to keep the United States a nation of small-scale enterprise has never flagged. At the same time the proportion of the national economy that small enterprise controls has steadily diminished. . . . One reason Congress has been losing the battle since the days when bewhiskered Senator John Sherman was scourging the trusts is that many government agencies ape the Civil Aeronautics Board. They protect the privileged from brash intruders. Some do it by design; some because it is the easiest way. . . .[33]

In his much-quoted work — *America's 60 Families* — Ferdinand Lundberg pointed out that members of the wealthiest families and other wealthy individuals have contributed funds to political parties. Taking up American history since the latter part of the 19th Century, Mr. Lundberg showed that *all* the presidents since that time, including Grover Cleveland, have had wealthy men in their cabinets and have had wealthy intimate acquaintances. He showed that various members of the wealthiest families and prominent corporation executives have favored opposing parties. To Mr. Lundberg, these associations suggested that this was a method whereby the big business plutocracy maintained control, whatever party won: "In this way the avenue of approach was kept open to the key men, the financial managers, in each party." [34]

[32] Ibid., pp. 12, 15–16.

[33] Ibid., pp. 241–242.

[34] Op. cit., see pp. 131–133, 154–157, 454–457, *et passim*.

The fear that big business has captured the Federal Government, or may, continues in 1953.

"In answer to questions on his opinion of President Eisenhower's Cabinet

Fifty years ago, Thorstein Veblen argued that quite apart from corruption and crude political favoritism, big business would inevitably dominate our institutions of government. Even a "learned, upright judge" on the bench will, because of the very nature of the law in a capitalist society — as Veblen conceived it — favor employers, owners, and property.[35] As for representative government, that also will inevitably favor big business, because even rank and file citizens accept the ideology of capitalism:

> Representative government means, chiefly, representation of business interests. The government commonly works in the interest of the business men with a fairly consistent singleness of purpose. And in its solicitude for the business men's interests it is borne out by current public sentiment, for there is a naive, unquestioning persuasion abroad among the body of the people to the effect that, in some occult way, the material interests of the populace coincide with the pecuniary interests of those business men who live within the scope of the same set of governmental contrivances.[36]

Big Business and Fascism

Some critics, including some of the more militant ones, tell us that big business is not content simply to *control* govern-

---

selections, Senator Morse [of Oregon] said they backed up his belief that 'big business has stolen the G.O.P.'" — *New York Times,* January 25, 1953.

"Businessmen will ride high and we can expect a deterioration in the cultural scene. There will be great pressure for conformity with the philosophy of business. . . . Never in history has an administration been so wholly staffed by businessmen. . . . It is the closest thing to a billion-dollar cabinet we have ever had." — Arthur M. Schlesinger, Jr., Professor of History at Harvard College, as reported in *The Boston Herald,* January 5, 1953.

"You and I and every American concerned with the future of the free world cannot fail to be greatly disturbed by the developments in our nation's Capital. Big business has moved in. They are taking over the government lock, stock, and barrel. They are sponsoring a program in which profits are being placed ahead of people, in which special privilege for the few has priority over the well-being of the many." — Walter P. Reuther, President, Congress of Industrial Organizations; address to the Fifteenth Constitutional Convention of the C.I.O., November 16, 1953.

35 *The Theory of Business Enterprise,* p. 286.

36 Ibid., pp. 281–282.

ment, while maintaining the *forms* of a democratic system. The rise and the power of big business threaten to undermine the democratic system altogether, and to *replace* the democratic form, as well as the substance, with an authoritarian one — with Fascism.

Sometimes, this fear is expressed in rather ambiguous and abstract terms, as it is in this passage by Professors Purdy, Lindahl, and Carter of Dartmouth College:

> . . . When control of economic affairs is concentrated in a few hands, democracy becomes a meaningless form. And even the form will not survive. The entrenched economic group will attempt to control the political organization of the country to protect its economic position, and injured interests will attempt to organize so as to improve their position. Political individualism will give way as the political unit becomes the group instead of the individual. Democracy will be succeeded by the forms and principles of authoritarianism.[37]

Sometimes the picture of big business leading the United States to Fascism is drawn in more concrete and militant terms — thus:

> . . . fascism in Italy and Germany has been subsidized largely by *heavy industry* – iron, steel, mining – and its bankers. *Light industry,* making consumers' goods for the most part – textiles, clothing, etc. – has played a reformist game and has, up to a certain point, opposed fascism. The barons of heavy industry must smash the labor unions and extend their dictatorial sway over the entire national economy. The light industrialists can afford class collaboration. . . .
>
> Much the same generalizations can be made about this country. The most implacable enemies of the New Deal have been heavy industrialists like the du Ponts (chemicals), Weir and Girdler (steel), the Mellons (oil, aluminum),

[37] *Corporate Concentration and Public Policy,* p. 300.

> and the Wall Street banks which finance their enterprises. . . .
>
> . . . The *content* of American fascism is the same as that of Europe: big business interests masquerading as anti-capitalism. . . .[38]

This is the kind of picture which is painted by those who say that big business, *knowingly, willfully,* and *intentionally,* fosters a Fascist revolution as a means to guarantee its control of political institutions. It has been suggested that it is a "Trotsky-ite" interpretation of history to hold that Fascism is a movement deliberately planned, financed, engineered, and controlled by big business.

There are other views among the critics as to what the relationship is between big business and Fascism. A principal one is that Fascism is the *unintended* but *inevitable* result of bigness in business. Fascism arises, according to this theory, quite apart from anything big business *intends,* but in consequence of the nature and, especially, in consequence of the *ordinary operations* of big business. This criticism of big business, as we shall see in the next chapter, represents an extreme degree of the criticism that bigness in business operates to undermine the structure of democratic society.

Conceivably, and logically, we might wait to deal with this particular argument until we get to the appropriate place in the next chapter. But it seems a bit more convenient if we take it up now, since the question of the relationship between big business and Fascism has been raised.

One view of this relationship — a view which has been labelled as "Stalinist" — holds that Fascism is a *"middle-class"* phenomenon. Under this view big business is only indirectly responsible. According to this version, the growth of big business has resulted in the economic disenfranchise-

[38] From the Introduction by Dwight Macdonald to Daniel Guerin's *Fascism and Big Business* (New York: Pioneer Publishers, 1939), pp. xiii and xviii. (The term "big business," Mr. Macdonald tells us, is "used in this book as roughly synonymous with 'heavy industry' and its banking connections"; p. xiv). (Italics in original.)

ment of the middle classes. The middle-class businessman — the small businessman — cannot compete with big business. He cannot maintain his independent business and his independent status. He is "proletarianized." In any case, the middle classes bear the brunt of cyclical as well as technological unemployment. Driven to desperation, the middle classes — not big business — turn to and support Fascism. In the eyes of some, this is the inevitable next step after capitalism has "matured," that is, after big business has appeared.

To pursue these two divergent, but equally critical, views much further would take us into the buzzing confusion of the theoretical subtleties and casuistry of dialectical materialism. For this we cannot spare the time.[39]

Other critics, who are perhaps less systematic and dogmatic in their thinking and who are, in any case, less clear and explicit in their analyses, simply link big business and Fascism by assertion and then go on to criticize that relationship.

A couple of passages from critics we have already quoted should be sufficient to round out this brief survey of the ways in which the relationship between big business and Fascism has been fitted in with other criticisms of big business.[40]

> When the history of our times is written, it may be decided that the greed and lust for power of captains of industry have been largely responsible for the growth of fascism which threatens to destroy the economy they control and profit from. First, as leaders they must take responsibility for the growing number of permanently unemployed. Second, as the failure of the capitalistic economies to absorb the unemployed became apparent, some of the more alarmed of these leaders sought to save themselves by financing a dictator who then set about to destroy the very system they hoped to maintain.

[39] For further views, see Lewis Corey, *Crisis of the Middle Class* (New York: Covici Friede, 1935), especially Chapter XII; Alfred M. Bingham, *Insurgent America* (New York: Harper & Brothers, 1935), especially Part III, Chapter XIII; and C. Wright Mills, *White Collar* (New York: Oxford University Press, 1951).

[40] In the next chapter, we shall come back, briefly, to this point.

The Thyssens little realized what they were doing when they helped Hitler come to power. . . . Judge Elbert H. Gary, former head of the United States Steel Corporation, probably never realized the full import of what he was saying when during the early twenties he proclaimed that what this country needed was a Mussolini. The leaders of American industry, more anxious to build bigger and bigger corporations than to allow the competitive democratic system to flourish, may yet feel that they must resort to another Frankenstein who may destroy them and those who have trusted them.[41]

* * *

. . . the central problem disrupting our world, the most dangerous issue democracy faces . . . is not basically created by Adolf Hitler and the Axis nations, but by the organized economic power backing the Hitlers in nation after nation over the industrial world as a device for shoring up for yet a while longer a disintegrating economic system. . . .

. . . Organized business enterprise is less and less willing to tolerate checks on its activities by the state; more and more it needs the state as active ally; and the national state, in turn, having delivered itself over by accepting the definition of its welfare as synonymous with the welfare of its business system, needs increasingly the utmost of aggressive efficiency from its businessmen. Business is in politics and the state is in business. . . .

And the public does not know what to do about this merging of powers up aloft over its head. As business has organized and has begun to state cogently and lavishly the case for its version of such an "ordered society," the popular challenge expressed earlier in the campaign to curb bigness by governmental action has become confused and blunted. Big business has carefully disseminated to the little man at the grass roots enthusiasm and pride as an American in the superefficiency of the marvelous assembly lines and other paraphernalia of giant technology that produces his automobiles and other daily conveniences. The little man is puz-

[41] Kemper Simpson, *Big Business, Efficiency and Fascism,* p. 6.

zled, hypnotized into inaction: if he is not to oppose *bigness* itself, the bigness of Henry Ford, Du Pont, and the other great corporations that make these characteristically American things possible, what *is* he to oppose about big business? The technique of dazzling, confusing, and dividing the opposition, used by Hitler, has been skillfully practiced by the propagandists for big business.[42]

Conclusion

In sum, critics of quite different ideological persuasions agree — superficially, anyway — in alleging that big business runs the country, or at least exercises a dangerously disproportionate power over its affairs. Views of this order are not confined to the more articulate critics. As we have seen, counterparts of these ideas show up often and widely throughout the public at large.

The critics differ greatly in their analyses as to how this alleged state of affairs came about and as to what should now be done. Some regard the situation, as they see it, as merely an aberration which can be remedied by relatively mild governmental measures and political action. They look to remedial action within the existing institutional framework.

Other critics see big business control as an inevitable consequence of large-scale private enterprise. The state of affairs which *they* perceive tends simply to demonstrate concretely to them that bigness in business is bad per se. These critics look for remedial action in the breaking up of big business where it is possible and the nationalization of large-scale enterprise where it is not.

Still others regard the alleged control of modern society by big business as inevitable, as implicit in capitalism itself. For these critics, it is not only big business which is bad per se, but capitalism itself. Big business, for these people, is simply the epitome of capitalism. Critics at this end of the spectrum

[42] Robert A. Brady, *Business as a System of Power,* Foreword by Robert S. Lynd, pp. vii and x–xi.

are accordingly led to the conclusion that the only appropriate course of political action in face of the situation, as it appears to them, is a series of profound structural changes in our system of institutions.

Having seen the range of the criticism to the effect that big business runs the country, we now come to the second major criticism of big business: it is incompatible with the economic basis of democracy.

CHAPTER 4

"Big Business Is Incompatible with the Economic Basis of Democracy"

THE IDEA that big business is incompatible with the basic premises and conditions of liberal democracy appears primarily among critics who are inclined toward a materialist philosophy and an economic interpretation of history. But the idea also appears widely, even if only implicitly, in many other critics as well.

Not only is this idea (and closely related ideas) very widely held, but it seems to have exceptionally great force. For there is as yet, so far as I know, no well developed political theory that meets the argument head on. The ideology of liberal democracy and free enterprise, as it is generally stated or commonly understood, seems not to make any allowance that the large business corporation may make any *positive* contribution toward the goals of liberal democracy. Small business is commonly referred to as the "backbone" or the "underpinning" of a democratic society. There seems to be no place at all for big business in the generally accepted political theory of democracy. Certainly, there is no political theory of wide acceptance which does more than recognize the "right"—a right of private property—of a corporation to be large; in other words, which *permits* or *tolerates* the existence of large corporations. And even that notion has been seriously attacked, with some success, in the federal courts. In short, the criticism gains in power because there is, as yet, no positive theory to the contrary.

No argument comes closer than this one to being an argument that big business is bad per se. In many other criticisms leveled at big business, it is often explained that the criticism is directed only at aberrations, perversions, misapplications, and the like. But the criticisms which draw upon *this* argument, when reduced to their essence, are criticisms based upon what is conceived to be the *intrinsic nature* of big business.

To get a grasp of this underlying theory as to why big business cannot be reconciled with democracy, it will be necessary for the discussion, in the next few paragraphs, to proceed at a highly theoretical and abstract level. But since that *is* the nature of the argument, there doesn't seem to be any way of avoiding it. I shall be as brief and clear as I can.

The Theory of Democracy, as Amended

The matter goes back to certain concepts and theories as to the importance of *power* and its distribution in society. A stream of political ideas with which all Americans are more or less familiar holds that democracy can be attained and can flourish only if the distribution and structure of *power* accords with one particular system. Essential points in this stream of ideas, it seems to me, are these:

1. In their political and social rights and status — power — all men are equal.
2. All power in the community must rest ultimately in individuals — in the people.
3. The people, as seems expedient, create agencies of government which have only such powers as are conferred upon them by the people. These units of power are responsible to the people. They derive their powers from the consent of the governed.
4. The power of government to act upon individuals is limited. The individual, for instance, is safe from bills of attainder and enjoys the equal application of law. Governments may act upon the individual only through the due process of law. The individual enjoys forever certain inalienable rights.

In this stream of ideas, the key to democracy was the distribution and structure of *political* power.[1]

But in the theories of democracy held by the critics we shall review presently, another premise commonly appears: There must be a substantial degree of *economic* equality among individuals, not just political and social equality. For, if there is not substantial equality in *economic* power, there can be no substantial equality in *political* power, which is the very essence of democracy.

An important corollary that scarcely ever appears in explicit form any more is that there must be no entities in the community which have material or economic power other than individuals — the people — and the responsible units of government which they create.[2]

Under this view, *the* key to democracy is the distribution and structure of *economic* power.

To explore all the thinking which lies back of this added premise would take a book in itself. But there are a few points which are essential to an understanding of this economic — materialist — interpretation of democracy. First, it is assumed that power does not inhere in the individual as a human being. Not in his individuality nor in his individual rights. The individual has power, it would seem, only in proportion as he has *economic* power.

In an extreme version of this materialistic philosophy, the

1 In totally secularized versions, these ideas appear to go so far as to hold to the notion that the distribution and structure – the formal organization – of *power* is the *sole* determinant of the political qualities of a society. Sometimes these ideas have become so preoccupied with the matter of *power* that they ignore the crucial importance, also, of the prevailing presuppositions within the community as to the dignity, responsibility, nature, and destiny of Man. In such versions it would appear that democracy has no *moral* base or premises – that it is amoral, morally indifferent, or morally neutral. Maybe just "objective."

2 In times past much was made of this idea. See Charles C. Abbott, *The Rise of the Modern Corporation* (Cambridge, Harvard University Press, 1936). The idea still persists in residual form even though the great battles for free incorporation seemed to have been won long since.

only *real* kinds of power are physical force and economic power. Power, it would seem, inheres in material things. And the human use of the power of force or consent is commanded by the use of economic power. (More of this in a moment.) Accordingly, the basis and the real determinant of political power is economic power. For some theorists, *economic* power is the *only* relevant power. Some use the ideas of "power" and of "economic power" interchangeably. At any rate, according to this view, if *economic* power is not diffused — "atomized" — among individuals in substantially equal shares, those with greater economic means will obviously command disproportionate economic power. Thus enabled to exercise disproportionate *economic* power, the few will be enabled, accordingly and in turn, to exercise disproportionate *political* power. Thus, will democracy be destroyed.

Underlying these ideas is the assumption that all individuals are economically motivated toward their own materialistic ends.[3] It is this assumption that provides the basis for the idea that the power of disposal over *things* provides the basis for a controlling power of disposal over *persons,* and, through them, over government and other institutions. He who controls what people are after can control what they do. A form of human "engineering."

Another step takes this theoretical analysis to the core concept of the political economy of materialistic individualism. Great in their powers, individuals are viewed as pursuing their materialistic ends irresponsibly — without regard to the consequences for society as a whole. Out of this individualistic and irresponsible pursuit of materialistic ends, the best possible state of affairs will result. Best, that is, from the point of view of society as a whole. Will result, that is, *if* there is substantial economic equality among all individuals.

[3] From such a notion, it is but a step to infer, as some have done, that the objective of the exercise of any form of power is material gain: People, and especially "classes," want political power, not as an end in itself, but as a means to economic gain.

For *if* there is, then *all,* in their individualistic and irresponsible pursuit of material ends, will — of necessity — hold *each* in check as they compete and deal with one another. If they are not substantially equal, they will not be able to check one another. Economic confusion, instead of order, will result. Inequality will grow. Democracy will wane.

Since, according to theories of this order, "atomized" economic power will hold each and all in perfect check and harmony in their economic life, and since, in a materialistic society *economic* life is pretty much to be identified with the whole of life, the relevance of political power and the need for the exercise of power by government is reduced to the vanishing point. Things will run by themselves. Government needs but a minimum of power to keep the machine running. All other power is safely dispersed. The problem of power is solved. And democracy is assured.

The application of this chain of ideas to *big* business is immediate, and if accepted, devastating. For a *big* business necessarily has "disproportionate" powers of disposal over things. Large corporations will have a disproportionate share of economic power, of that thing which is the ultimate basis of *political* power. Disproportionate power, great power, not in the hands of the people, nor yet in the hands of government, must necessarily — "by definition" — be incompatible with democracy.

That is the argument.

These ideas are the foundation of the economic, or materialistic, interpretation — or amendation — of the principles of democracy.

"Big Business Has Too Much Power"

The following statement illustrates and outlines the theoretical tie-in which critics make between the classical theoretical model of an economy of "atomized" private *economic* power and the model of liberal democracy based on restricted governmental, and widely diffused individual, *political* power. This statement was formulated recently by Professor J. K. Galbraith, a Harvard economist, in the course of presenting his own ideas as to what should be done about big business: [4]

> The competitive model provided an almost perfect solution of the problem of power. . . . Given its rigorous prescription of competition, there was very little scope for the exercise of private economic power and none for its misuse. And with the private exercise of economic power so circumscribed, there was no need for public authority to regulate it. Specifically, if no business is large enough to influence prices on the market in which it sells or on the market in which labor or materials are bought, no one can do anything very harmful to consumers, suppliers or wages of workers because no one has any power over prices charged or prices or wages paid. The man who is moved to exploit his consumers through unduly high prices will survive only long enough to discover that they have deserted him in favor of his numerous competitors. To pay a worker less than the going wage is to invite him to go where the going wage is paid. It requires only a moment's reflection to conclude that a businessman with power neither to overcharge his customers nor to underpay his labor (and for similar reasons his other suppliers) has very little power to do anybody ill.
>
> To minimize the exercise of private power, and especially the opportunity for its misuse, was to remove most of the justification for exercise of government authority over the economy. It is unnecessary for government to control the exercise of private power if it does not exist in any harmful form. . . .[5]

[4] In the narrow sense, Professor Galbraith is talking here mostly about *economic* power. But this *economic* power is clearly intimately interrelated with, if not actually identified with, *political* power and with "power" *in general.*

[5] *American Capitalism* (Boston: Houghton Mifflin Company, 1952), p. 30. Professor Galbraith suggests that this state of affairs was not only a theoretical ideal but also an actuality; but it has now been "superseded." (Ibid., p. 119.) To his way of thinking, the fact that it has been superseded is largely attributable to the rise of big business. His recommendation is that the growth of other large, powerful entities — consumer, farm, and labor groups, and

This concept which economic determinists have of democracy is sometimes merely held up as a conceptual ideal. But it is often said that society — or at any rate, the British and American societies — in fact actually looked like this in some ideal past; say, in the year 1800, 1860, or 1890.[6]

Such a picture was painted by Thorstein Veblen, whose acid ideas have unmistakably etched their imprint on many American intellectuals:

> . . . the efficient and autonomous factor in the days of the small industry ["whose development culminated in the eighteenth century"] was the individual workman, his personal force, dexterity, and diligence; similarly in the petty trade of the precapitalistic English situation the decisive factor was the discretion and sagacity of the small merchant and the petty employer, who stood in direct personal relations with their customers and their employees. In so far as trade and industry was not restrained by conventional regulations, statutory or customary, both trade and industry was in effect an open field of free competition, in which man met man on a somewhat equable footing. . . .[7]

In starting to daub out a gallery of sorry sordid pictures of a Modern America filled with pathos and inequity, not to say iniquity — not to say stereotypes — a contemporary sociol-

---

even, in particular situations, large private corporations — should now be encouraged (or at least permitted) in order to provide adequate "countervailing power" to hold large corporations in check.

[6] For instance: "As late as when the Sherman Act was passed, the normal structure of competitive business contained many firms, each controlling a small part of the market. . . ." The Council of Economic Advisers, *Third Annual Report to the President,* 1948, p. 16.

A Canadian economist, the late E. J. Urwick, went back to the English village of the 15th Century — the era, we might note, of the unending bloody Wars of the Roses and of the Hundred Years' War — to depict this ideal state of affairs: There, the power of the shoemaker, carpenter, and the rest, was easily checked, since they "were pretty much on a level. If [any] tried to extort more than his due, public disapproval would correct him, or in the last resort, a boycott, and the substitution for his services of those of the corresponding manufacturer in a neighboring village." *The Values of Life* (Toronto: University of Toronto Press, 1948), p. 178.

[7] Thorstein Veblen, *The Theory of Business Enterprise,* p. 270.

ogist looks back on the vision of the happier times of a simpler world:

> The small entrepreneur built his world along the classic lines of middle-class capitalism: a remarkable society with a self-balancing principle, requiring little or no authority at the center, but only wide-flung traditions and a few safeguards for property. Here the ideas of the political economist Adam Smith coincided with those of the political moralist Thomas Jefferson; together they form the ideology of the naturally harmonious world of the small entrepreneur.[8]

If this ideal, harmonious world has been superseded, what's the reason? The rise of big business. For big business doesn't fit in with the ideal distribution and structure of power which, the theory holds, is a prerequisite condition of democracy.

In the first place, to restate, the very existence of large corporations is at odds with the ideal of atomized power. For the economic power — the real foundation of all power — of the large corporation is obviously enormously greater than that of the individual. The power of any one individual entrepreneur is puny — negligible — relative to the bulk of the whole society. But the large corporation is in command of an absolutely large power — a power so great that it is relatively large even when measured against the bulk of society. This power is so large that it loses its private character. It is so great, the contention runs, that its exercise becomes a matter of public concern.

This is a point made by the Director of Research of the International Ladies' Garment Workers' Union in a statement before the "Celler Committee" in 1949:

> The subject of economic concentration is usually linked with the evolution of the giant corporations which dominate the economic scene and which, by their size and resources, dwarf their smaller counterparts. Despite the injunction of

[8] C. Wright Mills, *White Collar,* p. 3.

Jefferson penned in a 1785 letter to Madison, that "legislators cannot invent too many devices for subdividing property" and despite antitrust legislation, bigness has not been banned and corporate expansion, even after it has achieved the ability to oppress, has not been curtailed.

Massive concentration of corporate wealth, strengthened by interlocking connections of one sort or another and the right of one corporation to acquire and hold the stock of another, is definitely a matter of public concern. The larger the business unit or a group of business units acting in concert, the greater is the impact of their business decisions on the welfare of our whole economy.[9]

Not long afterward, essentially the same idea — coupled with the idea that the policy decisions of large corporations are arbitrarily and irresponsibly unilateral — was voiced by the Associate Director of Research of the CIO:

As we see it, by their very size and power corporations such as General Motors, United States Steel, General Electric and others are in a position virtually to shape the ultimate levels of national income and employment for the whole of the United States in any given period.

What U. S. Steel does about prices will influence almost the entire economy. What General Motors decides about its 1950 production budget will have national repercussions on total employment level and outlook.

I guess most of you are familiar with the fact that corporations like General Motors do not go into the markets and try to sell their products at the start of the given year, rather they will sit down and make up a budget and decide "Next year we are going to produce fifty per cent more than we did last year," or, "We will produce two-thirds of what we produced last year."

Decisions like that have simply staggering significance for what happens to all of employment and all of national income and the whole of our economy. And yet we find we are

[9] Statement by Lazare Teper, *Study of Monopoly Power,* Part 1, p. 300. See also the statement of T. K. Quinn, ibid., Part 2-A, p. 383.

in the curious position where these very important decisions which are virtually public in character are made in purely private channels by small groups of private individuals.[10]

"The Great Power of Big Business Is Irresponsible"

Second, not only is the power of big business perfectly enormous — it is unchecked. It cannot be checked by individuals and small business. Far from meeting the large corporation on a "somewhat equable footing," they are overwhelmed by it. The individual small business cannot effectively bring power to bear to check, or to compete with the large corporation. To be sure, it is sometimes said that the large corporations of the big business community do have adequate power to act as checks upon one another. But, it will be remembered, economic critics say that they are monopolistic or oligopolistic and will not do so.[11] Their actions, it is argued — or implied, as by Mr. Kassalow in the quotation above — do not reflect adaptation to the objective facts and pressures of the market, but deliberate, arbitrary, unilateral administrative decisions.

Nor are the enormous disproportionate powers of the large corporation really checked by government. Having been declared to be an "individual," at law, the corporation has powers that government cannot — up to now — curb by the constitutional means at its disposal.

[10] Statement by Everett M. Kassalow, "Panel Discussion on the Economics and Legality of 'Bigness'," *Current Business Studies,* No. 5, February, 1950, p. 40.

Compare: ". . . all power tends to develop into a government in itself. Power that controls the economy should be in the hands of elected representatives of the people, not in the hands of an industrial oligarchy. Industrial power should be decentralized. It should be scattered into many hands so that the fortunes of the people will not be dependent on the whim or caprice, the political prejudices, the emotional stability of a few self-appointed men. The fact that they are not vicious men but respectable and social minded is irrelevant. That is the philosophy and the command of the Sherman Act." Mr. Justice Douglas, dissenting, in *United States* v. *Columbia Steel Co.* 334 U.S. 495, 536.

[11] Professor Galbraith does say that large corporations do operate as mutual checks when they are buying from, and selling to, *each other.*

Nor, it has been said many times, can even the stockholders of the large corporation act as a check upon its irresponsibility. This argument was advanced long ago by Adam Smith. It was put forward forty years ago by Louis D. Brandeis.

> . . . numerous small stockholdings create in the corporation a condition of irresponsible absentee landlordism; that is, the numerous small stockholders in the steel corporation, in the tobacco company, and in the other trusts occupy a position which is dangerous to society. They have a certain degree of wealth without responsibility. Their only desire is dividends. Their demand upon the managers is at most to maintain or increase the dividends. They have no power or responsibility; they have no relations to the employees; they are remote, often thousands of miles from the people who are toiling for them. Thus we have reproduced in industry the precise conditions which brought all the misery upon Ireland and upon other countries where absentee landlordism has prevailed.
>
> Large dividends are the bribes which the managers tender the small investor for the power conferred to use other people's money.[12]

The "separation" of ownership and control in the large corporation was the central topic of discussion twenty years ago in *The Modern Corporation and Private Property* by Berle and Means.[13]

In his final statement before the Temporary National Economic Committee in 1941, Senator Joseph C. O'Mahoney of Wyoming painted this picture of the large corporation with enormous, irresponsible, unchecked power — power not in the hands of the people, nor yet in the hands of governments.

> . . . there are only ten sovereign states which have within their respective borders property valued at more than the assets of either the Metropolitan Life Insurance Company or

12 Hearings before the Senate Committee on Interstate Commerce, *Control of Corporations, Persons, and Firms Engaged in Interstate Commerce,* Vol. 1, pp. 1156–1157.

13 Supra.

the American Telegraph and Telephone Company[14] . . . none of the [48] states has the constitutional power to regulate the activities of the artificial agencies they launch upon the sea of national commerce. . . .

. . . . .

. . . private enterprise is threatened . . . by a general failure to comprehend the change that has taken place and a failure properly to coordinate Government and business in their relation to people. This failure, it has seemed to me, is principally due to the fact that we seem not to realize that modern business is no longer the activity of individuals, but is the activity of organizations of individuals and we have permitted these organizations to grow so large that people are actually helpless before them. We have persisted in treating these organizations as though they were clothed with natural human rights instead of having only the rights which the people, acting through their Government, see fit to bestow upon them. It will be impossible even to begin the task of adjusting Government to business until we realize that the modern business organization has grown to such proportions that neither the people, as individuals, nor through their local governments are able to cope with it. Local business, little business, private enterprise and local government, even the government of the states themselves, are in truth and in fact submerged by modern business organizations.[15]

In the words of Professor Theodore J. Kreps of Stanford, modern large corporations are so large, their powers so great, their activities so diverse, that they have become "states within the state":

[14] This fact achieves relevancy when, and if, the premise is granted that "power" is proportionate to the economic power of disposal over things. The premise being granted, the reasoning implicit here runs: Metropolitan Life and A. T. & T. have more power of disposal over things than ten sovereign states. Ergo, they are more "powerful."

[15] T.N.E.C., *Investigation of Concentration of Economic Power, Final Report and Recommendations,* 77th Cong., 1st Sess. (Washington, Government Printing Office, 1941), pp. 677, 675.

As these corporations grew, their structure, activities, and control methods acquired much of the power and the impersonal immunity of political corporations or the state. Not only did "company towns" multiply but the business corporation largely controlled its government, its police force, housing, taxation, and even education.

More and more the corporation began to look like a state.

It had a legislative body, an executive, an administration, a department of state or public relations, a law department, a treasury, a corporate bureaucracy or civil service with personnel divisions and pension plans, frequently a company police, "service employees," even an espionage system.

Many business corporations became so large as to constitute in essence *états dans l'état,* rule-making bodies which laborers, suppliers, and even competitors were compelled to placate and obey. Its penalties, — unemployment, blacklisting, withdrawal of sources of credit and capital, "freezing out," dumping, and the like — more drastically affected small business than any practicable sanctions within the power of government.[16]

[16] Theodore J. Kreps, "Preserving Free, Competitive Enterprise," pp. 520–521.

Compare: "A modern corporation is an economic society, a little economic state, — and not always little, even as compared with states. Many modern corporations wield revenues and command resources which no ancient state possessed, and which some modern bodies politic show no approach to in their budgets. The economic power of society itself is concentrated in them for the conduct of this, that, or the other sort of business. . . .

"Society, in short, has discovered a new way of massing its resources and its power of enterprise, is building up bodies economic outside its bodies politic which may, if we do not find the means to prevent them, the means of disclosing the responsibilities of the men who compose them, dominate bodies politic themselves. . . . Society cannot afford to have individuals wield the power of thousands without personal responsibility. It cannot afford to let its strongest men be the only men who are inaccessible to the law. Modern democratic society, in particular, cannot afford to constitute its economic undertakings upon the monarchial or aristocratic principle and adopt the fiction that the kings and great men thus set up can do no wrong which will make them personally amenable to the law which restrains smaller men: that their kingdoms, not themselves, must suffer for their blindness, their follies, and their transgressions of right.

"It does not redeem the situation that these kings and chiefs of industry are not chosen upon the hereditary principle (sometimes, alas! they are) but

The critics of big business can find no place in their theory of democracy for any such an entity — an entity which has the irresponsible powers of the individual, but on an incomparably vaster scale; an entity with great powers which are checked — as they see things — by no other agency, not even by the Federal government itself; an entity which is not responsible to the people, even though its powers rival those of the state itself.

"This Power Is Used for Antisocial Ends"

But for the critics, even this is not the end of the matter. Let's go back to the very concept of business enterprise which the critics entertain. Every business enterprise, it is assumed, seeks its own material gain. The pursuit of profits, they say, is its *sole* purpose. This activity is carried on in a completely irresponsible manner.

In this regard, critics see small business as being no different from big business. But the irresponsibility of the individual or of the small business firm is held in check by competition, and its actions are so channelled — willy-nilly — as to serve the best ends of society. And even if, in isolated cases, this irresponsible behavior isn't checked, it doesn't make much difference. For the power of the individual small business is so inconsequential relative to the bulk of the

---

are men who have risen by their own capacity, sometimes from utter obscurity, with the freedom of self-assertion which should characterize a free society. Their power is none the less arbitrary and irresponsible when obtained. That a peasant may become king does not render the kingdom democratic." — Woodrow Wilson, "The Lawyer and the Community," an address delivered before the American Bar Association, 1910, and reprinted in *College and State; Educational, Literary and Political Papers (1875–1913)* Ray Stannard Baker and William E. Dodd, Editors (New York: Harper & Brothers Publishers, 1925), Vol. II, pp. 255–257. [This address was reproduced as "Chapter I" of W. Z. Ripley's *Main Street and Wall Street* (Boston: Little, Brown, and Company, 1927); most of this passage was reproduced in Jerome N. Frank's, *Save America First* (New York: Harper & Brothers Publishers, 1938). Both of these authors, I think it is fair to say, can be counted among the critics of big business.]

whole society, that the effects of these aberrations can safely be disregarded.[17]

This line of argument we have been through. But in the hands of some critics it is taken a step further. *They* say that not only are all these things true. But, beyond this, they argue, the very purposes and objectives which are intrinsic to large corporations — and, consequently, to their effects on the community — are malevolent in nature.

This concept of the purpose and effects of business enterprise — especially *big* enterprise — runs all through the writings of Thorstein Veblen who has so profoundly influenced much of American critical thinking.

Veblen was a thoroughgoing materialist. The national income, in his view, was generated by impersonal, material forces. In his views, the national economy seems to be something like a vast clock-work — a machine which, left unhampered, would tick-tock away by itself to produce the ideal national product. To be sure, there is the aid of "available technical knowledge" (to which, Veblen notes, the businessman has contributed "less than his per capita quota") plus "expert knowledge, insight, and disinterested judgment" of "industrial engineers." But, in this materialistic, mechanistic world there is no place for any positive contribution for the "businessman" (or for the administrator) as distinguished — by Veblen — from the technician.

Within this mechanistic system, which — presumably — would run by itself, the object of business enterprise is not production, but profits. And profits come, not from production, but from the intervention of business in what would be the normal unfettered workings of the machine. Profits are made by *interfering* with what, apparently, would be the natural and inevitable ticking of the industrial mechanism.

Since the apparatus, with only the aid of engineers, would

17 Compare Corwin D. Edwards, *Maintaining Competition,* mentioned in footnote 47 on p. 94, above.

tick away by itself to produce the maximum and ideal national product, clearly there is no possibility of any positive contribution by "businessmen." Accordingly, any gains by them, anything they take out of the stream of income, must represent a loss to someone else — "the common man," Veblen tells us — who would otherwise have received it.

Indeed, there is a *net loss* to society — not merely a redistribution of income — since the production lost to society because of the "businessman's" tampering with the machine is greater than what he gains. Thus, Veblen tells us in *The Vested Interests and the State of the Industrial Arts:*

> The business man's place in the economy of nature is to "make money," not to produce goods. The production of goods is a mechanical process, incidental to the making of money; whereas the making of money is a pecuniary operation, carried on by bargain and sale, not by mechanical appliances and powers.
>
> . . . Business is a pursuit of profits, and profits are to be had from profitable sales, and profitable sales can be made only if prices are maintained at a profitable level, and prices can be maintained only if the volume of marketable output is kept within reasonable limits; so that the paramount consideration in such business as has to do with the staple industries is a reasonable limitation of the output. "Reasonable" means "what the traffic will bear"; that is to say, "what will yield the largest net return."
>
> . . . The highest achievement in business is the nearest approach to getting something for nothing. What any given business concern gains must come out of the total output of productive industry, of course. . . . [It is evident] that the owner or manager of any given concern or section of this industrial system may be in a position to gain something for himself at the cost of the rest by obstructing, retarding or dislocating this working system at some critical point in such a way as will enable him to get the best of the bargain in his dealings with the rest. . . . Sabotage of this kind is indispensable to any large success in industrial business. But it

> is also evident that the private gain which the business concerns come in for by this management entails a loss on the rest of the community, and that the loss suffered by the rest of the community is necessarily larger than the total gains which these manoeuvres bring to the business concerns; inasmuch as the friction, obstruction and retardation of the moving equilibrium of production involved in this businesslike sabotage necessarily entails a disproportionate curtailment of output.[18]

All this applies to all business, of whatever size — and, of course, applies with special strength to big business. Not only that, it is above all in "the larger mechanical industries" that control is in the hands of "persons who are highly skilled in the higgling of the market, the masters of financial intrigue." These "businessmen" have no technical knowledge and do not need it. Such matters are left largely to subordinates. The real directors of big business — "the businessmen" — merely approve or veto what the technicians propose. The control of the "businessmen" who constitute the directorate "does not effectually extend much beyond the regulation of the output with a view to what the traffic will bear." Indeed, having no socially useful — that is, no technical — skill, "there is very little that the 'businessmen' in charge can do except to keep the output short of productive capacity by so much as the state of the market seems to require." [19]

[18] New York: B. W. Huebsch, 1919, pp. 91–94.

[19] Ibid., pp. 91–92. Compare: ". . . As a university president, I learned that the men who dominate our manufacturing processes could not conduct their business for twenty-four hours without the assistance of the experts with whom the universities were supplying them. Modern industry depends upon technical knowledge; and all that these gentlemen did was to manage the external features of great combinations and their financial operation, which had very little to do with the intimate skill with which the enterprises were conducted. I know men not catalogued in the public prints, men not spoken of in public discussion, who are the very bone and sinew of the industry of the United States." — Woodrow Wilson, *The New Democracy; Presidential Messages, Addresses, and Other Papers (1913–1917)*, Ray Stannard Baker and William E. Dodd, Editors (New York: Harper & Brothers Publishers, 1926), Vol. 1, p. 16.

It is true, Veblen concedes, that business enterprise is not *wholly* taken up with "manoeuvres of restraint, obstruction and competitive selling." But in big business — "More particularly in the management of the greater industrial enterprises of the present day, the larger as well as the more lucrative part of the duties of those who direct affairs appears commonly to be of this nature." [20]

Fifteen years earlier, in his *Theory of Business Enterprise,* we find the same concept:

> . . . business men whose work is not simply routine constantly give some attention to manoeuvring . . . and to the discovery of new opportunities for putting their competitors at a disadvantage. This seems to apply in a peculiar degree, if not chiefly, to those classes of business men whose operations have to do with railways and the class of securities called "industrials." Taking the industrial process as a whole, it is safe to say that at no time is it free from derangements of this character in any of the main branches of modern industry. This chronic state of perturbation is incident to the management of industry by business methods and is unavoidable under existing conditions. So soon as the machine industry had developed to large proportions, it became unavoidable, in the nature of the case, that the business men in whose hands lies the conduct of affairs should play at cross-purposes and endeavor to derange industry. . . .[21]

Veblen's views, perhaps, are somewhat extreme. But we have already seen that a widely accepted view is that the companies of the big business community were put together, not for any sincere, socially sound objectives, but for purposes of predatory, monopolistic gain.[22] And in the large bulk of

[20] *The Vested Interests . . . ,* p. 96.

[21] Pages 34–35.

[22] There is certainly no suggestion in the following passage that the growth of large corporations could in any degree be attributed to a measure of success in a continuing quest for new products, new markets, improvement in product design or in production methods and equipment: "The increased volume of business necessary to permit [the growth of the large corporation] has been attained in part by price cutting; the largest firms, however, have more frequently attained their present size either by direct attacks upon

accepted economic theory, no constructive, dynamic purposes or effects are attributed to the business firm, large *or* small, and certainly not to the "monopolistic" or "oligopolistic" competitor. Underlying the theory of monopolistic competition as a basic premise, is a static view of business enterprise. Competitors are viewed, as they are by Professor Chamberlin and his many followers, as vying with one another to make sales against *given* wants. Production is viewed as being carried on by means of *given* techniques. Such views, inherent in static economic analysis, are not so very distant from the ideas of Veblen.

"Big Business Has Brought on Big Government and Big Labor"

A few critics make a further particular point in the argument that big business is incompatible with the economic and political bases of democracy. These people say that big business has caused the rise of big government and big labor. Big government and big labor, it is claimed, have arisen in direct and necessary reaction to the great and growing irresponsible and malevolent power of big business. Just the same, these critics say, these new entities of major political importance don't really fit in with democracy any more than big business. Like big business, they too represent a gross departure from the premises of democracy with regard to the ideal structure and distribution of power. In the eyes of some of these critics, these new enormous concentrations of power present just as great a threat to the future of democracy as big business, if not greater. In a sense, responsibility is placed upon big business not only for its own past, present, and future short-comings, but for those of big government and big labor besides.

The following passage from an article by the Honorable

---

rivals in the form of temporary or local price cutting aimed at destroying them, by defaming their products and the like, or by mergers." Arthur Robert Burns, *The Decline of Competition,* p. 8. See also Chapter 1, pp. [33–35], above.

Estes Kefauver, now Senator, then Congressman, from Tennessee, illustrates how the rise of big business is linked to the rise of big government and big labor.

> . . . Monopoly in industry long preceded the emergence of large labor organizations; in fact, it is the very existence of giant industrial corporations which has made almost inevitable the development of large labor organizations, and in turn, of big Government agencies to deal with the two of them.
>
> If we may learn anything from the history of other nations, it is that the time schedule reads: first, big business; second, big labor; third, big government; and fourth, collectivism. It appears that we in this country have long since passed the first stage; we have recently entered the second and now we are embarking upon the third. Can anyone be so blind as not to see what the fourth step will inevitably be? [23]

It is often said by critics, or implied, that if there were no big business there would be no big government and no big labor. If all business were small, power would be atomized. Small businesses, as we have heard, would hold each other in check, aided by local pressures as powerful as the business entities themselves. Since there would be no points of undue power, and since the economy would be a free-working and self-regulating mechanism, there would be no large role for government to play. Hence it would need no large powers.

But when business is big, it is monopolistic. Competition is not operative as a check. And local pressures are overshadowed by the power of the large corporation. The large corporation is not even responsible to its stockholders.

Since it is intolerable that there should be any such entities, and since their perverse workings make them even more intolerable, a new means must be found to check them. That means is big government — bitterly enough. For big gov-

[23] "The Coming Showdown," *The Progressive and La Follette's Magazine*, Vol. 11, No. 35, September 8, 1947, p. 1.

ernment is itself a still further departure from the traditional ideal of democracy.

Pretty clearly, ideas along these lines are embodied in the following passage:

> I believe that all those who fear Big Government should realize that Big Business not only is a curse in itself, but is the primary cause of Big Government. No one is disturbed about the size of government in its ordinary functions, such as those of judge, postmistress, soldier, sailor, diplomat, collector of taxes, educator of farmers, conservator of natural resources, or keeper of the peace.
>
> However, the difficulties arise when the private banks, insurance companies, big industrials, big utilities, big produce middlemen, are in such a position of domination as to wipe out virtually all competition or secretly join with competitors in antisocial moves. Then certainly the uncontrolled judgment of such interests cannot be allowed free play. And this is true for a very simple reason. Those with such power permit personal cupidity to override the commonweal. . . .
>
> The sure way to prevent too much power from being placed in the government is to prevent the concentration of private power.[24]

By analogous reasoning, critics say that big labor, also, has arisen as a reaction and as an offset to the great power of big business. Small business, labor could cope with. Small businesses competed freely for labor. If a man didn't like his employer, he could easily go elsewhere. In any case, the power of the employer was not appreciably greater than that of the employee — "man met man on a somewhat equable footing." But when business became big, and embodied concentrated, noncompetitive power, the only way for labor to get a fair shake was to become big too — big enough so that it could still meet business on an equable footing — and just as collusive. This is the historical analysis given by Professor Galbraith:

[24] Morris Ernst, *Too Big,* p. 278.

> . . . Not often has the power of one man over another been used more callously than in the American labor market after the rise of the large corporation. As late as the early twenties, the steel industry worked a twelve-hour day and seventy-two hour week with an incredible twenty-four hour stint every fortnight when the shift changed.
>
> No such power is exercised today and for the reason that its earlier exercise stimulated the counteraction that brought it to an end. In the ultimate sense it was the power of the steel industry, not the organizing abilities of John L. Lewis and Philip Murray, that brought the United Steel Workers into being. The economic power that the worker faced in the sale of his labor — the competition of many sellers dealing with few buyers — made it necessary that he organize for his own protection. . . .
>
> As a general though not invariable rule there are strong unions in the United States only where markets are served by strong corporations. And it is not an accident that the large automobile, steel, electrical, rubber, farm-machinery and non-ferrous metal-mining and smelting companies all bargain with powerful CIO unions. . . . By contrast there is not a single union of any consequence in American agriculture, the country's closest approach to the competitive model.[25]

According to a very common line of reasoning among the critics, big labor arose to protect the economic interests of the working man against the power of big business. As far as they can see, it may serve that purpose well enough. But, they go on, the protection of the general weal then requires a big government to protect the community against both big business *and* big labor and to place a check upon them both. Unfortunately, big government is the very opposite of an atomized power structure, the antithesis of liberal democracy.

It seems to me that this is the idea implicit in the quotation from Senator Kefauver. This is the analysis given in about so many words by Guido de Ruggiero, the eminent Italian

[25] J. K. Galbraith, *American Capitalism*, pp. 121–122.

philosopher, as we shall see in a moment. According to these lights, to repeat, liberal democracy can only survive where power is atomized. Where power is gathered together in big business and big labor, and in massive government over all, liberal democracy soon withers. Society becomes authoritarian, first in fact, later in form. This all stems back to bigness in business.

Thus, Professor de Ruggiero:

> [As "industry reached maturity"] . . . it became necessary to organize enterprises on larger and larger scales — thus limiting the initiative of the constituent elements. . . . In defense against concentration by capital labor inaugurated its own program of concentration as the only means for bettering its condition. Both types of concentration assumed dictatorial forms. . . . Liberalism thus found itself hemmed in between two opposed forces having in common only a basic antipathy to liberal tenets and technique. Individualism proved to be more and more inadequate for satisfying the new organic needs of society. While the political forms of liberalism still remained intact, the conflict for power between the forces of plutocracy and those of economic democracy threatened to distort them beyond recognition. The concept of a free sphere of activities with an impartial police state gave way to the concept of a state which should be conquered as a vehicle for the attainment of class objectives. Under this double set of forces the jurisdiction of the state was gradually extended far beyond the boundaries surveyed by liberalism. . . .[26]

[26] Article on "Liberalism," *Encyclopaedia of the Social Sciences* (New York: The Macmillan Company, 1933), Vol. 9, pp. 440–441. (Quoted with the permission of The Macmillan Company.)

Professor George J. Stigler, an ardent critic of big business, doesn't give much credence to the idea that big business has brought about big labor and big government. He does not give big business a clean bill of health, but he feels that "the scope and evils of big business are usually enormously exaggerated, especially with reference to labor and agriculture . . . more often than not these evils are merely a soapbox excuse for shoddy policies elsewhere." The public, he says, needs "extensive education" as to "how small a part of the economy is controlled by big business." Even so, since big business *is* guilty of "widespread monopolistic practices," "We have no right

"Something Must Be Done About Big Business"

Even though they might or might not accept the general gist of some of the more extreme views we have seen in this chapter and the last, many critics are prepared to conclude that big business is *so* incompatible with liberal democratic theory and practice — that it is, indeed, such a danger to democracy — that something must be done about it. That "something" varies enormously. But generally speaking it is likely to involve, if not nationalization, then either the dissolution of big business, or its control by government.

Thoroughgoing and minutely detailed government control was the solution of Theodore Roosevelt as he campaigned on the Progressive ticket in 1912:

> The people of this country are not afraid of the mere size of a business enterprise provided it is honestly organized and honestly managed. But they feel that such size carries with it a potentiality of wrong-doing that makes it necessary that the Nation, and if necessary the States, shall exercise over big business a control and supervision which are unnecessary as regards small business.
>
> . . . . .
>
> . . . Our proposal is to establish an administrative body which shall take absolute control over these big industrial concerns, just as the Inter-State Commerce Commission does with railroads or the Banking Department with banks – and a control such as will enable us to go in and inspect every big concern, inspect every practice, put a stop to rebates, put a stop to any issue of watered stock, put a stop to every practice which is not in accordance with the rules of decency and honesty, and then not to stop even there but to exercise such supervision over the big industrial concerns as will insure justice not only to the rival and the stockholders and the general public but to the wage-workers as well.[27]

---

to ask public opinion to veer away from big unions and big government – and toward big business." (See "The Case Against Big Business," pp. 158–162.)

[27] Theodore Roosevelt, *Progressive Principles*, pp. 185, 190.

A generation later Franklin Roosevelt, as for example in his letter which instigated the Temporary National Economic Committee, saw either dissolution or government control — or both — as necessary reactions to the great power of big business.

> The power of a few to manage the economic life of the Nation must be diffused among the many or be transferred to the public and its democratically responsible government. If prices are to be managed and administered, if the Nation's business is to be allotted by plan and not by competition, that power should not be vested in any private group or cartel, however benevolent its professions profess to be.[28]

The premise that modern technology requires large-scale production and organization, and that the breaking up of large-scale enterprise is neither possible nor tolerable from the point of view of social efficiency, is accepted by many social and political critics. But, in their way of thinking, since big business is incompatible with democracy, its growth and development necessarily produces an evolution away from traditional liberal democracy. This combination of ideas leads to the conclusion that big business will either become, itself, big government — Fascism; or big government will become big business — Socialism or Communism. In either case, liberal democracy is a thing of the past.

Here is this kind of thinking as expressed by Professor Robert S. Lynd, who has been quoted already in these pages:

> Liberal democracy . . . never solved the problem of bigness; but it alternately fought and condoned it in a confusion of inconsistent policies. A cultural system drenched with the artisan spirit of small enterprise found difficulty in accepting the facts that modern machinery demands integration and that productive enterprise, released from making a pair

28 T.N.E.C., *Investigation of the Concentration of Economic Power, Economic Prologue,* p. 188.

> of shoes for a known local customer and set to making standard goods for an impersonal and theoretically unlimited "market," likewise demands organization. Hence the recurrent efforts to curb bigness. But both bigness and monopoly are normal antecedents to the stage of planned provision for the needs of society which we are now entering, and there is no longer any point in attacking either. The only relevant questions today are: Who controls these productive facilities, and to what ends? and How effectively are they organized to achieve these ends? Or, stated in another way: Will democratic political power absorb and use economic resources, bigness and all, to serve its ends, or will big economic power take over state power? [29]

Other critics, like the English Socialist, Professor G. D. H. Cole, are somewhat more candid as to what their preferences are, or as to what their actual forecasts are, now that — according to their theories — liberal democracy is done for:

> A return to laissez faire is impossible. The concentration of capital needed for the full exploitation of modern productive resources is too great to be left uncontrolled by the state; for those who have this concentrated capital in their hands will assuredly control the state unless it controls them. . . .[30]

Whatever be the facts of the matter, and they are surely very complex, ideas like these do give, by themselves, an apparent credibility to the theory that big business does indeed bring about big government.

Conclusion

With this, we finish up with our review of the theoretical, the ideological, argument that big business is incompatible with the basic economic and political premises and conditions of liberal democracy. If this train of argument is accepted,

[29] From Professor Lynd's Foreword to Robert A Brady's *Business as a System of Power,* pp. xii–xiii.

[30] "Industrialism," *Encyclopaedia of the Social Sciences* (New York: The Macmillan Company, 1932), Vol. 8, p. 26. (Quoted with the permission of The Macmillan Company.)

anyone devoted to democratic values and ideals can scarcely avoid reaching the conclusion that big business is bad per se. Anyone looking forward with some interest and enthusiasm to a "New Order," to a wave of the future, or to an "inevitable" evolutionary next step, is likely to find that big business is bad, per se, in any case — even if on somewhat different grounds.

We shall now move on to the criticism that big business is incompatible with the social bases of democracy.

CHAPTER 5

"Big Business Is Incompatible with the Social Bases of Democracy"

THE THIRD major theme that runs through the political and social criticism of big business is that big business is incompatible with the *social* goals and premises of democracy. More. Not only is big business itself incompatible with the social goals and premises of democracy, critics say it is displacing and even driving out that form of economic organization which *is* compatible: *small* business. And the matter does not stop even there. For there are critics who say that big business generates gigantic pressures which, reaching out through liberal, democratic society, are operating to transform it into a totalitarian state.

More specifically, critics say that whereas democracy presupposes and cherishes a nation of independent property owners and individual "entrepreneurs," big business brings into the society simply "wage earners," "clerks," "mere agents," and "hirelings." Some say that big business is causing society to change from a commercial and manufacturing "yeomanry" of independent businessmen into a nation of payroll dependents. At best, it is a social loss that large numbers of people should lead the life of an employee rather than the life of an independent businessman.

More than this, it is said that such a society cannot for long sustain the substance of liberal democracy: salary and wage earners will not have the qualities society needs in order to cope democratically with the complex problems of civilized life. And the small businessmen who do remain will abandon the goals and methods of democracy in their effort to save themselves from the irresistible competitive pressure of big business. The new society will turn away from democracy and will give its loyalties and support to totalitarian government.

Altogether, critics say that big business is bringing about social changes of such a magnitude as to threaten the continued existence of democracy as we have known it — if, indeed, that democracy has not already been undermined beyond the point of collapse.

Clearly, these criticisms go far beyond those we have already seen, namely, that the large corporation is a new power entity which cannot be assimilated into our scheme of things, and that big business has captured and turned our institutions to its own advantage. What is alleged here is a subversion of democracy far more profound, if less direct, than the subversion which is involved in the corruption of voters, the manipulation of legislatures, or the infiltration of government.

The present strictures tend to hold that big business operates in such a fashion as to *destroy* the social structure which is the very foundation of democracy. To some of the critics, this characteristic of big business — as they see it — is a remediable defect. To some, it is inherent, either in large-scale production or in capitalism itself. But in any case, this is the ultimate in the political and social criticism of big business.

The "Mere Agent" vs. The "Entrepreneur"

The starting point of this criticism is the concept, the picture, which critics have of the corporate *employee* as contrasted to their concept, their ideal, of the independent businessman.

Viewed from the *outside,* the large corporation appears to critics as a huge, powerful entity — irresponsibly seeking its own gain, more often than not at the expense of the rest of the community. As they conceive how it looks viewed from the *inside,* the large corporation appears to critics as an authoritarian collectivism. Inside this organization the individual counts for little. He is a "clerk," a "mere servant." He needs but scant initiative, for he exercises none or but little. His responsibility, which extends only to his superiors in the organization, is to do as he's told. As a "mere agent" of a corporation, he has no individual responsibility toward society for his own actions as he goes about his daily toil. He is dependent on the organization for his livelihood. At most he has only the merest property interest in the material things with which he works. Even if he has a very high-ranking position in a large corporation, he is still only a "half-a-life" man. Clearly, such an individual has less than his full measure of human dignity.

The economically self-dependent individual is different. He owns the property with which he works. He is dependent for his livelihood only upon his own capacity to cope with the impersonal forces of the markets and upon his ability to compete with large numbers of other individuals like himself. He has unlimited scope for his initiative. Where society, through its government of limited powers, lawfully imposes responsibilities on its citizens, he is fully and individually responsible for his own actions. But, he is "beholden to no one." He is every man's equal. He is no man's man but his own. He is responsible to himself. As a human being going about his ordinary activities, he answers fully to his own conscience.

Such images of the individual as corporate employee and as independent entrepreneur occur commonly in the criticism of big business and the praise of small business. Sometimes they are set forth in considerable detail. Sometimes they are only implicit. They are widely encountered. They can be discerned in decisions and dissents of Supreme Court Justices.

A couple of quotations will serve as a beginning to show how, often in bits and snatches, these impressions of corporate and individualistic life crop up. These images will be rounded out as we go along.

Here is a fragment from the article on "Corporation" written by A. A. Berle, Jr., and Gardiner C. Means for the *Encyclopaedia of the Social Sciences:*

> . . . With the increase in the scale of business more and more individuals who might have been independent entrepreneurs have become major or minor executives without the independence and the full spur of business profits inherent in private enterprise. . . .[1]

Here, from the testimony of a one-time vice president of a large corporation, is a fuller development with obvious ethical and moral nuances:

> There is a deep moral and spiritual difference between the responsible president of an independent company and the dependent manager of a subsidiary factory. The manager is not part of the community in which he lives because his interest and attention is directed toward officials in New York or elsewhere. On them he is dependent for his job, his income, and his progress. He cannot have the same interest in the people employed in the plant. He operates according to rules made by others – handed down to him – and can hardly afford to be a good human being, which helps to explain the abuse of workers and the rise of unions. As a figurehead in position without authority he loses something essential within himself, like Kipling's description "some of him lived but most of him died." And I have seen this happen to company presidents and others – who became half-a-life men when they were merged into huge corporations.[2]

Not only department and division heads, but even presidents and chairmen of the boards of directors of large corporations — it is suggested — may have less scope for individual action, self-expression and fulfillment than the humblest independent businessman. Thus, again from Berle and

1 New York: The Macmillan Company, 1931, Vol. 4, p. 422. (Quoted with the permission of The Macmillan Company.)

2 Testimony of Mr. T. K. Quinn, *Study of Monopoly Power,* Part 2-A, p. 382.

Means — this time from *The Modern Corporation and Private Property:*

> Group activity, the coordinating of the different steps in production, the extreme division of labor in large scale enterprise necessarily imply not individualism but cooperation and the acceptance of authority almost to the point of autocracy. . . . At the very pinnacle of the hierarchy of organization in a great corporation, there alone, can individual initiative have a measure of free play. Yet even there a limit is set by the willingness and ability of subordinates to carry out the will of their superiors. In modern industry, individual liberty is necessarily curbed.[3]

It is, I take it, concepts like these which underlie the implicit identification of "channels of opportunity for young men and women" with *small* business. *Big* business, presumably, may offer them "employment," but not "opportunity." For — we are told — even at the very peak of the large corporation, there is only a *measure* of free play for individual initiative.

As often conceived and portrayed, the way of life and the opportunities for self-expression and self-realization offered to the individual by small business are vastly richer than those held out by the large corporation. In this light, the

[3] Op. cit., p. 349. (Quoted with the permission of The Macmillan Company.)

Many critics in attacking the large corporation seem to be reflecting rather absolutist ideals in their concept of individualism. The idea seems to be lurking in the background that individualism or individual freedom means the *absolute,* unrestricted expression of the self. Berle and Means seem to be suggesting here that man is indeed an "island," incapable of working in a group spontaneously, harmoniously, democratically, and with satisfaction. For them, group activity *necessarily* implies acceptance of authority almost to the point of autocracy. The need of the individual for "individualism" seems to be so absolute that only by the pressure of authority to the point of autocracy can he be reconciled with the group.

Upon such misanthropic assumptions and notions as this is the police state based.

Of such notions as this comes the idea that administration is necessarily an authoritarian process, and that the relationships inside the large corporation — a *large* group — are *necessarily* authoritarian.

rise of big business appears as much more than an evolution in the form and structure of economic organization. It appears as a large-scale growth of an inferior way of life. It appears as a socially and morally undesirable movement.

As many of the critics see things, this growth of an inferior way of life for the individual is a matter for public dismay. For, to them this process is not only deplorable from the point of view of the individuals actually involved. It must also be — they indicate — a matter of general distress in a society whose primary communal objectives are devoted to assuring the well-being of the individual. From such views, the idea flows naturally that society can properly — and should — use its collective powers to foster small business and to discourage the growth of big business. Under this philosophy, such a course of public action to protect individuals from this inferior way of life is in the interest of the community at large.

This is the chain of reasoning and philosophy which, as I interpret it, underlies the oft-cited dictum of the Supreme Court in the *Trans-Missouri* decision:

> . . . ["trusts" or "combinations"] may even temporarily, or perhaps permanently, reduce the price of the article traded in or manufactured, by reducing the expense inseparable from the running of many different companies for the same purpose. Trade or commerce under those circumstances may nevertheless be badly and unfortunately restrained by driving out of business the small dealers and worthy men whose lives have been spent therein, and who might be unable to readjust themselves to their altered surroundings. Mere reduction in the price of the commodity dealt in might be dearly paid for by the ruin of such a class and the absorption of control over one commodity by an all-powerful combination of capital. . . .
>
> . . . the result in any event is unfortunate for the country, by depriving it of the services of a large number of small but independent dealers, who were familiar with the business, and who had spent their lives in it, and who supported them-

> selves and their families from the small profits realized therein. Whether they be able to find other avenues to earn their livelihood is not so material, because it is not for the real prosperity of any country that such changes should occur which result in transferring an independent business man, the head of his establishment, small though it might be, into a mere servant or agent of a corporation for selling the commodities which he once manufactured or dealt in; having no voice in shaping the business policy of the company, and bound to obey orders issued by others. . . .[4]

Of the concepts which are implicit here as to the roles of the individual in small and large business enough comes through to suggest their outlines. The individual in big business is a "mere servant or agent." He has "no voice" in what goes on. His job is simply to "obey orders issued by others." Clearly, it is visualized that he works for something like an authoritarian collectivism.

In passing, we might remark that this concept here and the concept of Mr. Justice Brandeis which we saw in Chapter 1, that administration is, by definition, an authoritarian process, are essentially one and the same. One is the obverse of the other: Looking down in the organization, the administrator exercises judgment, makes the decisions, issues orders, and, with his own "master's eye," checks up to see that his will is done. Looking up in the organization from the levels below, the individual accepts the direction of his superiors and obeys orders, and does what he's told. There is responsibility and initiative — "voice" — only at the top.

To return to the passage from the *Trans-Missouri* decision. In this expression of social philosophy, there is also a value judgment that is especially noteworthy: The exchange of small independent businessmen for employees of big business entails a *moral* loss to society in terms of the initiative, liberty, and dignity of individuals. Even if greater economic efficiency should result, the *economic* gains to society would

[4] *United States* v. *Trans-Missouri Freight Association* (1897), 116 U.S. 290.

not offset this *moral* loss. Such a gain would be too dearly paid for.

In one of the most notable cases of recent years, *United States* v. *Aluminum Company of America,* Judge Learned Hand of the Circuit Court of Appeals harked back to ideas of this order. He gave it as the opinion of the court that Congress, in passing the Sherman Antitrust Act, was acting primarily out of social and moral motives. The objective, it appears from this viewpoint, was to preserve small business as an ideal way of life, as part of an ideal *social* order.

In the Court's opinion, speaking through Judge Hand, Congress

> . . . did not condone "good trusts" and condemn "bad" ones; it forbad all. Moreover, in so doing it was not necessarily actuated by economic motives alone. It is possible, because of its indirect social or moral effect, to prefer a system of small producers, each dependent for his success upon his own skill and character, to one in which the great mass of those engaged must accept the direction of a few. These considerations, which we have suggested only as possible purposes of the Act, we think the [relevant] decisions prove to have been in fact its purposes.[5]

A few paragraphs below, Judge Hand again emphasized the Court's belief that Congress has had other than just "economic reasons" in passing the Antitrust Acts. There are, he said, other reasons

> . . . based upon the belief that great industrial consolidations are inherently undesirable, regardless of their economic results. . . . Throughout the history of [the Antitrust Acts] it has been constantly assumed that one of their purposes was to perpetuate and preserve, for its own sake and in spite of possible cost, an organization of industry in small units which can effectively compete with each other. . . .[6]

[5] *United States* v. *Aluminum Company of America, et al.* (1945), 148 F. 2d. 416, 427.

[6] Ibid., pp. 428 and 429.

These passages from notable court decisions clearly convey the idea that big business is bad per se — is "inherently undesirable." And the evil of big business — to this way of thinking — lies in its *social* consequences, regardless of its *economic* consequences. The evil of big business lies in the supplanting of a "system of small producers, each dependent for his success upon his own skill and character," by a system in which the individual has "no voice" and is "bound to obey orders issued by others."

This is a profoundly significant line of reasoning. It is so significant, it seems to me, that we will do well to stay with it for a few minutes even though this means digressing from the main line of thought. For this idea, logically extended, implies that there is *no* defense to the charge of "bigness" except to show that a corporation is *not* "big."

A Digression on Big Business and the Sherman Act

If big business is "inherently undesirable," if small business should be preserved "for its own sake," then there is *no* pragmatic defense of big business to be made. It would do no good to show, even *if* it can be shown, that in practice and in particular cases big business has operated to give economic satisfaction. For — by basic presuppositions — the evil of big business lies in its nature: It represents a departure from an ethically and morally ideal social pattern.

This philosophy has immediate bearing on the interpretation and application of the Sherman Act. According to this philosophy bigness in business is a state of affairs, an *end* result, which is evil in itself. The *end* being evil, it is — in strict logic — of little consequence what the *means* are by which it is reached. To be sure, particular means may be declared unlawful, per se. But it is of comparatively little moment *how* an evil end is attained. Given the basic ideas we have seen, it is only of legalistic and sentimental moment, for example, whether the growth of big business is due to conspiracy and contracts in restraint of trade or to something else — say, like superior efficiency, or active and imaginative enterprise.

Some court decisions, notably the "Steel" decision, seem to have held that the Sherman Act "did not make mere size an offense." In that leading case even a minority opinion agreed that a large corporation "is entitled to maintain its size and the power that legitimately goes with it, *provided no law has been transgressed in obtaining it.*"[7]

Such a doctrine would seem to imply the thought that, in passing the Sherman Act, Congress was motivated in the direction of outlawing as evil certain *means* by which big business might come into being, but *not* the *end* result of bigness itself.

Many critics of big business believe that this doctrine subverted the intent of Congress. *They* say that the *end* — bigness in business — is the evil that Congress struck at, and that the *means* by which bigness comes about are only of incidental consequence.[8]

For instance, it would seem there is more than just the germ of this idea in the "Alcoa" decision. Apparently, the Court didn't see much evidence to suggest that conspiracy and contracts in restraint of trade played any important part in the growth of the company. The Aluminum Company had, however, diligently, zealously, and with foresight, exploited its opportunities. Ordinarily the diligent exploitation of opportunity would not appear as an evil. Not in this country. Nor was it condemned as such here. However, it led in this case — the Court said — to an evil result. For the energetic and unfailing exploitation of opportunity by a

[7] *United States* v. *United States Steel Corporation* (1920), 251 U.S. 417, 451, and 460. (Italics added.)

[8] We have seen, in Chapter 1, that a common view of critics is that the *means* of big business growth *have* been antisocial. Many of them, apparently, would disallow the possibility that business *can* become big by anything but antisocial means.

company which was already large had the evil end *result* of foreclosing opportunities to "newcomers":

> . . . It was not inevitable that it [the company] should always anticipate increases in the demand for ingot and be prepared to supply them. Nothing compelled it to keep doubling and redoubling its capacity before others entered the field. It insists that it never excluded competitors; but we can think of no more effective exclusion than progressively to embrace each new opportunity as it opened, and to face every newcomer with new capacity already geared into a great organization, having the advantage of experience, trade connections and the élite of personnel.[9]

Given the philosophy we have seen, the exploitation, by a large company, of opportunities which conceivably *might have been* exploited by "newcomers" is, per se, an undesirable state of affairs. For, in this view of things, it is in the social and moral interest of society that economic opportunities should be exploited by a system of independent small businesses, and not by large corporations with their mere servants and agents.

If this philosophy be accepted as being the philosophy of the Sherman Act, as opposed to that of the "Steel" decision, then it indeed follows that, under law, there could be no such thing as "good" large corporations. It would mean that an unequivocal and energetic national policy of checking and dissolving *all* large corporations would be in order.

"Big Business Is Driving Out Small Business"

Returning to the main stream of discussion, we come to the argument that not only is big business arising and bringing into our society vast numbers of mere servants, agents, and "half-a-life" men, not only is it pre-empting opportunities which might have been exploited by independent small businessmen, but that it is literally displacing small business

[9] *United States* v. *Aluminum Company of America,* p. 431.

and driving it out. This is not merely hurting the individuals involved; not merely bringing an increasingly large undesirable element into the society. This injures the social, as well as the technological advance of society. It injures communal life at the grass-roots level. Ultimately this process of the displacement of small business results in changing the basic structure and the basic quality of society.

No criticism of big business carries a greater emotional impact than that which charges that big business drives out small business. None carries a greater political charge. None strikes closer to some very deep-seated and deeply felt ideals.

This criticism compounds all the criticism we have reviewed up to this point. It is insufferable that large business organizations should be guilty — it is said — of the various separate counts reviewed up to now: That big business should erect large organizations which are inefficient and monopolistic. That in our society, where power should be widely and safely diffused, there should coalesce huge, irresponsible, malevolent entities of power. That big business should run the country — its political apparatus and its economic organization. It would be bad enough that organizations are growing up in our midst which do these things.

But *on top of all this* big business — it is widely believed — is snuffing out small business, the one form of business enterprise which does *not* do these things. Big business, it is said again and again, is driving from the scene that form of business organization which is the ideal of economic and political theories. Given this combination of ideas, it is easy to appreciate what critics must feel when presented with the contention that small business is being trampled down and devoured by big business.

But this picture causes distress in more than just economic and political dimensions. The idea that small business is being destroyed carries an unbearable poignancy all its own. For small business, as an ideal, is closely linked to some deeply held sentiments as to the ideal way of life for the individual. The destruction of small business, accordingly, has more than just an economic or a political meaning. It means that opportunities for individuals to pursue this ideal way of life are being extinguished.

This thought traces back to the concepts which critics have of the role and circumstances of the individual in small and large organizations. For many of the critics, the ideal human role is that of the independent individual — the independent farmer, artisan, professional man, the small businessman. To them, the role and circumstance of the corporate employee are basically incompatible with a full, human, life. This criticism of big business, obviously, has strong ethical and moral overtones. It is ideas along these lines which account for much of the depth of feeling and the sense of urgency which underlie the insistence that "relief" be given to small business and that the expansion of big business be halted.

The most casual effort could dig up a score or more statements of this order, which take it as fact that big business is driving small business to the wall:

> Close financial control, through interlocking spheres of influence over channels of investment, and through the use of financial devices like holding companies and strategic minority interests, creates close control of the business policies of enterprises which masquerade as independent units.
>
> That heavy hand of integrated financial and management control lies upon large and strategic areas of American industry. The small-business man is unfortunately being driven into a less and less independent position in American life. You and I must admit that.[10]

* * *

[10] Franklin D. Roosevelt, *Message from the President of the United States Transmitting Recommendations Relative to the Strengthening and Enforcement of Antitrust Laws,* 75th Cong., 3rd Sess., reproduced in T.N.E.C., *Investigation of the Concentration of Economic Power,* Part I, *Economic Prologue,* p. 186.

No great stretch of the imagination is required to foresee that if nothing is done to check the growth in concentration, either the giant corporations will ultimately take over the country, or the Government will be impelled to step in and impose some form of direct regulation in the public interest. In either event, collectivism will have triumphed over free enterprise, and the theory of competition will have been relegated to the limbo of well-intentioned but ineffective ideals. . . .

> "The capitalist system of free initiative is not immortal, but is capable of dying and of dragging down with it the system of democratic government. Monopoly constitutes the death of capitalism and the genesis of authoritarian government." [Hearings before the T.N.E.C., 76th Cong., 1st Sess., Part 5, p. 2200.]

. . . Either this country is going down the road to collectivism, or it must stand and fight for competition as the protector of all that is embodied in free enterprise.

Crucial in that fight must be some effective means of preventing giant corporations from steadily increasing their power at the expense of small business. . . .[11]

The thesis that big business is obliterating small business is a major premise for numerous contemporary works on political and social theory. Authors state the proposition and go on from there. This sort of thing is well illustrated by the following passage from a recent work by a well-known British professor of political theory who has spent considerable time in the United States:

[Over the past "three-quarters of a century"] the individual business man has been ousted by the company, the company by the cartel and the trust, the trust by the super-trust. In this process the sky is the limit; nothing short of monopoly, first national, then in favoured cases, international, is the ultimate goal. The general pattern is hardly affected by the survival of a host of small men in out-of-the-way places or in

[11] Federal Trade Commission, *Report on the Merger Movement,* pp. 68–69.

other than key industries; these are now no more than the hangers-on of modern economic society, directly or indirectly dependent on the big concerns, tolerated in lines of business where no large profits are to be earned and debarred by their isolation from exercising any real economic power. The continuous and progressive replacement of the smaller by the larger unit has been the typical trend of economic organization in our time.[12]

The idea that small business finds it difficult to survive in the modern economy — especially in competition with big business — is the basis of proposals for a variety of government actions to assist it. The platforms of both major political parties in the campaigns of 1952 implicitly accepted the idea that small business is so endangered that it needs special assistance and protection:

> . . . Small and independent business is the backbone of American free enterprise. Upon its health depends the growth of the economic system whose competitive spirit has built this nation's industrial strength and provided its workers and consumers with an incomparably high standard of living. . . .
>
> . . . We are alarmed over the increasing concentration of economic power in the hands of a few. We reaffirm our belief in the necessity of rigorous enforcement of the laws against trusts, combinations, and restraints of trade, which laws are vital to the safeguarding of the public interest and of small competitive businessmen against predatory monopolies. . . .[13]

* * *

> We will aid small business in every practicable way. . . . We will maintain special committees in Congress whose chief function will be to study and review continuously the problems of small business and recommend legislation for

[12] E. H. Carr, *The New Society* (London: Macmillan & Company, Ltd., 1951), p. 25.

[13] Platform of the Democratic Party, 1952, as given by *United States News & World Report,* August 1, 1952, p. 87.

their relief. We shall always be mindful of the importance of keeping open the channels of opportunity for young men and women.[14]

Public officials who urge Draconian measures against big business start with the idea as a major premise that the imminent extinction of small business is threatened because of its rapid displacement by big business.

Thus the nation was warned by a high-ranking official of the Department of Justice:

> . . . We may be sure that the increasing concentration of American industry is spreading so rapidly that no half-measure can stop it. . . .[15]

A former high-ranking official of the Federal Trade Commission conceded that "the pros and cons of big business" are "inadequately known." And he listed a number of crucial topics on the subject of big business about which little or nothing is known, including "the nature and extent of the contribution made by bigness to the prosperity of our economy." And he agrees that research "into the problem of bigness should be undertaken promptly on an ambitious scale." But he urged, nevertheless, that "a tentative policy of attack is needed even before the research is completed," —

> . . . what is known about the problem indicates that such delay would be unduly dangerous. Our large enterprises are growing by accretion, and their power appears to show increasing momentum. There is a substantial risk that, before the diagnosis of big business is completed, the independence of small enterprise will have been destroyed and the time for effective remedial action will have passed. Indeed,

[14] Platform of the Republican Party, 1952, as given by *United States News & World Report,* July 18, 1952, p. 84.

[15] Sigmund Timberg (Chief, Judgment and Judgment Enforcement Section, Antitrust Division, Department of Justice), "Some Justifications for Divestiture," *The George Washington Law Review,* Vol. 19, December, 1950, p. 146.

some observers of the American business system assert that already the competitive policy has ceased to be practicable.[16]

"Big Business Blights Social Advance and Communal Life"

So much for the general picture which critics draw of the displacement of small business and its dire consequences. The conceptions which critics have of big and small business, that the one is made up of mere servants and that the other is made up of enterprising and responsible individuals, leads them to see other particular consequences in the displacement of small business by big business. Technological advance, which has obvious social significance, is slowed down. So is broad social advance, as well. Worse, local communal life is actually blighted.

We have seen in Chapter 1 that a major theme in the economic criticism is that big business restrains technological advance. Part of this baneful effect — we are told — is due to the monopolistic character of big business. But the explanation also runs in terms of the supposed necessarily authoritarian nature of the large corporation as contrasted to the small business. The top administrators of a big business cannot be present everywhere in the organization at all times; and in their absence, developmental activity flags. Moreover, since employees have little or no ownership interest in the company, it is supposed that they are not eager to push these activities. There is no incentive for them. Such a view follows logically from the dour materialistic presupposition that the sole motivation of human beings is economic gain. It flows also from the dour moralistic presupposition that hu-

[16] Corwin D. Edwards (until recently Chief Economist and Director of the Bureau of Industrial Economics, Federal Trade Commission), *Maintaining Competition*, p. 109.

When the Queen of Hearts cried, "Sentence first — verdict afterwards," Alice said loudly, "Stuff and nonsense — The idea of having the sentence first!" Dr. Edwards' idea, apparently, is that there isn't time to go through due process, i.e., to try the case first, and *then* reach a verdict, and *then* pass sentence. He apparently hankers after a sort of martial law for big business.

man beings have no sense of responsibility toward the interests of others. In any case, these ideas lead to the conclusion that important technological advance cannot be expected of big business.

When ideas like these are combined with static and mechanistic ideas such as Veblen's, big business necessarily appears far more interested in hampering the workings of the nation's economic machine and in exploiting *given* opportunities, *given* wants, *given* markets, *given* techniques than in pushing technological advance.

With such ideas by way of foundation, it is quite logical that critics should accord the accolade for technological advance to small business. It is entirely logical, given the premises, that they should hold that the growth of the economic system depends upon the health of *small* business and that it is *small* business which has provided America with its incomparably high standard of living.

A few critics do not stop there; they see in a widely diffused property interest in small business the basis not only for *technological* advance, but for the *general* advance of society: in learning, in responsible attitudes among its citizens, and in moral values. This idea is especially to be found among critics of the school which is sometimes called the "Distributivists."

In America, one of the prominent persons of this persuasion is Mr. Fred I. Raymond. He has proposed that the size of business enterprise be sharply limited. In his book, *The Limitist,* he advances the idea that the *general* progress of society comes from small, independent business, and that big business retards this progress:

> Many persons have come to the basic conclusion that the general welfare of a whole people is highest when the ownership of property is widely distributed among the people. . . . Through this widespread ownership the great majority of the people gain opportunity, independence, security and a dignity, which make them contented, law-abiding, peaceful

> citizens. This ownership creates in many the desire to preserve and improve. One person's improvement leads to the adoption of this improvement by others. The desire to improve also leads to study, and study leads to the exchange of thought which becomes teaching. Thus this widespread ownership leads to progress in making man's life more enjoyable and more fruitful. . . . [But now] it can be said without much danger of dispute that new enterprise, which was relied upon so strongly as a force of wealth distribution, not only fails to accomplish this result under present day conditions but must fail as long as we permit the unlimited size and growth of our existing giant corporations.[17]

The social criticism of big business also makes the point that its displacement of small business injures communal life. Independent small businessmen provide civic activities with generous, active, competent, well-intentioned leadership. The employees of large corporations do not. Accordingly, when small independent businessmen are driven out or taken over by big business, the employees of large corporations do not take their place. In this leadership vacuum, civic spirit wanes, and programs of civic improvement falter. Or these programs may come to be dominated by the local "clerks" of the absentee management. In this case, civic programs will be carried out only on the sufferance of the large corporation. The programs will no longer be expressions of real local interest, desire, initiative, or sense of responsibility.

This view is implicit in the dissent of Mr. Justice Douglas in the *Standard Oil of California* case.[18] As I interpret this dissenting opinion, Mr. Justice Douglas did not want the Standard Oil Company of California to enter into exclusive supply contracts with independent dealers. He believed that such contracts would impair the genuine independence of

[17] Op. cit., pp. 9–10 and 40.

[18] *Standard Oil Company of California and Standard Stations, Inc.* v. *United States* (1949) 337 U.S. 293.

the dealers and would injure competition. However, he seems to have feared that if the company were enjoined from entering into such contracts, it would establish gasoline stations of its own. That would be worse. From a community point of view — Douglas intimates — even a semi-independent small-businessman is preferable to a fully dependent employee:

> The lessons Brandeis taught on the curse of bigness have largely been forgotten in high places. Size is allowed to become a menace to existing and putative competitors. Price control is allowed to escape the influences of the competitive market and to gravitate into the hands of the few. But beyond all that there is the effect on the community when independents are swallowed up by the trusts and entrepreneurs become employees of absentee owners. Then there is a serious loss in citizenship. Local leadership is diluted. He who was a leader in the village becomes dependent on outsiders for his action and policy. Clerks responsible to a superior in a distant place take the place of resident proprietors beholden to no one. These are the prices which the nation pays for the almost ceaseless growth in bigness on the part of industry.[19]

The thesis that civic spirit and social welfare must wilt in the shadow of big business was set forth in considerable detail by a report of the Smaller War Plants Corporation to the Senate Small Business Committee.[20] This report was written by C. Wright Mills, author of *White Collar,* who was quoted briefly in Chapter 4.

This report summarized the findings of sociological studies of three small-business and three big-business cities. Sociological statistics were compiled for these unidentified cities and interviews were had with individuals in the several com-

19 Ibid., pp. 318, 319.

20 Smaller War Plants Corporation, *Small Business and Civic Welfare,* 79th Cong., 2nd Sess. (Washington: Government Printing Office, 1946).

munities. In general, Mills found that civic and social welfare were perceptibly higher in the sample of small-business towns than in the sample of big-business towns:

> It appears that in the small-business cities is found the most favorable environment for the development and growth of civic spirit. A more balanced economic life and greater industrial stability is provided in small-business cities. There the employment is more diversified, the home-owning middle class is larger, and self-employment greater. Public health is better in the small-business communities investigated; the study reveals that a baby has a considerably greater chance to survive his first year in the small-business city than in the one dominated by a few large firms. In small-business cities public expenditures for such facilities as libraries and education are substantially above such expenditures in big cities. Where big business predominates slums are more prevalent. The small-business cities studied provide for their residents a more balanced economic and social life and on the whole a higher level of civic welfare than big-business cities.
>
> . . . . .
>
> Enterprises ["to improve parks, obtain better schools, make the streets broader, etc."] are carried on extensively only if there exists an active civic spirit. In the communities studied, it was found that civic spirit did not have firm roots in the big-business cities, and insofar as it existed it was of a different, and less active type than that which prevailed in the small-business cities. Essentially, it was found that big business tends to dry up civic spirit. . . .[21]

The differences in the two sets of towns are ascribed to differences in one variable and no other — the presence or absence of big business.

A number of reasons are given for the blighting effect of big business. They add up to the idea that in the big-business towns the sturdy, responsible, independent, small-business *class* has been displaced by a *class* of corporate em-

[21] Ibid., pp. v, 22.

ployees. Both "classes," it seems, are motivated equally by materialistic values. But, it is said, "the small businessman may participate actively in civic affairs if for no other reason than civic progress and improvement may redound to his own self-interest." But this "cannot be expected of executives of large corporations." There is nothing in it for *them*. In the absence of material incentive, they withhold their support. "This fact that there is no economic incentive for officials of absentee-owned corporations 'to be someone civically' is among the most important causes of the lower levels of civic welfare in the big-business cities." [22]

This lack of material incentive stems back, apparently, to the fact that corporations — like individuals — are in business solely to make money. Accordingly, when the time comes for higher officials in large corporations to consider local employees for promotion, there is no reason for them "to include among the standards used for promoting subordinates any contributions made to local civic welfare." Such contributions, it follows logically from this basic concept of the objectives of a corporation, are relevant only "if, by chance or design, they happen to benefit the profit position of the corporation." [23]

Other reasons are given here, and in Mills' *White Collar* as well, which amplify his ideas. Most are along philosophical lines of stern and rigid economic determinism. However, he does sketch a charming vignette of the wives of big business: The wives of big business play a part in undermining civic welfare. More — they play an important sort of dialectical role in the undermining of the "middle class."

The wives of big business aren't interested in civic activities. "They are usually concerned, rather, with trips to metropolitan centers, parties and other functions, journeys to the country, the very latest fashions, celebrities, etc." [24] "The often glamorous women of the firm's officials come and

22 Ibid., p. 23.
23 Ibid., p. 26.
24 Ibid., p. 28.

go between the metropolitan center and their exclusive suburb in the small city." [25]

The small business wives of the "middle class" are excluded from this brilliant, glamorous, peripatetic social whirl. Working hard on civic activities won't get "middle-class" wives "in" with the corporate smart set. "A typical middle-class woman in a big-business city could work herself to the bone on civic matters and never be noticed by the executives' wives." [26] On the other hand, "if it became known that, by some chance, she happened to be well acquainted with a metropolitan celebrity, she might well be 'in.' " [27] This set of manners and morals, it appears, diverts small business wives from civic activities and sets them to emulating — unsuccessfully, alas, — the glamorous wives of big business.

More is involved, however, than frustrated social ambition or even the decline of civic welfare. For, "In the eyes of the small businessman's wife who has Not Been Invited one sees the social meaning of the decline of the old middle class." [28]

This brings us to the last point under the criticism that big business displaces small business: The displacement of small

[25] C. Wright Mills, *White Collar,* p. 48.

[26] *Small Business and Civic Welfare,* p. 28.

[27] Ibid., p. 28.

[28] C. Wright Mills, *White Collar,* p. 48. Actually, apart from external "glamour," life inside the large company, it appears, is pretty dispiriting and dehumanizing for all concerned. (Ibid., Chapters 11 and 12.) It might be noted that Professor Mills' unflagging pessimism leads him to some deep misgivings about even the classic form of small business — the family-run store, where "economic life . . . coincides with family life." Human life there is scarcely more tolerable and meaningful than life in big business, it would seem. "In the hole-in-the-wall business, also known as a Mom-and-Pop Store, the parents can keep a constant eye on each other and on the children. Such economic freedom as the family enterprise may enjoy is often purchased by lack of freedom within the family unit. It is, in fact . . . a feature of such petty bourgeois life that extreme repression is often exercised in its patriarchal orbit. Child labor, often sweated child labor, has its home in the lumpen-bourgeoisie." Life on the farm, we are to gather, is equally somber and crushing. (Ibid., p. 30.) The "lumpen-bourgeoisie," be it said, *can* take comfort — if they like — from the fact that life in America, seemingly, is a pretty grim business for doctors, lawyers, and professors, too. (Ibid., Chapter 6.) Things, it seems, are tough all over.

business is simply one aspect of the destruction of the "middle class." With the destruction of the property-owning, entrepreneurial "middle class," democracy itself is being undermined, and the way is being prepared for the rise of totalitarianism. Some of the critics we have seen believe we have already reached this stage.

Before we go on to that final point, we really should pause to consider the basic premise of the criticisms under review in this chapter: that it is a *fact* that big business *is* driving out small business.

Some Facts about "Concentration"

Is it really true that the increasing concentration of American industry is spreading so rapidly, and has spread so far, that the independence of small enterprise is likely to be destroyed in the very near future? Many critics have no doubt whatever on this score. There have been numerous statistical studies which show considerable "concentration" in many industries. Other studies go on with the intent to show that the degree of concentration is greater now than at various times past.

We shall not here look into any of these studies. All the major studies have been reviewed incisively — and, in some cases, devastatingly — by Professor Morris A. Adelman of the Massachusetts Institute of Technology. His own skillful and painstaking analysis of available data and of the data presented by these studies leads him to a quite different kind of conclusion. This, he summarizes, himself:

> This article may be summarized in three statements. (1) The American economy is highly concentrated. (2) Concentration is highly uneven. (3) The extent of concentration shows no tendency to grow, and it may possibly be declining. Any tendency either way, if it does exist, must be at the pace of a glacial drift.[29]

[29] "The Measurement of Industrial Concentration," *The Review of Economic Statistics,* Vol. XXXIII, No. 4, November, 1951, p. 295.

Professor Adelman goes on to say:

> . . . References to "the growth in economic concentration," or statements that "during the past 16 years [1932–48] big business has been getting bigger and little business littler," or that "the forces of concentration [are] growing stronger by the hour," or that "concentration of industry is increasing so fast that no half-measures can stop it," and many others of like tenor – these must now be dismissed as unfounded. Concentration may be a problem, but for better or worse it is not threatening to engulf the economy. . . .[30]

But all such studies, whatever they show — as Professor Adelman is aware — are entirely superfluous anyway, so far as the hard core of the criticism of big business is concerned. They are *all* beside the main point. For most of the critics it is only a matter of minor detail whether or not, in statistical fact, the business world is more concentrated in the hands of big business nowadays than in, say, 1940, 1933, 1929, 1914, or 1900. Even if it can be demonstrated that it is not, the only consequence would be to cause the attack to re-emphasize its *basic* point: there is more big business and less small business than there *should* be. As measured against the ideals of an atomized economic structure, an atomized power structure, and a society of individual entrepreneurs, there is *too much* bigness. Not only is there too much bigness relatively, there is too much absolutely. Ideally, there should be none.

Now we return to the main stream of the argument.

"Big Business Is Transforming Society"

We have already seen something of the argument — that which has been called a "Stalinist" Theory — that big business is operating to bring about Fascism because of the pressures which it brings to bear on society, especially on the "middle class." We shall now take a further look at ideas along the line that the rise and spread of big business brings about a fundamental change in the nature of society.

30 Ibid., p. 296.

In displacing small business, big business — it appears — is transmuting the atom of society. Under the vast and irresistible energy of big business, the atom is being transmuted from an independent individual into a dependent employee. Or the individual is being transformed from a liberal, independent small businessman who wants little by way of government, into a political reactionary who seeks to capture and use total political power to remake society to his advantage and liking. As its atoms become transformed from one kind of unit into another, the character of the society changes accordingly. In particular, society is being turned from a liberal, humane, democracy into a monolithic, inhuman, totalitarianism.

That's the gist of the argument we shall now look at. With this we shall bring to a close the survey of the political and social criticism of big business.

The theory now before us is a logical extension of ideas we have already seen. If the atoms of society are changed in their basic characteristics, does it not seem natural to conclude that the character of society — the collective mass of atoms — will be changed also? Granting this line of reasoning, it remains only to specify clearly the nature of the change in the atom and then to work out, by logical deduction, what the specifications of a social mass composed of such atoms will be.

Pre-eminent among the critics of modern times who have worked through this deductive process is the late, internationally esteemed German sociologist, Karl Mannheim. Mannheim's ideas — or ideas like them — have considerable currency. His theories have had enormous influence. Because of this, we shall examine them at some length. We can take them as typical, if only a little extreme, of ideas often encountered among the social and political critics.

Central to Mannheim's ideas are concepts of the individual in small and large organizations much akin to those we have seen. The economy, according to him, and the society, have come to be less and less made up of virile, self-reliant, self-responsible individuals who interact with each other and the impersonal forces of the market to produce the material goods and services of the community. These are coming more and more to be supplied by large organizations.

An outstanding characteristic of these large organizations is coordinated, synchronized planning — in Mannheim's own phrase, "functional rationalization." This functional rationalization is the means whereby large-scale business applies scientific advance and improved techniques to production. Functional rationalization is the means whereby the economies of production made possible by scientific and technological progress are converted into realities.

A fundamental of this functional rationalization, according to Mannheim, is centralization of planning. This involves the centralization of decision-making and the centralization of administrative responsibility. This centralization of planning, deciding, and taking responsibility means that rational thinking under the pressure of responsibility is also centralized. All this, it seems, is necessary if technological progress is to be exploited and maximum economies are to be obtained.

This theory of administration Mannheim apparently took over from the precepts of so-called "scientific management." There is an abundant literature — much of it American, unfortunately — that holds that (whether they are in fact, or not) organizations *ought* to be administered in this fashion.

Accepting these ideas as to what administration of large organizations is — or ought to be — Mannheim went on to think through some of the implications of authoritarian, "scientific" centralization. He pondered what this would do to the individual. His conclusions parallel closely the critics' concept we have already seen of the individual in the large organization: The individual is reduced to an unthinking, irresponsible, taker-of-orders. All individuals, that is, except a few key planners and deciders. This is what functional rationalization entails.

This is how Mannheim himself puts the point.

> . . . functional rationalization is, in its very nature, bound to deprive the average individual of thought, insight, and responsibility and to transfer these capacities to the individuals who direct the process of rationalization.[31]

This, says Mannheim, is what happens to the individual *inside* the large modern organization. This is one consequence of "scientific" management, of centralized authoritarian administration. But there is another, more far-reaching consequence.

This process of what might be called the "down-grading" of the individual — the social atom — so changes him that he will not, he cannot, support a democratic system. A democracy is not composed of atoms which are unaccustomed to thought, self-motivation, and responsibility. A totalitarianism *is*.

Says Mannheim,

> The fact that in a functionally rationalized society the thinking out of a complex series of actions is confined to a few organizers, assures these men of a key position in society. A few people can see things more and more clearly over an ever-widening field, while the average man's capacity for rational judgment steadily declines once he has turned over to the organizer the responsibility for making decisions. In modern society not only is the ownership of the means of production concentrated in fewer hands, but . . . there are far fewer positions from which the major structural connections between different activities can be perceived, and fewer men can reach these vantage points.
>
> This is the state of affairs which has led to the growing distance between the élite and the masses, and to the "appeal

[31] *Man and Society* (London: Kegan Paul, Trench, Trubner & Co., Ltd., 1940), p. 58.

> to the leader" which has recently become so widespread. The average person surrenders part of his own cultural individuality with every new act of integration into a functionally rationalized complex of activities. He becomes increasingly accustomed to being led by others and gradually gives up his own interpretation of events for those which others give him. When the rationalized mechanism of social life collapses in times of crisis, the individual cannot repair it by his own insight. Instead his own impotence reduces him to a state of terrified helplessness. . . .[32]

Only a monolithic, centrally planned society can be composed of such atoms.

But the transmutation of the atoms of society does not stop with the individuals actually digested into large authoritarian organizations. Even those who remain outside — the struggling small businessmen — are affected. They cannot compete with, and survive in the midst of the technological changes generated by big business and its greater efficiency.[33] To save themselves from being displaced and annihilated they must, and do, strive to save themselves from big business by stopping technological advance:

> The petty entrepreneurs, who direct their own tiny individual economic units, the small shopkeeper and the artisan, whose enemies are technical invention and large-scale production, have a quite different attitude towards further industralization and rationalization. To maintain their independence they must destroy the big concerns, the great factories, and the department stores. If they were to have things

[32] Ibid., pp. 58–59.

[33] Compare: "The lower strata of the middle class — the small tradespeople, shopkeepers and retired tradesmen generally, the handicraftsmen and peasants — all these sink gradually into the proletariat, partly because their diminutive capital does not suffice for the scale on which modern industry is carried on, and is swamped in the competition with the large capitalists, partly because their specialized skill is rendered worthless by new methods of production." — Karl Marx and Friedrich Engels, *The Communist Manifesto,* 1848.

their own way, technical rationalization would be brought to a standstill. . . .[34]

But, if natural evolution is to be stopped, the whole of society must be remoulded through and through. This can be done only if government is captured and converted into an instrument of total power. This, the embattled "new middle class" of small business undertakes to do. This is the natural course of democratic society, given technological progress and "functional rationalization":

> . . . Just as the industrial proletariat strives to alter the form of the class system by turning everybody into a proletarian, so the "new middle class" attempts to rescue itself by using all the political techniques at its command in order to reverse the process of industrial development, to restrict the extension of rationalized industry, and to prevent the development of the modern rational type of man with all his humane ideals. . . . it is clear that a change in social order according to the wishes of these groups or classes will not take place of itself, but must be brought about by force. . . . or, at any rate, planned intervention. . . . The unorganized growth of democratic society culminates in dictatorship.[35]

The impact of big business on the individual, both within and without, transforms society from a liberal democracy into a totalitarian dictatorship.

An only slightly different version of what is going on in the world is put forth by "Distributivists" and, especially in Europe, by a number of "Catholic Socialists." They hold the view, rather common among critics of big business, that widely diffused ownership of productive resources and correspondingly small business enterprise is the indispensable base of democracy. Bigness in business erodes that base.

[34] Karl Mannheim, *Man and Society,* p. 105. Mannheim's picture of big business as the organizing force behind technological development and advance, and of small business as a technologically reactionary force, is obviously at odds with the picture drawn by many of the other critics.

[35] Ibid., pp. 105–106.

Hilaire Belloc, the well-known British author and Catholic layman, for a long time, until his recent tragic death, was a principal spokesman for this point of view:

> It has been found in practice, and the truth is witnessed to by the instincts in all of us, that such widely distributed property as a condition of freedom is necessary to the normal satisfaction of human nature. In its absence general culture ultimately fails and so certainly does citizenship. The cells of the body politic are atrophied and the mass of men have not even, at last, an opinion of their own, but are moulded by the few who retain ownership of land and endowments and reserves. . . . Ownership is not a general feature of our society, determining its character. On the contrary, absence of ownership, dependence on a precarious wage at the will of others is the general feature of our society and determines its character. . . . Hence our society has fallen into the diseased condition known as "Industrial Capitalism." In this state the control of the Means of Production is vested in a comparatively small number; consequently economic freedom has ceased to be the note, giving its tone to society. . . . The only economic difference between a herd of subservient Russians and a mob of free Englishmen pouring into a factory of a morning, is that the latter are exploited for private profit, the former by the State in communal fashion.[36]

The corrective for this condition, Belloc stated frankly, is a program of political *reaction* to undo what has been done by economic, legal, social, and industrial evolution over the past century or more:

> In other words, you must . . . reverse the present current of economic life; you must do the opposite of what was done by those who began the industrialization of the modern world — you must act in a fashion which *they* would have called reactionary. *That spirit of reaction must run through*

[36] From *The Restoration of Property* by Hilaire Belloc (Copyright 1936 by Sheed & Ward, Inc., New York), pp. 17–18 and 134.

all our effort at the restoration of property if there is to be any chance of its even partial success.[37]

Thus it is that critics contend that big business — perhaps the inexorable evolution of capitalism itself — has caused society to change from a structure of "classless individualism" — where man met man on equable footing — into a society of economically unequal, politically conscious, and militant classes.[38] This development, they say, forebodes the end of liberal democracy. Indeed, some say this *is* the end of democracy.

Conclusion

With this, we complete our survey of the political and social criticism of big business. This is the stream of criticism, as it even now flows on. We have now seen the views of a number of "social-welfare advocates" whose "groping for a rationale of public interference in private capitalistic enterprise" found "glorious realization" in the theories of monopolistic and imperfect competition.

The administrators of big business may already be well impressed by the number of their critics and the range of their strictures. But we have not yet done. There is more. And this remainder, looking ahead over the decades, may be more significant than anything we have yet seen.

* * *

In the last chapter or so we have been dealing more and more with ideas which have ethical and moral overtones — with ideas of good and evil. In starting out on this survey of the criticism of big business, we commenced — at the economic level — with ideas which ostensibly relate to questions

[37] Ibid., p. 93. (Italics in original.)

[38] For some further views, see Maurice H. Dobb, *Capitalist Enterprise and Social Progress,* especially pp. 151–153; and the article by G. D. H. Cole, on "Laissez-faire," *Encyclopaedia of the Social Sciences* (New York, The Macmillan Company, 1932), Vol. 9, pp. 15–20.

of fact. And in passing along the scale of the criticisms of big business, we have now reached a new stave. From here on, the ideas we shall be dealing with relate primarily to ethics and morals, to virtues and vices, good and evil. From here on, there is a shift in the key of the criticism: moral values and value judgments now become the outstanding notes. Ideas from the realms of economics and politics now become the overtones.

The discussion ascends to even higher levels of abstraction.

PART III

The Ethical and Moral Criticism of the Civilization of Big Business

Introduction

O weariness of men who turn from GOD
To the grandeur of your mind and the glory of your action,
To arts and inventions and daring enterprises,
To schemes of human greatness thoroughly discredited,
Binding the earth and the water to your service,
Exploiting the seas and developing the mountains,
Dividing the stars into common and preferred,
Engaged in devising the perfect refrigerator, . . .

—T. S. Eliot.[1]

CRITICISMS of the basic ethical and moral character of our industrial, big business civilization have been made by men who come from most dissimilar backgrounds and who look upon the world from vastly differing standpoints. The particular expressions of these criticisms are as varied as the individuals making them. But despite the particular differences of viewpoint and the variety of emphasis, and the differing amounts of charity, pessimism, and vehemence with which these criticisms are made, there is a basic uniformity which runs through them: Our society is *rich* enough — or so at least many of the critics concede. Some of them, indeed, say it is too well off. And our society may be *democratic* enough. But we are not a *good* society. In terms of human and spiritual values — not economic and political values — our society, *these* critics say, is destitute. Some of them say we suffer from "weariness." Some say we are barbarous. Some say "Satanic."

If one could cast up a consensus of these views — a sort of a "sense of the meeting" — it might run something like this: Our civilization, at best, is beset by spiritual and moral doubts. It is an "Age of Anxiety." Or, it is empty of those

1 Quoted by permission from "Choruses from 'The Rock.'" Reprinted in *The Complete Poems and Plays* (New York: Harcourt, Brace and Company, 1952), p. 104.

ethical and spiritual values which are necessary to the good society — to "Peace of Mind," or "Peace of Soul." Some critics speak of a Lost Generation, a Disillusioned Generation, or a Beat Generation.[2] We are told that we live in "an age starved for spiritual values." [3] At worst, our civilization is a literal hell on earth in which mankind can live only an animal life, not a human life.

The present Pope, Pius XII, asks, "What age has been, for all its technical and purely civic progress, more tormented than ours by spiritual emptiness and deep-felt interior poverty?" And His Holiness speaks of ". . . the spiritual and moral bankruptcy of the present day. . . ." [4] Albert Schweitzer, in 1923, spoke of the "decay of civilization." [5] In 1949, in one of the most powerful and moving fables ever written, C. Virgil Gheorghiu (a Roumanian novelist, now a refugee in France) likened present-day industrial civilization to a submarine, hopelessly sunken and with enough oxygen to sustain life for only a few more hours:

> "The atmosphere in which contemporary society lives. Man cannot endure it much longer. Bureaucracy, the army, the government, central and local administration, everything is conspiring to suffocate man. Contemporary society is suitable for none but machines and mechanical slaves. It was created for their benefit. But for human beings it is asphyxiating. As yet they are unconscious of it. They believe that they are living normally as they did before. They are like those sailors in the submarine who go on working in the poisonous atmosphere for another six hours. But I know we are nearing the end." [6]

[2] E.g., Clellon Holmes, "This is the Beat Generation," *The New York Times Magazine,* November 16, 1952, p. 10.

[3] Francis Henry Taylor, Director, Metropolitan Museum. (As reported in *Time,* December 29, 1952, p. 50.)

[4] Encyclical, *Summi Pontificatus* (October, 1939).

[5] *The Decay and Restoration of Civilization* (London: A. & C. Black, Ltd., and New York: The Macmillan Company, 1923).

[6] *The Twenty-fifth Hour* (New York: Alfred A. Knopf, 1950), p. 122.

This is the kind of ethical and moral questioning which is encountered beyond the economic, political, and social criticism of big business.

One of the interesting things about this underlying criticism of modern industrial civilization is that it is not, for the most part, directed explicitly at "big business" as such. Indeed, in the criticism we shall review in the next three chapters the term "big business" appears only occasionally. Even the word "business" doesn't crop up as often as in the material we have sampled up to now. Essayists, playwrights, poets, and theologians simply express themselves in terms and frames of reference which are different from those of, say, economists, business administrators, social theorists, or presidential candidates. For this reason, it is possible to let the point occasionally slip away that this criticism applies every whit as much to big business as anything we have seen so far.

I'll try to nail this point down.

First of all, let's consider the terminology and concepts of the ethical and moral critics. They often express themselves in highly abstract terms. They speak with dismay or vehemence about "life in the twentieth century," "industrial civilization," "the Machine." These high-level abstractions and most broadly generalized ideas and concepts simply represent the far end of a series which begins at about where the terminology of the political and social critics leaves off. Retracing back down to the lower levels of abstraction and to the less generalized concepts of the ethical and moral critics, the terms encountered become again those of the more familiar order: "the modern trust," "the corporation," "businessmen," "the businessman."

Basically, and especially *concretely,* the target of the ethical and moral critics is the same as that of the economic and the political and social critics.

Here, for instance, in roughly ascending order of abstraction and generality, is a sample of the terms that ethical and moral critics use to label what it is *they* are attacking:

> "the modern trust . . . the consolidated corporate monopoly . . . [which] are the practical realization of the commercial spirit in its most despotic form";
> "corporations for private profit," "the corporation";
> "the prevailing forms of business enterprise";
> "men of business," "businessmen";
> "the expansion of investment," "the commercial community";
> "private interests";
> "private enterprise," "private capitalism";
> "capital," "capitalistic enterprise," "the capitalist system," "capitalism";
> "the modern economic order";
> "the spirit of capitalism," "the ethos of capitalism";
> "capitalist morality," "business morality";
> "the profit motive";
> "decent godless people";
> "men who turn from GOD . . . Engaged in devising the perfect mechanical refrigerator";
> "power . . . wielded by the irresponsible private owners of the sources of production, or their agents";
> "accumulation of power";
> "immense power and economic domination . . . concentrated in the hands of a few";
> "industrialism," "mass-production industrialism," "modern industry";
> "modern technics," "our present industrial set-up," "the new industrial structure";
> "our world of commerce and finance and mass production";
> "our sensual and materialistic generation";
> "industrial enterprise," "industrial capitalism";
> "uniformity and standardization," "the factory system";
> "the Factory," "the Machine," "the assembly line";
> "industrial civilization," "capitalist civilization,"
> "business civilization";

"the neotechnic phase of civilization," "our civilization," "civilization";
"a world . . . ruled by men of business";
"industrial culture," "asphalt culture";
"modern society," "a mechanistic society," "the acquisitive society";
"the City," "soulless giant cities," "city existence";
"this age of industrialism," "the present age," "the Age of Anxiety";
"modern times," "the world today";
"life in the twentieth century."

To the extent that such high-level abstractions as "life in the twentieth century," "capitalistic enterprise," "the modern economic order," and "this age of industrialism" can be related back down to things which are concrete, it is to the techniques, the workings, the products, and the consequences of "big business" — of the very same thing the economic and the political and social critics are after: "the corporation," "the trust," and "men of business."

Truly, it stands to reason that this should be so. For "industrial civilization," and "life in the twentieth century" *are* very largely distinguished, for better or worse — I believe for better — from the civilizations of other times and places by the workings, the products, and the consequences of large-scale private enterprise. Of big business.

And by "big business" I mean here just about what most of the critics mean. Not merely such large corporations as the Union Pacific Railroad Company, American Telephone and Telegraph Company, General Motors Corporation, General Electric Corporation, United States Steel Corporation, and Standard Oil Company (New Jersey) — all of whose influences on American civilization are so very obvious. But also all businesses employing as many as 1,000 or even 500 people. For, relative to the individual "atoms" of economic and political theories, and as compared to the run of productive units of other times and in most of the rest of the world today, even companies employing a mere 500 are *big*. And it is precisely the methods, the processes, the products — the total impact — of business concerns of this size and up, which have done so much to bring about the revolutionary changes which now distinguish this civilization from others of the past and present.

As much as anything else, modern American civilization *is* the civilization of "big" business. Whatever may have been their contributions to our welfare and our progress — and these contributions in the aggregate surely have been enormous — it is not "little workshops," "small merchants," "petty employers," and "tiny individual economic units" which have generated those characteristics which now palpably *distinguish* America from other civilizations.

Simply consider the modern development and exploitation of natural resources; our transportation and communication methods and systems; consider how our food is farmed and processed; how our clothing is made; consider the materials of which our buildings are constructed. Consider how we treat and cure ourselves when we are sick. Consider how all these things contrast to their counterparts, say, of the Europe of the 17th Century, or of the countries of Asia and the Middle East even in this century. The ways and the means of life in our industrial civilization are obviously and profoundly different. Consider that modern industrial civilization is the only civilization in which large-scale private enterprise has evolved as a *general* and *commonplace* method of organizing cooperative productive effort. The point need not be labored. Industrial civilization and big business have evolved hand in hand in a close, reciprocally influencing relationship. Industrial civilization *is* the civilization of big business.

Again, lest there be any doubt in the mind of the reader, if you fall in the category of "men of business," "businessmen" or even of "the ordinary businessman," or if you are an executive of a "private enterprise," even if you are not exactly engaged in devising the perfect mechanical refrigerator — when it comes right down to it, the critics are still talking about *you*. It is *you* whom they hold responsible for the civilization they do not like, its way of life, its values, its objectives, its mores.

Gentle reader, they are talking about what they think you stand for, about what you have done and do, about the way you do it, about what they think you hope to do — about all the things they associate with *you,* about *your* civilization.

This brings us to the second major point to be taken up in this introduction to Part III. The ethical and moral critics often seem to be suggesting that spiritual poverty, acts of sin, and evil are characteristics unique to business civilization rather than timeless characteristics of the human race. Oftentimes critics in this vein lay the evils they perceive in modern life to the unique circumstances, conditions, and features of industrial, urban, business civilization. By implication, they hold blameless the erring individual. The individual is exculpated. They place responsibility for his inadequacies and errors upon the unique environment in which he lives, upon the material basis of modern life. And this is, precisely, the environment, the material basis of life, which has been brought about by business. By implication, if not in so many words, moral shortcomings and human sin are, first, suggested to be unique to business civilization; second, ultimately attributable to business. By this chain of inference, business and businessmen are held responsible for creating a world which leads the individual into sin.[7]

[7] A homely, if heart-rending, example of this way of thinking:

"America's Plenty Blamed"

"Israel Lichtenstein, thirty-seven, stabbed his attractive wife, Analise, twenty-eight, while she was asleep in their seventh-floor room at 601 W. 160th St. at 7:30 a.m. and then dashed up three floors to the roof and plunged to his death. She died shortly after she was brought to Mother Cabrini Hospital.

" 'He did it,' according to a physician who had been treating Mr. Lichtenstein for nervousness, 'because his wife had a domineering attitude about

Perhaps this needs to be spelled out.

All civilizations have had their critics. Massachusetts Bay had the Mathers. Florence was scourged by Savonarola. Athens had its Socrates. Judah and Jerusalem had Isaiah and Jeremiah. Humanity still not having achieved perfection, we must in our age as well expect our own due measure of ethical and moral criticism. But in our day such criticism very often takes a turn which is not to be found in earlier critics — say, in the prophets of the Old Testament. And it is this turn, with its implicit message, which brings so much of the ethical and moral criticism of *our* civilization to bear so heavily on big business.

Isaiah and Jeremiah cried dreadful warnings aloud to the sons and daughters of Zion. As I read their words, they were decrying the willful waywardness of fully and individually responsible human beings of free will. These great critics, I think, did not attribute the spiritual and moral shortcomings of their audience to the facts that they were an essentially rural people, with a tribal political and social order, employing the productive techniques of the late Bronze or early Iron Age. To these still stirring prophets, the evils which they deplored and their correction were — it would seem — matters of individual human will and responsibility.

In contrast, throughout much of the criticism of modern times there is an unmistakable implication that the spiritual and moral shortcomings in industrial civilization are due to economic, political, and social institutions and organization structures; to the predominantly urban way of life; and to the use of the products, techniques, and equipment of large-scale production. A goodly amount of modern criticism seems to hold that the sins of contemporary society arise

---

everything and considered herself physically, mentally, and spiritually superior to her husband. Had they stayed in Europe where there are not as many beauty parlors, nylon stockings and other such things, they would have been happy and this never would have happened.' . . ." — *New York Herald Tribune,* January 27, 1954, p. 17.

because it is possessed of demons — in the form of private entrepreneurs, businessmen.

It is upon the external circumstances, conditions, and arrangements of modern life that many critics now seem to lay the burden of blame for human error and sin, not upon the individual — and on a small demonic "class." There is an unmistakable tendency in many of the critics who will now be cited *not* to attribute the evils *they* decry to an everlasting capacity for error and sin on the part of individually responsible beings with free will.

In a sense, this is something of a counterpart to political theories which hold that power is not inherent in individuals, but in their relationships to property, to things. Virtue and vice seem to be seen by many of the ethical and moral critics not to be internal matters of the spirit — of individual will — within people themselves. Rather, the spiritual nature and content of life seem to be seen as determined by the relationship of individuals to things of the external world — to property; to the physical circumstances of life; to the techniques of the productive activity they are engaged in — and by the prevailing political and social institutions.[8]

That is to say, many of the economic, political, and social critics see human attitudes and behavior as shaped by material environment and by organization mechanisms and structures. And so do many of the ethical and spiritual critics of our day. In this, they are unlike the prophets of the Old Testament from Isaiah to Malachi.

But we are in danger of wandering off.

The point is that the implication is often all too clear that many critics believe that if big business were eliminated, along with the conditions which it has brought about and with those conditions which have given rise to it, we *would* be able to achieve a *good* society.

The *goodness* of the envisioned society would be the result

[8] E.g., Fred I. Raymond, who seems to think ownership of property gives people dignity, contentment, desire to create, etc. See pp. 183–184 above.

of a different material environment, different institutions, and different organization structures and mechanisms which would take the place of those associated with big business.

I come now to the third point.

It is probably true, although I know of no way of proving it, that many of the fervid but statistically ungrounded assertions — *pro* as well as *con* — as to what various economic and political facts relating to big business "must" be, are simply rationalizations and manifestations of ethical and moral convictions. As with presuppositions concerning matters of fact, so too is it likely that the patent limitations or illogic of unrealistic theories as to the economic behavior of large corporations and as to their administration can be regarded as a kind of wishful thinking tracing back to moral conviction, faith, assumption, or preconception. Especially is this likely since many of these theories do not even purport to be generalized descriptions of situations minutely, systematically, and clinically observed at first hand. They are nothing more than chains of deductive reasoning — more or less rigorous — based upon assumptions picked up from goodness knows where.

Of the three planes of criticism of big business, it is this one concerned with ethical and moral values, this one which expresses ethical and moral convictions and assumptions, which is the most basic. It is in this stratum of thought and feeling, surely, that many of the criticisms of the other levels have their roots, from which they draw inspiration and emotional nourishment.

As the fourth and related point, I would hazard a guess that the role, if any, which large-scale private corporations are to play over the course of the next century or so will be just as much — if not far more — determined by the direction of the preponderance of convictions on ethical and moral issues as by even the most iron-clad, incontestable factual demonstrations as to the efficiency and effectiveness of their operations, or as to their political impact.

For only the smallest minority of the people are well versed in economic and political theories. Nor are we always moved to decision by the facts presented in argument by the protagonists of various courses of political and social action. But, more or less deeply, we all of us do have ethical and moral convictions about the world we live in. Moreover, these convictions govern *which* facts — say, about big business — we will be willing to admit as relevant to our judgment, and how important we gauge them to be. History seems to suggest that political movements and actions are more often the consequences of moral conviction — and indignation — than of arid, factual analysis.

Now to move on to the fifth introductory point, a summary sketch of what ethical and moral critics say about the civilization of big business. The criticisms we shall review seem to fall under three major headings. And it is under these headings that we shall take them up in the next three chapters.

First, it is said, the only values which big business civilization prizes are materialistic ones; values of the spirit are ignored. This inversion of values, as the critics see matters, results in individual emptiness and frustration, for men cannot live by material values alone.

Second, it is said that the fundamental individualism of our big business society amounts to an immoral irresponsibility. Such individualistic irresponsibility, it is said, is immoral in itself. In one set of terms, it amounts to a denial of the moral, the Christian, duties incumbent upon all human beings.

Third, critics say that the materialism and the irresponsible individualism of modern big business civilization have combined to produce a crassly materialistic, chaotically irresponsible, and basically inhuman order of things — in short, an *evil* society in which a good *human* life can scarcely be lived.

How did civilization come to this sorry state? There is no simple consensus among critics as to cause and effect relationships; and, again, there are differences as to emphasis. But there is considerable agreement as to the major aspects of the evolution of the present culture from earlier times. Since the Reformation — so this agreement might run — and especially from the end of the 18th Century, the West has turned more and more away from moral and human values, and has embraced materialistic and mundane values. The debasement of what should be the primary values of human life, and the enhancement of what should be secondary values, are what account for the spiritual emptiness and moral confusion critics see in modern life. Such values, as the basis of human motivation, and as criteria for decisions, lead to inhumanity.

At the same time — the analysis might continue — men have become free to pursue, without responsibility to Divine Law, to natural moral law, or to the community, their own individual materialistic ends. Political, social, and economic theory have become thoroughly secularized. Economic expediency for private material gain has become, at first, a permissible consideration, and later, the prevailing, if not the sole, criterion for conduct and decision. Indeed, it is said that economic expediency has, itself, achieved the status of the *ethical* norm for action by individuals as they exploit the institutions of private property, freedom of enterprise, freedom of contract, freedom of exchange, and the right of inheritance.[9] This individualistic irresponsibility is immoral in and of itself, in the eyes of critics. For it is based upon the immoral and inhuman idea that man *is* an "island," and in no sense whatever his brother's keeper.

Motivated and guided by material values, it is said, and freed from responsibility to the community and to law, natural or Divine, large-scale private enterprise — big business — has brought into being a morally intolerable civilization. As critics see matters, the rising and now dominant "class" of

[9] See, e.g., Max Weber, *The Protestant Ethic and the Spirit of Capitalism* (New York: Charles Scribner's Sons, 1930), especially pp. 50–51; and R. H. Tawney, *Religion and the Rise of Capitalism* (New York: Harcourt, Brace and Company, 1926) and "Penguin Edition" (New York: Penguin Books, 1947), especially pp. 13–16 in the latter edition.

businessmen has converted practically all production to factory, that is to say, mass-production processes. In the factories, men and women are no longer craftsmen whose skills and personal responsibility for a good product give them dignity, status, and satisfaction. Instead, they are unskilled and interchangeable. Some say the worker in the factory has become a dehumanized, "robotized," irresponsible "unit." [10] These individuals not only derive no satisfaction from their work. They are so debased that they cannot enjoy and will not sustain a high level of culture.[11] Having no esthetic sensibilities or refinement of taste, they are content with the ugly products poured out by these factories. This amounts to a *moral* transmutation of the "atom" of society.

Another major product of the industrialization of society at the hands of big business, so it is widely agreed among the critics, has been the concentration of humanity in large population masses through the upbuilding of cities. Relatively fewer people now live on the soil. The city dweller is believed not to have the intimate human relationships and communal responsibilities which are felt to be so meaningful and satisfying to the country man. This "unnatural" urban life, in contrast to the more "natural" way of life on the farm, is held to be incompatible with the attainment of the highest moral and spiritual values. This is an evil in itself. Moreover, in the eyes of some, the city sets an ethical tone which drags down the level of civilization of the whole community.

Finally, it is said repeatedly, and often implied, that because of the sweeping impact of materialistic, irresponsible individualism, the current level of civilization is at a point on a downward trend. The state of civilization — it is said

[10] See, e.g., Wilfred Wellock, *A Mechanistic or a Human Society?* (Birmingham, England: Published by the author, date unspecified). Compare Alexis de Tocqueville, *Democracy in America,* as cited below, Chapter 8, p. 261.

[11] José Ortega y Gasset, *Revolt of the Masses* (New York: W. W. Norton & Co., Inc., 1932, and Mentor Books, The New American Library of World Literature, Inc., 1950.)

— has been, and is now, retrogressing. The present big business, industrial civilization carries implicit within it — critics hold — worse things than have yet been seen, including war, the end of democracy, and, even, a new age of barbarism.

The following passage by a British pamphleteer brings together in about as succinct a summary as is to be found a vision of the moral consequences of "mass-production industrialism":

> . . . Mass-production industrialism has almost obliterated the worker's responsibility, also his opportunities for creative self-expression, and thus robbed him of social status and personal dignity. At the same time transference from rural to urban conditions has deprived him of vital social relationships. In the new conditions the only interest which a worker has in his labour is that of drawing wages, whence an ever-increasing emphasis is laid on money and money values and a decreasing emphasis on spiritual values. Quantitative, standardised production supersedes quality and distinction, while monotonous, uncreative labour starves both heart and mind and kills or poisons the spirit. Men cease to be whole persons and become sub-human robots with fragmented minds. This mass-manproduct of mass-production industrialism fittingly and timely appears, to become the foundation of the totalitarian era into which we are now passing with a momentum no one seems able to check.[12]

Thus, in outline, the ethical and moral criticism of industrial civilization.

Now to the first charge: modern civilization — the civilization of big business — is built upon an inverted system of values.

[12] Wilfred Wellock, *Gandhi as a Social Revolutionary* (Birmingham, England: Published by the author, September, 1950), p. 3.

CHAPTER 6

Excessive Materialism

FOR MANY of the critics of modern big business industrialism, its basic defect is its enhancement of materialistic values and the corresponding subordination of spiritual, moral, or human values. This concept of the nature of the value system of modern society is a fundamental premise and a starting point of much of their writings. As a corollary, but not often stated in just so many words, there is also a premise that the ordering of values was different in other societies of older times and in societies of other places. There often appears the suggestion that in, say, the New England of the 18th Century, or the France and Italy of the Middle Ages, or the India of the 20th Century, values of the spirit were ranked higher than material values. It appears from what many critics say that they believe that the ethical and moral level of life — inner life, at any rate — was higher then and there than it is here and now.

These critics also proceed from the basic postulate that the *prime* end of human existence is the perfection of the personality, spirit, or soul of the individual person. Or, as seen from a different standpoint, that the *prime* objective of human life is conformity to moral, natural, or Divine law. Some, in varying degrees inclined to asceticism, insist that this is the *only* proper end. Others countenance varying degrees of worldliness. They concede the permissibility, albeit in far inferior status, of other objectives such as material welfare or esthetic satisfaction.

Despite the differences among them, the critics are as one in the belief that in big business civilization the scale of values has been inverted. They charge that material welfare, which should be regarded as a secondary value, or accepted only to the extent that it is a *means* to the good life, or which should even be shunned as inherently evil, has achieved a status of primacy which is incompatible with the good life or the good society. In the eyes of these critics, it is this inversion of values — or, as some say, confusion of means and ends — that is the fundamental error or inadequacy which lies at the bottom of the many specific evils which they observe.

Roughly speaking, this excessive materialism, as it is treated in critical writings, appears to have immediate consequences of two sorts which blend into one another. First, such a scheme of values results in a contorted and empty life for the individual. Second, it is said, such a false ranking of values by the community at large results in a society which is ugly, or perhaps just overly utilitarian, at best and, at worst, thoroughly inhuman and depraved. In any case, both the individual and the society as a whole lose sight of the true purposes and joys of life.

"Materialism Blights the Individual Life, Today"

To take up the immediate consequences of a false ordering of values for the individual himself: It is visualized that the individual who places materialistic, worldly values ahead of spiritual and moral values is foredoomed to frustration and unhappiness; at best — to an empty life without real human joy or meaning. The emptiness of life and frustration of the spirit are even — or, perhaps, are especially — the inevitable destiny of those who are "successful" according to materialistic worldly values. This is held to be true particularly when material gain and social status become identified with each other, as they are said to be in our industrial culture.

This theme of the frustrating nature and emptiness of these false values recurs again and again, and finds its way into popular literature. This idea, I take it, is at least part of the "message" of Sinclair Lewis' *Babbitt*.[1] The hero of this best-

[1] New York: Harcourt, Brace and Co., 1922.

selling novel, George Babbitt, has come to be a popular stereotype of a "successful," but a callow, and, below the effusive exterior, a deeply sad and confused member of the "middle-upper" class — of the "typical" American businessman.

The theme appears in J. P. Marquand's more recent best-seller, *Point of No Return.*[2] This, of course, is the story of a young banker who attains a long-standing goal — promotion to a vice presidency of the bank — with the substantial increase in income which goes with the position. This increase in income, as Charley Grey and his wife Nancy recognize, will enable them to do, and to acquire more *things:* to buy a bigger (hence "better") house; to belong to a more expensive (hence "better") country club; to maintain a larger (hence "better") boat; to send the children to private instead of public (hence "inferior") schools. In consequence of being able to do and to have these more costly things — from a materialistic point of view, "better" things — their social status will be enhanced. A rise in social status automatically follows a rise in wealth in a society which puts material values first. "Everything" turns on getting more wealth, more *Things.*

The pathos of this nationally popular story, as I read it, lies in the fact that at the very moment of attaining his goal, our young friend comes to a realization that the values that he and his wife, and their associates, live by are essentially superficial and without real significance. He comes to realize — too late; beyond the "point of no return" — that the *true* values in life, values in terms of real meaning to the inner human spirit, are not determined by the values put upon them by a materialistic scheme of things. He comes to see that the things he has gained are without *true,* deep value, especially relative to their spiritual cost to him in the mode of his life. They do not have values which will satisfy the yearnings of the spirit. Charley and Nancy and their asso-

[2] Boston: Little, Brown and Company, 1949.

ciates come through this story, and its popular dramatization, as prototypes of individuals whose values are confused and empty. The story, it seems to me, can be taken as a parable of the deep sadness which Marquand sees in a kind of corporation executive Everyman in a materialistic society.

An explicit statement of the proposition that the materialistic values of business society lead to unhappiness and frustration is to be found in *The Acquisitive Society* by the eminent British historian, R. H. Tawney. The masses who labor in such a society, he holds, are not happy because they "come to be regarded, not as the ends for which alone it is worth while to produce wealth at all, but as the instruments of its acquisition. . . ." They are not happy, despite their wages, for they know that their culture does not esteem "the dull and sordid business of labor" nor those who so give their lives to making this civilization. The rich in Tawney's society of stereotypes are no better off, for they have "abolished the principle [of service and social purpose] which makes activity significant, and therefore estimable." For Tawney, the rich are "more truly pitiable than some of those who envy them. For like the spirits in the Inferno, they are punished by the attainment of their desires." [3]

The pathos of *Point of No Return,* I take it, is closely related to the truly pitiable lot which Tawney visualizes for the rich in modern materialistic culture.

As suggested in the passage from Tawney, critics of industrial civilization hold that materialistic values are so enhanced that the pursuit of wealth is seen as becoming an *end* in itself, or even *the* end objective of the life of the individual. When this happens — it is said — material welfare and the carrying on of business are no longer as they should be, at most, mere means to the development of the human personality, soul, or spirit. The means and ends of life are then confused. This confusion, commentators contend, has become a keynote of our society.

[3] New York: Harcourt, Brace and Company, 1921, pp. 35–36.

According to Max Weber, the German historian, and to a number of other Europeans he quotes and refers to in his very influential book, *The Protestant Ethic and the Spirit of Capitalism,* this inversion of values is the very *"spirit* of capitalism." *They* say that under capitalism the production and amassing of material things is *the* objective of human existence. As they conceive the "spirit of capitalism," it is a scheme of things where material values, and material values alone, provide the motivation of activity, the criterion of choice, judgment, and decision, and the objective of action. This is the point of view they even trace back to the philosophy of Benjamin Franklin. Franklin's writings, *Necessary Hints to Those That Would be Rich* and *Advice to a Young Tradesman,* are cited by Weber as exemplifying the quintessence of the materialistic spirit and *"ethos"* of capitalism.[4]

When material welfare becomes *the* objective of life, so the moral critics of capitalism say, the individual becomes morally bankrupt — or, even, corrupt — and that which is human in the individual is extinguished. To Weber, the "Alpha and Omega of Franklin's ethic" is the earning of money. Franklin's morality is described as exclusively utilitarian. As Weber sees Franklin's "capitalistic" morality — which he takes as the spirit of modern capitalism to this very day — human virtues have ceased to be ends in themselves. Virtues are no longer virtues because they are morally *right.* Weber says that in capitalistic morality, as enunciated by Franklin, such virtues as honesty, punctuality, industry, frugality, and modesty are virtues only because and *only in so far* as they are actually *useful* to the individual. This being so, "the surrogate of mere appearance is always sufficient when it accomplishes the end in view." As Weber interprets this philosophy, which he says is epitomized in Franklin, "unnecessary surplus" of such a virtue as honesty is "unproductive waste."[5] Capitalistic virtues are thus seen as being subordinated to the level of expedients. They are "morally"

4 Op. cit., pp. 48–54.

5 Ibid., pp. 51–54.

right only in so far as they are useful — as means for attaining the prime objective, material wealth. This represents carrying the confusion of values to the point of corruption.[6]

Thus, in the varying points of view represented in the range of criticism from Marquand to Weber, the mis-ordering of basic values by the individual in modern industrial society has consequences for the individual ranging from pathetic sadness to a pretty thorough corruption. In the passage from T. S. Eliot which appears a few pages back, the consequence is "weariness."

It is not only in his inner life that the unfortunate individual is portrayed as being affected by his inverted values. His perceptions and understanding of the world about him become warped. Accordingly, he is unable to relate himself realistically and satisfyingly to his environment. Really *human* relationships with others cease to be possible, even with members of his own family. More drastic than a touching pathos or even than moral corruption, the consequence is a total blighting of personality, degradation of human dignity, and even physical destruction.

All these ideas seem to me to be present in Arthur Miller's "smash hit" play, *Death of a Salesman*.[7] Willy Loman, the salesman, the play's central figure, bids fair to become a stereotype of the confused, tragic, and unsuccessful materialist and business go-getter who clings to his empty, frustrating values right down to the ultimate end.

Because of his distortion of basic values, Willy's life loses its flavor. It becomes a lie. Willy, not only just as an individual, but above all as a product of business civilization, becomes a completely tragic character: an object of pity to

[6] Weber's broadside tract, I say, gives less than a full picture of the whole Benjamin Franklin. The portrait of venality and insincerity he would have us accept scarcely captures, for instance, the likeness that still shines through the record of the proceedings of the Constitutional Convention. See James Madison, *Journal of the Federal Convention;* for example, the entries for June 2, June 11, August 7, August 20, 1787.

[7] New York: The Viking Press, 1949.

his wife, of scorn to his sons. For Willy, the true values of life, and its true meaning become so lost in his confusion that even death becomes a means to empty material ends. Or, at least, so I interpret this sell-out drama.

So much for the de-spiritualizing effect of excessive materialism on the individual in modern society, which, in the case of Willy Loman is seen as being carried to the point where human life, no longer an end in itself, becomes meaningless. This is the effect of materialism on the "atom" of the industrial culture.[8]

"Materialism Blights the Whole Society, Today"

The second count which is directed at industrial civilization under the heading "Excessive Materialism," is that the frustration, de-spiritualization, dehumanization, and corruption of materialistic individuals carry over to the society as a whole. This corruption is said to show itself in such things as the false ranking of goods, the false ranking of people, and an attenuation or absence of social justice and human charity. Depending on the point of view of the critic, the charge is made that industrial, big business capitalism has not, in fact, produced a "good society"; or, that there are inherent difficulties in the way of achieving a "good society" in a capitalist industrial setting; or, by way of extreme criticism, that a capitalistic society must *necessarily* be a "bad" society. Because of its supposed materialistic, utilitarian values, the civilization of big business is characterized in terms which range from "superficial" to "brutal."

In the paragraphs which follow, we shall examine a sampling of the range of these criticisms in a roughly ascending order of intensity, beginning with milder protests and closing the chapter with more vehement attacks on modern society.

[8] In a recent article, "Literature and the Businessman," Howard Mumford Jones, noted literary critic and Professor of English at Harvard College discusses "the businessman" as portrayed in popular literature. The picture which he finds drawn is much like that given in these paragraphs. (*Harvard Business Review,* Vol. 31, No. 1, January–February, 1953.)

The mildest of the criticisms are of the sort which express an esthetic distaste for modern civilization, its products and its way of life. These tend to characterize — to stereotype — life in our culture as devoid of "finer" or "higher" elements. By way of example, we can take a passage from Albert Schweitzer.

Albert Schweitzer — doctor, philosopher, theologian, musicologist, musician — is a critic of industrial civilization who has become something of a legend among intellectuals on two continents even during his lifetime. Schweitzer fitted personal action to words, apparently finding life, or escape, in the remoteness of the Congo more to his taste than life in his native industrialized Alsace-Lorraine. As he sees things, the improper subordination of spiritual values in industrial civilization is seen in the way individuals allocate their time. Most effort goes to productive work and the quest for gain, little or no time is allocated to the pursuit of any "higher ideal." In consequence of this inversion of values by individuals — Schweitzer says — modern civilization is deteriorating. The individual has come to live merely as a worker, a producing unit, not as a human being, and he devotes practically all his time and energy to work. Esthetically and spiritually, life has become sterile:

> . . . To spend the time left to him for leisure in self-cultivation, or in serious intercourse with his fellows or with books, requires a mental collectedness and a self-control which he finds very difficult. Complete idleness, forgetfulness, and diversion from his usual activities are a physical necessity. He does not want to think, and seeks not self-improvement, but entertainment, that kind of entertainment, moreover, which makes least demand upon his spiritual facilities.
>
> The mentality of this mass of individuals, spiritually relaxed and incapable of self-collectedness, reacts upon all those institutions which ought to serve the cause of culture, and therewith of civilization. The theatre takes a second place

behind the pleasure resort or the picture show, and the instructive book behind the diverting one. . . .

When once the spirit of superficiality has penetrated into the institutions which ought to sustain the spiritual life, these exercise on their part a reflex influence on the society which they have brought to this condition, and force on all alike this state of mental vacuity.

How completely this want of thinking power has become a second nature in men to-day is shown by the kind of sociability which it produces. When two of them meet for a conversation each is careful to see that their talk does not go beyond generalities or develop into a real exchange of ideas. No one has anything of his own to give out, and everyone is haunted by a sort of terror lest anything original should be demanded from him.

The spirit produced in such a society of never-concentrated minds is rising among us as an ever growing force, and it results in a lowered conception of what man should be. In ourselves, as in others, we look for nothing but vigour in productive work, and resign ourselves to the abandonment of any higher ideal.[9]

It should not be inferred from this relatively quiet passage that all of Schweitzer's criticisms are equally so. Elsewhere, he has more vigorous things to say, as might be expected of a man who speaks of the "decay of civilization."

T. S. Eliot, it seems to me, makes much the same point in his famous lines about the lost golf balls:

In the land of lobelias and tennis flannels
The rabbit shall burrow and the thorn revisit,
The nettle shall flourish on the gravel court,
And the wind shall say: "Here were decent godless people:
Their only monument the asphalt road
And a thousand lost golf balls." [10]

The symbolism, of course, is of superficiality; harmless, even "decent." But "godless," also. The contrasting gentleness

[9] *The Decay and Restoration of Civilization,* pp. 19–20. (Reprinted by permission of The Macmillan Company.)

[10] "Choruses from 'The Rock'," p. 103. (Reprinted with permission.)

of the judgment acts as a foil to the envisioned destiny of this superficial "godless" — materialistic — society: decay and rot to the point of obliteration.

Religious leaders, of course, have been especially vocal among the ethical and moral critics of industrial civilization. They, above all, are most concerned with what they visualize as the inversion of values in modern society. There is no mistaking the vigor of some of their criticisms; but, while their strictures are often vigorous, they are not as strident and abrasive as those of some of the lay critics.

Apart from what these leaders have to say, perhaps the most interesting thing about their criticisms is the degree of similarity among them despite underlying doctrinal differences, especially on matters of theology. It is possible that Protestant criticism is, on the whole, somewhat more tempered than Catholic. On the other hand, while Catholic opinion opposes what it sees as extremes of materialism and individualism, it does not oppose capitalism as such, and is quite categorical in its general support of the institution of private property. Some Protestant leaders, on the other hand, do seem to express misgivings about what seems to them *inherent* defects in capitalism; and a number are quite prepared to endorse social in preference to private ownership.

Aside from these few comments, we shall not be able to explore further the topic of religious criticism in our day. We shall have to be content with only a few illustrative samples.

Emil Brunner of Switzerland, an intellectual world leader among the Protestant theologians of our day, is one of those who, while not absolute pessimists, see *inherent* difficulties in constructing a "good society" on the basis of a capitalistic, business system. Brunner takes issue with Karl Marx — as a staunch Christian, Brunner stands four-square opposed to Communism — by arguing that "Capitalism" in Marx's sense hardly exists any more in Western society. But Brunner does go on to say:

> . . . All the same, the moral dangers inherent in the capitalist system have become and still are sinister realities: tremendous intensification of the profit motive, increased inequality with regard to property and power, social disintegration. There does exist what Karl Marx calls a "proletariat," i.e., enormous masses of men living under conditions unworthy of and detrimental to human personality, as well as to true community and spiritual cultural life.[11]

Another example of the view that there are *inherent* tendencies for capitalism to be at variance with the development of the "good society" is found in the *Findings and Decisions* of the First Assembly of the World Council of Churches, an agency, of course, with a world-wide constituency of Protestant denominations. After making clear the points of conflict between Christianity and "the atheistic Communism of our day," the Assembly went on to point out conflicts which it saw between Christianity and capitalism:

> The Church should make clear that there are conflicts between Christianity and capitalism. The developments of capitalism vary from country to country and often the exploitation of the workers that was characteristic of early capitalism has been corrected in considerable measure by the influence of trade unions, social legislation and responsible management. But (1) capitalism tends to subordinate what should be the primary task of any economy — the meeting of human needs — to the economic advantages of those who have most power over its institutions. (2) It tends to produce serious inequalities. (3) It has developed a practical form of materialism in western nations in spite of their Christian background, for it has placed the greatest emphasis upon success in making money. (4) It has also kept the people of capitalist countries subject to a kind of fate which has taken the form of such social catastrophes as mass unemployment.[12]

[11] *Christianity and Civilization* (London: Nisbet & Co., Ltd., and New York: Charles Scribner's Sons, 1949), Part II, pp. 90–91.

[12] Geneva, London, and New York: The World Council of Churches, 1948, p. 45.

There have been no more consistent and energetic critics of materialism in business, industrial society than the Popes of the Roman Catholic Church. Perhaps one of the most influential documents of our times was the Encyclical *Rerum Novarum* which Leo XIII addressed to the world in 1891. Leo XIII categorically denied that the organization of economic life on the basis of private property was inherently wrong and that, for instance, conflict was inherent in the relationship between capital and labor, between employer and employee. But he was concerned about industrial inhumanity. This he traced to erroneous emphasis of materialistic values and corresponding neglect of Christian duties such as charity and justice. His impressions of the state of industry led him to protest that "it is shameful and inhuman to treat men like chattels to make money by, or to look upon them merely as so much muscle or physical power." [13] Such inhuman treatment of human beings is a consequence of a materialistic outlook which comes to view human beings as means to ends only — instruments of production.

In his first Encyclical, written in 1922 shortly after his election, Pope Pius XI ascribed the many social, political, and international problems of modern society very largely to the enhancement of material values and the corresponding subordination of the "eternal and spiritual," both by individuals and by nations. "It is in the very nature of material objects," said Pius XI, "that an inordinate desire for them becomes the root of every evil, of every discord, and in particular, of a lowering of the moral sense." Materialism can lead only to dissatisfaction, "division among men," "vexation of the spirit," and to evil. In our materialistic civilization, "Men today do not act as Christians, as brothers, but as strangers, and even enemies. The sense of man's personal dignity and of the value of human life has been lost in the brutal domination begotten of might and mere superiority in numbers.

[13] *Rerum Novarum* (New York: The Paulist Press, Pamphlet Edition, 1939), p. 13.

Many are intent on exploiting their neighbors solely for the purpose of enjoying more fully and on a larger scale the goods of this world." [14]

We shall see in the next chapter that religious leaders have also had strong criticisms to make of the irresponsible individualism they discern in modern society.

Now to take up some sample comments of laymen who express not mere distaste for industrial civilization, nor even deep concern, but ardent outrage. Among such critics there appears not only the idea that the society brought into being by large-scale industry *is* inhuman, but, generally speaking, there are strong suggestions of a thesis that it is *inherently* so. Inherent inhumanity is quite a different matter from "superficiality," or even "weariness."

Plenty of examples of this point of view are to be found in rather dull, tedious prose essays of limited circulation. But more interestingly and more importantly it is to be found in popular writings. During the 1920's and 1930's there was quite a spate of proletarian novels — a number of which had some considerable success — which contained implicit attacks on modern society on moral grounds. One of the most noted writers in this vein, to name but one, is Upton Sinclair. His concept and portrayal of inhumanity in *The Jungle* [15] of the meat-packing industry had an undoubtedly great impact on American feelings in the decade prior to World War I. And a generation later, the United Automobile Workers, C.I.O., distributed 200,000 copies of his grim picture of the automobile industry, *The Flivver King.*[16]

Charlie Chaplin, in his popular and hilariously pathetic film, *Modern Times,* seemed to be portraying a concept of a very human industrial Everyman who is pushed around by the inhuman forces and agents of modern big industry. In

14 Encyclical, *Ubi Arcano* (Translation by James H. Ryan; publisher unspecified), p. 9.

15 New York: Doubleday, Page & Company, 1906. Also, New York: The Vanguard Press, 1926 and 1927.

16 Detroit: The United Automobile Workers of America, 1937.

this view, as it strikes me, there is no suggestion of optimism: that Charlie's crushing defeat, after all, may not be suffered by all people, nor that the forces which crush him may be remediable defects. It looks to me as though this is intended as a picture of the *essence* of modern large-scale industrial capitalism. But that, of course, is a matter of interpretation.

The view that the materialism of life in our society is incompatible with what is most human and humane is seen, for further instance, in this passage from Alexis Carrel's *Man the Unknown,* a pre-World War II best seller:

> The brutal materialism of our civilization not only opposes the soaring of intelligence, but also crushes the affective, the gentle, the weak, the lonely, those who love beauty, who look for other things than money, whose sensibility does not stand the struggle of modern life.[17]

This passage suggests that in industrial civilization a kind of Darwinian struggle for survival is going on, and that those who have thrown off what is most human in the human being are winning out. Inhumanity and brutality, apparently, are on the ascendant, growing and triumphing in a self-generating degenerative process.

In his viciously witty *Brave New World* [18] — again, something of a best seller — Aldous Huxley has painted a revoltingly amusing picture of a society whose system of values gives pre-eminence to *things* up to a point where production literally becomes the end of life and humans the means only. In Huxley's inverted materialistic "utopia," all other considerations — love, the family, sexual morality, and even human reproduction itself — have given way as values and ends in themselves to the expediencies of efficient production, which had become *the* end of human existence. In this polemic — it is not a satire — Huxley makes it abundantly clear that he is drawing out what are to him the ultimate implications —

[17] New York: Harper & Brothers, 29th Edition, 1935, p. 317.
[18] Garden City, New York: The Sun Dial Press, 1932.

even if they may be the *reductio ad absurdum* — of the system of values he perceives in the big business civilization of industrial America.

Conclusion

On this note we complete our sampling of ideas to the effect that industrial civilization is not *good* because its values are of the wrong order. Not only are they of the wrong order, in the eyes of the critics; but, as we have seen, a number of them conceive that there are no values of consequence in this society other than material ones. Not only inside the individual business, but throughout society as a whole the quest for material gain is taken to be the sole motivating force. Economic expediency is taken to be the sole criterion of decision. The result, they say, is evil. Clearly, this criticism is on an entirely different plane from those we saw on the economic and on the political and social levels.

One cannot help being impressed with the range of these critics — poets, novelists, scholars, world-eminent religious leaders and spokesmen. Going beyond the written word, samples of criticism on this plane could have been drawn also from the works of artists. Explicitly embodying clearly different overtones — those of avowed Marxism — but equally critical of the moral values which are seen in industrial capitalism, examples could have been drawn, for instance, from the widely known and much admired works of the Mexican artists José Orozco and Diego Rivera.

The critics are not confined to any one political "school."

Finally, the emotional impact of much of this criticism and the popular response which it receives must also be noted. The fact that several items from which examples were drawn were in the best-seller class attests to their ability to strike a responsive chord in large numbers of people. The thought that our society and its people are dehumanized through the inversion of basic values is very obviously one to stir many people very deeply — more deeply, say, than pages of statistics relating to differential costs of production of large and small cement mills.

We shall now move on to the second major point in the ethical and moral criticism of the industrial civilization of big business: that it is premised upon an irresponsible individualism. Like excessive materialism, this aspect of the culture of big business is seen as an evil in itself, and as a cause of moral defectiveness in the society.

CHAPTER 7

"Irresponsible Individualism"

INDIVIDUALISM — especially irresponsible individualism — is the second major focal point of the ethical and moral criticism directed at industrial civilization.

"Individualism," like other concepts of a high order of abstraction, means different things to different people. As it appears to be conceived by its moral critics, it seems to amount to a rather literal interpretation of ideas which were systematically set forth long ago by Adam Smith and others, mostly Englishmen, who followed him.

There is a famous passage in Smith's plea for laissez-faire in foreign trade which is often cited as containing key ideas of the philosophy of Individualism. It will be helpful to have these words in mind as we review what critics have to say. "Every individual," said Smith,

> . . . is continually exerting himself to find out the most advantageous employment for whatever capital he can command. It is his own advantage, indeed, and not that of the society which he has in view. But the study of his own advantage naturally, or rather necessarily leads him to prefer that employment which is most advantageous to the society. . . .
>
> . . . He generally, indeed, neither intends to promote the public interest nor knows how much he is promoting it . . . by directing [his] industry in such a manner as its produce may be of the greatest value, he intends only his own gain, and he is in this, as in many other cases, led by an invisible hand to promote an end which was no part of his intention. . . .[1]

[1] *An Inquiry into the Nature and Causes of the Wealth of Nations,* Vol. II, pp. 32 and 35 ("Modern Library Edition," pp. 421 and 423.) (It is fair to say that Adam Smith personally was by no means the advocate of a policy of unqualified "laissez-faire" he has sometimes been represented to be on the strength of these passages.)

This passage, literally construed, contains two ideas which critics have taken as of the essence of individualism. Of these, they are profoundly critical. First, that the individual engaged in economic activity has *gain* — material gain — as his *sole* motive. Second, that the gain he seeks is "his own" — exclusively — and "not that of the society." It is these two aspects of individualism, as the critics conceive it, that to their way of thinking lead to a host of evils.

It is hard to disentangle these many evils one from another. But, in a very rough way, these criticisms seem to make two broad points:

First, that individualism is a morally defective scheme of things. It is defective on two planes:

It is defective as a way of life for the individual himself. And it is defective as a basis of social organization. For most of the critics, man is *not* an "island"; he *is,* at least to some extent, his brother's keeper. Individualism is at odds with the moral concept that the individual has moral obligations, or Christian duties, towards others and toward the community at large. Meeting these obligations is a requirement of the moral life. Moreover, individualism is at odds also with the moral vision of society as an organically harmonious entity. Individualism is conceived of as being the negation of this vision. Under individualism, according to this view, there is no whole, but only atomic fragments — "islands." These fragmented particles do not operate to fulfill the requirements of the social whole — not so much the material requirements as the spiritual requirements. For under individualism, the individual units of society do not work toward the requirements of the whole, but are engaged in unqualified competition, if they are not actually working at cross-purposes and in strife with one another.

Second, and this is clearly an extension of the first point, critics visualize that competitive, irresponsible individualism not only does not work to meet the requirements of the whole, but actually produces a social order which is chaotic rather than harmonious. Individualism is seen as the basic cause of much of the internal strife of modern society. Irresponsible individualism, moral critics say, has undermined democracy and has brought authoritarian elements into modern society. These views are reminiscent of the charges which political and social critics have made directly against big business.

Looking ahead to the topic of our next chapter, irresponsible individualism, combined with materialism, is said to have worked to produce the business civilization which many critics find repugnant on moral, ethical, or spiritual grounds. It is repugnant to them in its essential concrete aspects and manifestations: in the allocation of its resources; in its mechanized factories; in its large cities, and in its way of life.

Individualism shares the animus of the moral critics equally with materialism.

The Moral Defectiveness of Individualism

The following rather lengthy excerpt from Tawney's *The Acquisitive Society* conveys a good general idea of what critics conceive to have been the major moral consequences of the rise of individualism: the sluffing off of moral obligation and responsibility by the individual and the dissolution of the vision of society as a harmonious moral whole. This is a common interpretation of the *moral* meaning of the continuing political and social evolution of the Western world since the beginning of the 17th Century:

> . . . The essence of the change was the disappearance of the idea that social institutions and economic activities were related to common ends, which gave them their significance and which served as their criterion. . . . Opinion ceased to regard social institutions and economic activity as amenable, like personal conduct, to moral criteria, because it was no longer influenced by the spectacle of institutions which, arbitrary, capricious, and often corrupt in their practical operation, had been the outward symbol and expression of the

subordination of life to purposes transcending private interests. . . . But what was familiar, and human and lovable — what was Christian in Christianity had largely disappeared. . . .

The natural consequence of the abdication of authorities which had stood, however imperfectly, for a common purpose in social organization, was the gradual disappearance from social thought of the idea of purpose itself. Its place in the eighteenth century was taken by the idea of mechanism. The conception of men as united to each other, and of all mankind as united to God, by mutual obligations arising from their relation to a common end, which vaguely conceived and imperfectly realized, had been the keystone holding together the social fabric, ceased to be impressed upon men's minds, when Church and State withdrew from the center of social life to its circumference. What remained when the keystone of the arch was removed, was private rights and private interests. . . . [After the 18th Century, these private rights and private interests came to be regarded as "absolute and indefeasible" and as] the ultimate political and social reality; and since they were the ultimate reality, they were not subordinate to other aspects of society, but other aspects of society were subordinate to them.

. . . . .

The result of such ideas in the world of practice was a society which was ruled by law, not by the caprice of Governments, but which recognized *no moral limitation on the pursuit by individuals of their economic self-interest. . . .*[2]

To this way of thinking, individualism is clearly equated to *irresponsible* individualism. More — it is equated to a scheme of things in which there are *no* moral limitations. Material gain is the *only* consideration. The concept of individualism thus becomes irresponsible, materialistic individualism.

Ideas along the same line, it seems to me, are contained in

[2] Pages 10–14. (Italics added.)

the following passage from *The Age of Jackson* by Arthur M. Schlesinger, Jr., Professor of History at Harvard. Here, these ideas are more specifically related to America, to more recent history, and to the rise of the large corporation in particular:

> . . . industrialism brought the growing depersonalization of economic life. With the increase in size of the labor force, the master was further and further removed from his workmen, till the head of a factory could have only the most tenuous community of feeling with his men. With the development of manufacturing and improved means of distribution, the seller lost all contact with the buyer, and feelings of responsibility to the consumer inevitably diminished. The expansion of investment tended to bring on absentee ownership, with the divorce of ownership and management; and the rise of cities enfeebled the paternal sentiments with which many capitalists had regarded their workers in towns and villages. Slowly the vital economic relationships were becoming impersonal, passing out of the control of a personal moral code. Slowly private morality and business morality grew apart. Slowly the commercial community developed a collection of devices and ceremonials which enabled businessmen to set aside the ethic which ruled their private life and personal relations.
>
> Of these devices the most dramatic and generally intelligible was the corporation. For a people still yearning for an economy dominated by individual responsibility, still under the spell of the Jeffersonian dream, the corporation had one outstanding characteristic: its moral irresponsibility. "Corporations have neither bodies to be kicked, nor souls to be damned," went a favorite aphorism. Beyond good and evil, insensible to argument or appeal, they symbolized the mounting independence of the new economy from the restraints and scruples of personal life.[3]

The juxtaposition here of these excerpts from Tawney and Schlesinger prompts a parenthetical comment. As we saw earlier, a host of critics hold a fervid animus toward big busi-

[3] Boston: Little, Brown and Company, 1945, pp. 334–335.

ness because it is not consistent with *their* ideal of "real," well-nigh literal individualism. Most of the critics now under review are no less resolute in their attack on the supreme moral *errors* of irresponsibility and individualism. Schlesinger here, like many other critics, is directing the same charges at "the corporation" — chiefly at its depersonalization of relationships and increasing irresponsibility — that theologically inclined critics have levelled at individualism since long before Adam Smith and the "Manchester School" ever came along.[4]

These thrusts on quite different flanks put big business in an interesting, if somewhat taxing, tactical position. On the one side, it is attacked because it is crushing down and stamping out individualism. On the other, it is attacked because it is chargeable with the profound moral errors of that very same individualism, of which it is held to be the apotheosis, the heir, the successor, or the perversion, as the case may be.

It really *is* a dilemma to be attacked by the different sets of critics for almost diametrically opposite reasons. It's — well, perplexing.

But we must get on.

As moralist critics tend to see individualism, it is a doctrine which not only frees the individual to lead his own life and to carry on his affairs in his own way. (Some of the religious critics favor individual freedom, and responsibility, within very wide limits, even if — interestingly enough — some of the lay critics seem not to.) But — and here is where the objection comes in — they say that individualism is in fact a scheme of things which frees the individual from *all* moral

[4] Professor Schlesinger, it will be noted, in addition to corporations also does not like factories and cities. This, as we shall see later on, is often, naturally enough perhaps, part of the syndrome – cluster of symptoms – of dissatisfaction with big business and its civilization.

Another interesting point is that Schlesinger's stereotyped pre-corporate capitalist was apparently more paternalistic than he was individualistic. In giving us this rather warming sketch of the responsible, pristine individual entrepreneur, Schlesinger is somewhat at odds with many other students, including Adam Smith and R. H. Tawney.

obligations or even compunction. In their eyes, the concept of individualism, as it has evolved, has provided a *rationale* and an institutional framework to aid and abet the individual to pursue materialistic ends and to live by materialistic values alone. Individualism, as they see it, has given institutional status to a *sinful* way of life. It is not that individualism has merely legalized for the individual his freedom to pursue this sinful way of life. Individualism has made this sinful, irresponsible way of life the very basis of the social order.

Pope Pius XI in explaining the opposition of the Roman Catholic Church to individualism did so, it seems to me, in terms much like these. He stated that under individualism, "free rein was given to human avarice." Individualistic materialism is referred to as a "mere sordid selfishness," and it is castigated as "the disgrace and the great crime of the present age." [5]

Because of the great authority, to say nothing of the influence and prestige of the Vatican, we may well explore these ideas further.

In condemning individualism, the Popes have tried to make it clear that the Church is not condemning individual freedom, the institution of private property, or the idea of "capitalistic economy." Pius XI affirmed that "a just freedom of action should be left to individual citizens and families." [6] The Holy See has insisted that private property is in accordance with natural law and Divine Law, and has defended the institution of private property against the attacks of Socialism.[7] Pius XI also stated that Catholicism stood in contradiction to Socialism because Socialism is ignorant of, or unconcerned about "the sublime end both of individuals

[5] Encyclical, *Quadragesimo Anno* (1931) (New York, The Missionary Society of St. Paul the Apostle, Pamphlet Edition, 1939), pp. 36 and 37. [The title of this encyclical denotes that this encyclical appeared forty years after the encyclical *Rerum Novarum* of Leo XIII.]

[6] Ibid., p. 7.

[7] Leo XIII, *Rerum Novarum,* pp. 7–8; and Pius XI, *Quadragesimo Anno,* p. 12.

and of society." [8] Capitalistic economy, however, he said, "is not vicious of its very nature." [9]

But the position of the Church on these matters is qualified. First, the freedom of action which, according to the Pontiffs, should be left to individual citizens and families, is a "just" freedom; *but* it is subject to the interests of the community as a whole and the duty of justice. The principle of freedom of individual action is specifically qualified: ". . . this principle is only valid as long as the common good is secure and no injustice is entailed." [10]

Second, the rights to property, including the disposition of one's income, in the view of the Popes, cannot be regarded as unqualified and absolute. These rights are subject to the Christian duties of justice and charity.[11] And, while the State has no right to *abolish* private property, or "to exhaust the means of individuals, by crushing taxes and tributes," private property *is* subject to the right of the State "to control its use and bring it into harmony with the interests of the public good." [12]

Third, so far as "Individualism" as a systematic body of theory and practice is concerned, and especially its *rationale* as set forth by the "Manchester School" of English economists, that *is* expressly condemned by Pius XI as an "evil" and a "danger" along with its opposite, "Collectivism." [13] For "Individualism" of this tradition is seen as denying or minimizing the social or public aspect of the use of property. This contrasts to the Church's view of "Collectivism," which is seen as erring through its rejection or diminution of the private or individual character of ownership.[14] The unity of human society, the Church holds, cannot be built upon class

[8] *Quadragesimo Anno,* pp. 31–32.

[9] Ibid., p. 27.

[10] Ibid., p. 7.

[11] Leo XIII, *Rerum Novarum,* p. 15 and Pius XI, *Quadragesimo Anno,* pp. 13–14.

[12] Leo, XIII, op. cit., p. 29 and Pius XI, op. cit., p. 14.

[13] Pius XI, op. cit., pp. 15, 12, 21, and 28.

[14] Ibid., p. 12.

warfare. But neither can the proper ordering of economic affairs be left to a free competition alone which ignores the interests of society as a whole. For holding the contrary, the " 'Individualistic' school," according to Pius XI, has fallen into error:

> This school, ignorant or forgetful of the social and moral aspects of economic matters, teaches that the state should refrain in theory and practice from interfering therein, because these possess in free competition and open markets a principle of self-direction better able to control them than any created intellect. Free competition, however, though within certain limits just and productive of good results, cannot be the ruling principle of the economic world. This has been abundantly proved by the consequences that have followed from the free rein given to these dangerous individualistic ideals.[15]

Irresponsible individualism has also been criticized by Protestant leaders, although, of course, they do not speak with a single voice nor do they speak to Protestants with the authority of the Popes when *they* address the Catholic world. Accordingly, as on other matters, there is hardly a Protestant viewpoint, as such, on individualism. But the statement of the Executive Committee of The Federal Council of the Churches of Christ in America on *Basic Christian Principles and Assumptions* probably can be taken as more or less representative of ideas widely, if not uniformly, held among Protestant leaders in the United States.

According to this statement, there are three objectives and norms by which economic institutions should be judged: order, freedom, and justice. "An economic system that neglects any one of those values will soon become intolerable." In the view of this statement, one-sided devotion to one or another of these objectives and norms is characteristic of present controversies between economic systems. But since *all* these values have a "rightful claim upon the Church and

[15] Ibid., p. 24.

the Christians," "there can be no Christian sanction for one-sided support of either economic individualism or economic collectivism." Accordingly

> . . . Christians should be guided by their ethic to seek the economic institutions which will in a given set of circumstances serve most fully the three positive values of justice and order and freedom. This means that there must be a perpetual Christian struggle in behalf of whatever values are most neglected in the predominant economic institutions. Under capitalism the emphasis should be on the need for justice, and under any form of collectivism the emphasis should be on the need for freedom.[16]

The statement of the Executive Committee of the Council did not, apparently, reject individualistic motivation absolutely, for it stated that economic institutions should make constructive use of such motives as the individual desire for economic security, the desire to improve the economic condition of one's family, the desires for scope for one's capacities and for social approval. But it did go on to set forth these qualifications to the pursuit of individual interest:

> . . . under Christian influences these motives should be kept in harmony with concern for the welfare of the community and with the individual's sense of Christian vocation. The Church should keep under the strongest criticism those economic institutions which increase the self-interest of men and which develop a moral climate within which money is regarded as the chief good and in which success in acquiring it is most highly honored.[17]

Thus, this Protestant group also, it would seem, sees untempered individualism as defective from the point of view of the morality of the individual and from the point of view of the moral interests of *social* justice.

[16] *The Church and Economic Life: Basic Christian Principles and Assumptions* (New York: The Federal Council of the Churches of Christ in America, 1948), p. 5.

[17] Ibid., pp. 6–7.

Albert Schweitzer, who has had a deep influence on the thinking of both religious and intellectual leaders also has been critical of individualism. In the following passage he argues — clearly from a moral standpoint — that individualism ignores the needs of the social whole, of the "community."

> Civilization is, it is true, furthered to a certain extent by the self-regarding ideals produced by the groups of people who unite and co-operate in defence of their similarly threatened interests in so far as they seek to obtain an improvement in their material, and thereby also in their spiritual, environment. But these ideals are a danger to the idea of civilization as such, because the form which they assume is either not at all, or very imperfectly, determined by the really universal interests of the community. The consideration of civilization as such is held back by the competition between the various self-regarding ideals which go under its name.[18]

Interestingly enough, the political Left, in addition to criticizing modern capitalism on *materialist* grounds, has also been critical on grounds of traditional *morality*. Such ideas are to be found in the works of Sidney and Beatrice Webb, whose influence on British thought has been enormous and some of whose influence, it would appear, has also traversed the Atlantic.

In their book, *The Decay of Capitalist Civilization,* the Webbs argue, among other things, that capitalism has failed to provide the maximum production of commodities. Even more important, to the Webbs, capitalism is "inimical to national morality and international peace; in fact to civilization itself." This is because it places "exclusive reliance on the motive of pecuniary gain to individual owners."[19]

[18] *The Decay and Restoration of Civilization,* pp. 17–18. (Quoted with the permission of The Macmillan Company.)

[19] Sidney and Beatrice Webb, *The Decay of Capitalistic Civilization* (New York: Harcourt, Brace and Co., 1923), p. xvii.

Individualism, for the Webbs, recognizes materialistic gain as the exclusive motive for the individual.

And, to the Webbs, individualism is irresponsible. In fact, to them it is an "amazing arrangement" that the land, along with other instruments for the production of wealth, "should be the private property of a relatively small class of individuals, with hardly more public responsibility attached to it than to the possessor of a watch or a walking stick." [20]

As the Webbs interpret history, private capitalism has undertaken "to secure the livelihood of the people, not as its aim, but as an incident of its devotion on principle to the art of getting rich quickly." Far from being of prime concern, the interests of the social whole are clearly — to this way of thinking — given a lowly subordinate status. To make matters worse, private capitalism has entered this undertaking on "the frankly buccaneering terms" that Church and State were not to interfere, and that "its operations were to be godless and lawless." [21] Thus, individualism appears not only as totally irresponsible, but totally without moral compunction.

It follows — given these ideas — that such an institutional arrangement is "fundamentally inconsistent with the spiritual advancement of the race." [22] Individualism fails to provide for the moral needs of the social whole.

"Individualism Undermines Democracy"

We shall now move along to look at some examples of moral criticism to the effect that individualism has operated to undermine democracy and to bring in elements of authoritarianism.

The institutions of individualism confer powers upon the individual which in earlier times resided elsewhere: in church, feudal, municipal, and guild authorities. It is logical that critics who hold that individualism is irresponsible

20 Ibid., p. xi.
21 Ibid., p. xii.
22 Ibid., p. xvi.

should also hold that there is now no responsibility in the exercise of these powers. In the eyes of some of the critics, this aspect of individualism, combined with unequal distribution of wealth (immoral in itself) has given rise to great private extragovernmental power being vested in a few individuals. This idea, it seems to me, underlies the representation of the administrators of big business as "princelings," "earls," and "grand seigneurs." It is also consistent with this way of thinking that this irresponsible power should be seen as being exercised solely in accordance with the economic interests of those who possess it.

As critics interpret events, individualism has brought about a new power structure which is *morally* blameworthy. For one thing, it is said that this power structure is incompatible with the maintenance and furtherance of a harmonious social whole. It is said that this power is distributed unequally and that this is a cause of social injustice and discord. As seen by various critics, political inequality ranges from unequal access to the instruments and protection of governmental power to *de facto* control of constitutionally democratic governments by the "wealthy classes" and the "vested interests." These charges are reminiscent of some made by the political and social critics.

Moreover, individualism is seen as introducing a one-sided element of power into the relationship between employer and employee. Because this power is irresponsible and because the employer is materialistically oriented, the relationship of employer to employee tends to become impersonal and distant, or even inhuman and immoral. At best, this relationship is authoritarian.

The Holy See of the Roman Catholic Church has expressed deep concern over the impact of the institutions and operations of individualism on other institutions. On account of the "evil of Individualism," Pope Pius XI said, "things have come to such a pass that the highly developed social life which once flourished in a variety of prosperous institutions organically united with each other, has been damaged and all but ruined." Social life has lost its organic form. Virtually all that is left, following the extinction of many local associations and other bodies, are "individuals and the state." Under the circumstances the state became encumbered with burdens once borne by associations and has become "submerged and overwhelmed by an infinity of affairs and duties." And, so Pius XI held, it is an "injustice, a grave evil, and a disturbance of right order" for a larger and higher organization like the State to take over functions which can be, and used to be, performed efficiently by smaller and lower bodies.[23]

The inequality in the distribution of private power is seen by the Vatican as an important factor in bringing about a morally deplorable state of society. For, Pope Pius XI asserted, "the vast differences between the few who hold excessive wealth and the many who live in destitution constitute a grave evil in modern society"; further,

> . . . the immense number of propertyless wage-earners on the one hand, and the superabundant riches of the fortunate few on the other, is an unanswerable argument that the earthly goods so abundantly produced in this age of industrialism are far from rightly distributed and equitably shared among the various classes of men.[24]

As to inequality, Leo XIII believed that, because of the concentration of so many branches of trade in the hands of a few individuals, "a small number of very rich men have been able to lay upon the masses of the poor a yoke little better than slavery." [25] Picking up this point forty years later, Pius XI asserted that "immense power and despotic economic domination is concentrated in the hands of a few." He stated also that "accumulation of power" is the "characteristic note of the modern economic order." [26] The devel-

[23] *Quadragesimo Anno,* pp. 21–22.
[24] Ibid., p. 17.
[25] *Rerum Novarum,* p. 4.
[26] *Quadragesimo Anno,* p. 29.

opment of this inequality, it is to be gathered from the Vatican's pronouncement, is a consequence of the neglect of the Christian duties of justice and charity. Its continuation represents further neglect.

Moreover, this concentration of power, in the view of the Holy See, has led to a morally distressing struggle for domination, first for dictatorship in the economic sphere itself; second, to the fierce battle to acquire control of the state; and, third, to clash between states themselves.[27] This set of ideas as to the consequences of individualism is developed from a moral basis. Yet, despite some deep differences, these ideas recall those of such writers as Veblen, de Ruggiero, and Mannheim which stemmed from secular, materialistic concepts.

Looking at the relationship between employer and employee, the Vatican has perceived much immoral "inhumanity." The inhumanity which the Popes see in modern industry they lay largely to the selfishness, materialism, and irresponsibility they impute to individualism. Leo XIII observed that "working men have been given over, isolated and defenceless, to the callousness of employers and the greed of unrestrained competition"; again, he noted that working men "cannot but perceive that their grasping employers too often treat them with the greatest inhumanity, and hardly care for them beyond the profit their labor brings. . . ."[28] Pius XI stated that very many employers "treated their workmen as mere tools, without any concern for the welfare of their souls, indeed, without the slightest thought of higher interests."[29]

Returning to lay critics, we have already seen how many of them feel that big business, the lineal descendant of individualism, sired by modern technology, has operated to bring about a power structure which is incompatible with democracy. Having explored ideas of this sort already, we shall not

[27] Ibid., p. 28.

[28] *Rerum Novarum*, pp. 4 and 36.

[29] *Quadragesimo Anno*, p. 36.

look into them further. However, a couple of general comments are in order.

Likenesses are apparent between the ideas of lay and specifically moral critics on the political consequences of big business and of individualism. But there are also important differences, and it is these we shall note before going on.

In the first place, many of the lay political and social theorists, especially those with a mechanistic orientation, seem to be unclear in their own minds as to *why* the alleged undermining of democracy by big business is a *bad* thing. That it is bad is just taken for granted as an unexamined presupposition. The religious critics, in contrast, are quite explicit in their thinking on this aspect and are able to draw upon a fully elaborated system of moral theory to explain *their* position.

Second, it will be recalled that the political and social critics have been disturbed because they believe that it is impossible to reconcile the existence of big business with their *ideal* power structure in which there are only the responsible State and irresponsible individuals. On the other hand, morally oriented critics, especially those whose ideas parallel those of the Vatican, deplore the disappearance under individualism of intermediate entities because it *has* brought about a system in which there are left only individuals and the State. *Their* ideal power structure is of a vastly different sort.

As conceived by both sets of critics, modern developments — including the emergence of large corporations — are at odds with opposing ideals as to social structure. Big business is caught in a cross fire.

Lay as well as religious moral critics blame materialistic industrialism for introducing an element of authoritarianism into modern industrial society. This element of authoritarianism they see in the relationship of employer to employee. In looking at a couple of examples of ideas along this line we shall bring this chapter to a close.

James J. Gillespie, a British management consultant and

author of books on management methods, is among those with a moral slant who see authoritarianism in industry and connect it with the evolution of materialistic individualism. Following the fall of feudalism and the Reformation — says Gillespie — man became free from bondage, but he also became free from protection and security. In "the new industrial structure" and "our present industrial set-up," he says, the worker passed from the control of the feudal lord to that of the individualistic and authoritarian capitalist intent upon making his own way:

> With the new goal of status through power and money seeking and with the loss of religious discipline, the new rulers [the "bourgeoisie"] replaced the familiar relationship of Lord and serf by the compulsory relationship of master and wage slave; and this new relationship found its bitterest expression in industry where the wage slave, small child, adolescent, man and woman had a poorer life "than a donkey in a costermonger's barrow." The person was not now a dear child of God, the person was now an economic unit in the employer's search for status through power.[30]

As Gillespie sees it, the worker in the plant — this "economic unit" — is subject to the autocratic rule of an imposed "headman." He is subject to an imposed "institutional discipline which must be obeyed." The authoritarian control and management implicit in — as Gillespie calls it — the "headmanship system in industry" is a "life frustrating and anxiety creating cultural technique" which "hangs on, a relic of the early factory age, in modern industry." Gillespie ascribes a considerable amount of prevalent industrial unrest to the contrast between the responsible freedom and democratic participation which workers have in their social and political life and the state of "childish dependency and irresponsibility," without democratic participation, in which they find themselves in their work situation.[31]

These views of Gillespie on authoritarianism in industry

[30] *Free Expression in Industry* (London: Pilot Press, Ltd., 1948), p. 27.
[31] Ibid., pp. 28 and 31.

are less stringent than those of Sidney and Beatrice Webb who saw the power of the "capitalistic owner" as absolute. As the Webbs saw things, the division of labor and the rational planning, scheduling, and operation of an industrial enterprise of natural necessity create a situation in which workers must come under the orders of those who must manage and who, by the nature of things, have some measure of power. These ideas, obviously, are closely related to those of Karl Mannheim. This power stemming from natural necessity, combined with the irresponsibility of individual ownership, say the Webbs, makes for authoritarianism or worse in modern industry:

> . . . This natural necessity places a power in the hands of these few persons which, unless it is controlled in the general interest, as it is in the public services, can and does become a tyranny compared to which the worst political tyrannies are negligible. When it is wielded by the irresponsible private owners of the sources of production, or by their agents, the disparity of effective freedom . . . is such as to amount to the practical subjection of the mass of the people. . . . The capitalistic owner and director is entirely insubordinate, whilst his employees are helplessly subordinate. . . .[32]

Ideas of this order are reminiscent of the concepts regarding the nature of relationships within the modern corporation which are implicit in such critics of big business as Supreme Court Justices Louis D. Brandeis and William O. Douglas.

Conclusion

To summarize what we have seen in this chapter: The moral critics of industrial civilization see in its traditional individualism — carried forward in the day of business corporations — not merely the institutional freedoms to engage

[32] Sidney and Beatrice Webb, *The Decay of Capitalist Civilization,* pp. 182–183.

in enterprises chosen freely and to operate without let or hindrance, the freedoms to buy and sell freely, to enter freely into contracts, and to acquire, use, and dispose of property. They see not merely the freedom of the individual and of freely organized groups to pursue such ends and to live by such values as appeal to *them*. In these institutions the critics see and emphasize the freedom of the individual to seek his own, and the freedom of the corporation to pursue its own individual *selfish* ends and to disregard those of the community. In this scheme of things, critics see the individual and the corporation as having no responsibility, beyond the limits of legal torts, for the consequences and effects of actions upon others, and especially, no responsibility for their impact on society as a whole. They see the individual and the corporation as having no responsibility to work positively toward the needs of the community as a whole.

To them, accordingly, individualism necessarily becomes more or less synonymous with *irresponsible* individualism. Some of them equate individualism with irresponsibility. Some identify individualism with the unswerving, dedicated, single-purposed, and selfish pursuit of material gain. Individualism, is thus not only irresponsible, which, they would hold, would be immoral in itself. The immorality of individualism is compounded by the unalloyed materialism of the basic values with which they see it conjoined.

Materialistic, irresponsible individualism is held accountable for engendering an immoral or even inhuman system of relationships within modern industry. Over all, it is held accountable for the rise of an immoral and politically troubled social order.

In the next chapter we shall see that the moral and ethical critics of big business industrial civilization go on to say that materialism and individualism have combined to produce a society which is immoral in some of its most distinguishing characteristics and manifestations.

CHAPTER 8

"The Baneful, Inhuman Civilization of Big Business"

IN THE PRECEDING two chapters we have seen how present-day culture has been denounced on the grounds that its fundamental values and its institutions are morally defective. In this chapter we shall take up the kind of moral criticism which is directed primarily at the outward concrete manifestations of the industrial civilization of big business — at its works and effects.

The outward aspects of the civilization of big business which have drawn the most fire from moral critics are four in number: First, the allocation and use of economic resources under the initiative and direction of private enterprise. Second, the concentration of many of the gainfully employed in large, mechanized industrial establishments characteristic of so much of big business. Third, the concentration of a substantial fraction of the population in large urban centers which have been built up and made possible by the works of big business. Last, the behavior and social relations of people in the environment and culture of the civilization of big business. Each of these has been criticized on moral, ethical, and spiritual grounds.

As critics see things, the concrete aspects and manifestations of this civilization are in very large measure the inevitable, if unintentional, end-product of the actions of a materialistically and selfishly motivated and socially irresponsible class — businessmen. As seen by these critics, it has been the institutions of individualism which have permitted this irresponsible class to organize the economy and to exploit technological progress for its own gain.[1] The re-

[1] As noted in Parts I and II, technological progress often seems to be viewed as a mechanistic, well-nigh self-generating, impersonal process occurring independently of the activities of business enterprise.

sulting consequences, it is said, are morally and spiritually deficient.

In seeking its own gain, so critics say, business is led to allocate and use resources — to produce — in ways which neglect, or at best inadequately serve the moral and spiritual welfare of the community as a whole. In the pursuit of profit, business — especially big business — has constructed large, highly mechanized factories and commercial establishments which, so it is contended, are incompatible with satisfying human relationships, with the enjoyment of work, and even with human dignity itself. The actions of private business enterprises, each motivated by an individualistic desire for gain, have resulted — so critics have said — in the building up of large cities in which a fully and richly human life can scarcely be lived.

Finally, as a sort of sum total, it is said that the social relations of the people of this civilization are not humanly satisfying. Indeed, it is often argued that these relations are nonhuman and even inhuman. And the behavior of the people is criticized as adolescent, primitive, and even barbarous.

The bent of many critics to lay moral deficiency to particular institutional arrangements, organization structures, and to a particular set of material conditions of life, is clearly apparent in much of the criticism of this vein.

To the first of these four topics.

"Immoral Production"

Moral criticism of production, of the allocation and use of resources, under industrial capitalism has two points of focus. First, as part of the criticism of industrialism, objection is raised that the allocation of productive resources is not governed by the requirements — especially the spiritual requirements — of the community *as a whole*. It is governed, critics hold, by the activity of business concerns irresponsibly seeking their own materialistic ends. Accordingly, the welfare of the harmonious social whole is neglected. Such neglect is immoral, since its welfare *should* be a prime moral objective of human life.

Second, objection is raised that the *composition* of the national product, which results from the private direction of economic activity, has important moral defects. Individual and social morality, it is implied, would require that the economy should produce a different, and *morally better* pattern of goods and services for the people.

These two points are often inseparably intertwined in the writings of critics. This is natural enough. For, given the first as a premise, the second flows from it naturally.

Moral criticism of the allocation and use of resources under industrial capitalism is essentially different from strictly *economic* criticism. And it may help to clarify the nature of this moral criticism if the two are contrasted.

A utilitarian economist might argue that the actual allocation of resources and the composition of the national product do not correspond closely enough to what the people *in fact want* in terms of their willingness to pay. This discrepancy — larger or smaller, depending on the inclinations of the particular economist — would be ascribed by such an *economist* to such factors as lack of knowledge and imperfect foresight on the part of businessmen and consumers, errors of judgment, the immobility and nonconvertibility of productive agents such as specialized machines, and to institutional blocks such as "monopolistic competition" and government restrictions. The economist might say that if all imperfections and blocks were removed, the private enterprise economy *would* function to fulfill *existing* individual wants in the mechanically perfect manner described by the economic theory of pure and perfect competition. If this came to pass, we could expect the strictly *economic* critic to be satisfied and to become silent.

But not the *moral* critic. For the moral critic has standards of judgment other than whether the economic system perfectly satisfies existing individual wants.

To be sure, moral critics have charged, among other things, that the private enterprise system fails to function in the mechanically perfect manner set forth in the economic theory of pure and perfect competition. But that is not the *essence* of *their* criticism. Even if the economy did work precisely as blue-printed in classical economic theory, their essential criticism would still stand: to their way of thinking, the very processes of individual initiative and responsibility by which the economy is directed would still be morally defective; and so, too, would be the composition of the national product.

As these critics see matters, the private enterprise system, conceived as being individualistic, irresponsible, and materialistic, will not serve moral and spiritual needs which cannot compete successfully in the market place for the products and resources of the economy. In their eyes this will be a moral defect of the private enterprise system no matter how perfectly it might function. It will not — they say — provide for such needs as education and communal social activity. It will not serve those moral and spiritual needs of the community as a whole — especially the intangible ones — which have no effective institution for their expression or for making themselves felt in the allocation of resources and in the distribution of the national product. On the contrary, people critically inclined will hold that private enterprise will always give rise to *social costs* in terms of things of the spirit, costs which society does not really want to incur. For instance, they say it will make the pleasant countryside ugly and will pollute its clear air and charming streams. It will give rise to sordid industrial areas which blight the human spirit. Matters like these relate to the first point of focus of this kind of criticism.

In the second place, and this is implicit in the opinions of many of these critics, the existing individual wants of the people in industrial civilization, which private enterprise tries to serve for its own profit, are *themselves* morally and spiritually deficient. It seems that under industrial capitalism people *want* to consume morally inferior goods and to spend their leisure in morally inferior ways. It seems that the people's wants and desires, in other circumstances, would be different from what they are now: Under some other economic system, it appears, people would want, or in any case, they would *get,* a morally superior national product to consume. They would spend their leisure time in morally more edifying ways.

Now to some examples of how these points are made and developed.

Sidney and Beatrice Webb, who have already provided examples of criticism on moral and ethical grounds in other connections, also provide illustrations of the moral charges made as to the allocation and use of resources. As they viewed matters, these processes in industrial civilization are fundamentally antisocial and immoral. For them "the tremendous stimulus" of the profit motive "is undiscriminating." Hence, there is no reason, as they saw it, that resources should not be wasted, if that is profitable to individualistic capitalists, nor why commodities should not be subject to "insidious worsening." Again, under capitalism as it appeared to them, even the "smuggling of opium into China or whiskey into the United States," the "manufacture of cocaine" and the "organization of gambling" in countries other than the capitalist's own "are as legitimate sources of gain as the growing of wheat." The physical environment of the society, the "devastation of the pleasant countryside, the pollution of the streams and atmosphere, the creation in the slums of the new urban centers of all the conditions of disease and premature death," are all consequences of "the irresponsible determination" by the "propertied class" of what shall be done. In short, for the Webbs, "there is no such 'invisible hand,' as Adam Smith suggested, always guiding the dictatorship of the capitalist, even without his being aware of it, so that it promotes the economic welfare of the community." [2]

Similar but more obviously emotional views have been expressed by Eric Gill, an English type-designer, internationally-known sculptor, and religious enthusiast. His writings — especially his *Autobiography* — have enjoyed considerable popularity in the United States, as well as in England, among people of rather divergent, but always strong, religious convictions. To Gill, the free enterprise system was an abomination. And his views are particularly interesting in that they suggest the degree of passion which can underlie moral criticism of big business industrial civilization.

Gill believed that the spiritual needs of the social whole could not be met by the private enterprise system and that, under it, the composition of the national product could not be morally good. These defects, in Gill's thinking, clearly trace back to the fact that the private enterprise system relies upon the initiative of irresponsibly individualistic, materialistically motivated businessmen:

> . . . We live in a world which is ruled by men of business, and ruled therefore according to businessmen's notions of what is good. This is a simple fact and it seems to me, and to the few who think likewise, that it is an insufferably monstrous, iniquitous and vile state of affairs. It seems to us incomparably more horrible that men of business should rule us and impose their foul point of view on the world than it would be if the whole race of men and women should rot their bodies with lechery and drunkenness. There is no idolatry so destructive of charity, so desolating; there is nothing which so certainly obscures the face of God as the desire of money — the root of all evil. . . . And yet we, in our world of commerce and finance and mass-production, regard it as the very flower of virtue. We place those who have successfully amassed money in the highest seats of govern-

2 *The Decay of Capitalist Civilization,* pp. 183–187.

ment and give honour to the rich as to the saints of God. . . . Hence it is that we must go down into the dust disgraced and infamous, with no monument to our prowess but the filthiness of our cheap idols; for even our idols are filthy, having no reason for existence but the money profit of those who sold them. Saleability is the business man's criterion of good.

If a thing cannot be sold, it is no good to the man of business. This is right and proper. I am not complaining or cursing about that. The man who buys in order to sell can only judge of good by the saleability of what he has bought. What will sell is good, because it is good for him. . . . From the human and normal and godly point of view the merchant is not purely a man of business; he is the carrier, the purveyor, the conveyor and he is paid for the service he renders in carrying. But the man of business, is the man who, by definition, is only concerned to buy cheap and sell dear, for that is his nature; that is his reason of being; that is what he is for; that is how he makes his living. And it doesn't matter one jot to him what he buys and sells, provided only that the transaction yields him a profit on his investment. The man of business, as such, is a parasite. . . . There is no reason whatever why there should be any men of business at all. But, be that as it may (and any civilization can endure a certain small proportion of pimps and thieves without succumbing – just as a man can endure a few warts and spots on his body without dying) what is truly monstrous and disruptive and corrupting to our life and virtue is that such persons should be our rulers – that they should have usurped the seats of kings, that their hideous teaching should have replaced the Gospel. That is what is unendurable; that is what is unforgivable; that is what God will neither endure nor forgive.[3]

Oftentimes what is essentially moralistic criticism appears in the ideas of people who are not usually considered to be moralists. Lewis Mumford, the lecturer, author, and town

[3] Eric Gill, *Autobiography* (London: Jonathan Cape, 1940), pp. 194–196. (Reprinted with permission.)

planner, is well known for his many-faceted condemnation of the civilization of big business capitalism. Many of his criticisms have a moralistic base, stemming as they do from a particular set of values which is affronted by that civilization as he perceives it. The allocation and use of resources in the free enterprise economy, and the consequent national product which is generated thereby, are among the many aspects of industrial civilization of which he does not approve in his widely read *Technics and Civilization.*

In a passage reminiscent of the Webbs, Mumford states that under capitalistic enterprise, the "service of the consumer and the support of the worker" are "entirely secondary" as claims upon productive enterprise. The "reward of capital" is the "dominating one." Mumford concedes that, to be sure, "sometimes profits were obtained by lowering the costs and spreading the product." But, he goes on to argue, "if [profits] could be had only by offering inferior or adulterated goods — as in the sale of medical nostrums or the slum housing of the underpaid worker — health and well being were sacrificed to gain." The private enterprise system, that is, produces what is profitable, not necessarily what is *good.*[4]

In a passage reminiscent of Karl Marx's theory that profits have their origin in the appropriation of "surplus value" through the exploitation of labor by capitalists, Mumford also charges that "the community, instead of receiving a full return for its goods and services, permitted a portion of the product to be diverted for the private gratification of the holders of land and capital." Not only is the composition of the national product immoral, so also — apparently — is its distribution among the people.

Mumford gives voice explicitly to the theme that the allocation and use of resources are irresponsibly determined by capitalists whose sole motivation is materialistic:

[4] *Technics and Civilization* (New York: Harcourt, Brace and Company, 1934), pp. 373–374.

> . . . These holders of land and capital, backed up by the law and all the instruments of government, determined privately and solely in accordance with the canon of profit what should be produced and how much and where and how and by whom and on what terms.[5]

Mumford also sets forth implicitly the frequently-met thesis that mal-allocations of resources occur because the over-all needs of the society as a whole have no institutions for their expression:

> . . . what are called gains in capitalist economics often turn out, from the standpoint of social energetics, to be losses; while the real gains, the gains upon which all the activities of life, civilization, and culture ultimately depend were either counted as losses, or were ignored, because they remained outside the commercial scheme of accountancy.[6]

Mumford goes on to hold that the present "crude state" of industry in time will be superseded by the "advanced state."[7] And in this "advanced state," the national product will be qualitatively—at any rate—quite different from what it is nowadays. In the "advanced state," apparently, consumption will be "normalized." Mumford seems to mean by that, that consumption will not be so irrational, capricious, individualistic, and improvident as it now frequently is. He points out that the poorer inhabitants of Professor Robert Lynd's "Middletown" spent their money for automobiles and radio sets even though "the houses they lived in during their period of putative prosperity often did not have ordinary sanitary toilet facilities." Even the rich now live in "great cities lacking in sunlight and open spaces," whereas in a society with a "normalized standard of life," they would be "healthier and happier" than they are now. Under this "normalized standard of life," it seems, individuals will not necessarily have more *things*, in any event not necessarily

[5] Ibid., p. 374.
[6] Ibid., p. 375.
[7] Ibid., p. 387.

more money-income. But they will have more leisure, health, "biological activity," and esthetic pleasure. Some of the objectives of the "normalized standard" will include "handsome bodies, fine minds, plain living, high thinking, keen perceptions, sensitive emotional responses, and a group life keyed to make these things possible and to enhance them." [8]

In the "advanced state," according to Mumford, industry will rest upon "rational organization, social control, physiological and psychological understanding." This "advanced state," we are assured, will be efficient and will meet the requirements of society as a whole. There will be, I gather, no nonsense about individualistic activities motivated by the desire for gain, which he earlier refers to as ". . . the sordid motives of profit-making and self-seeking that govern the prevailing forms of business enterprise. . . ." In the "advanced state," Mumford says portentously:

> . . . the goal is no longer as much production as is compatible with the canons of private enterprise and private profit and individual money incentives: it is rather efficient production for social uses no matter how drastically these sacred canons must be revised or extirpated.[9]

Unfortunately, Mumford does not go into detail to tell us how this process of extirpation is to be carried out by the "Big Brother" of his "advanced state." Perhaps George Orwell has already told us in *1984*.[10]

These examples give the gist of the moral criticism of the allocation and use of resources under private enterprise. We now move along to the moral criticism of one of the most obvious and most unique manifestations of industrial civilization: "the Factory."

[8] Ibid., pp. 397–399.
[9] Ibid., pp. 309 and 387.
[10] New York: Harcourt, Brace & Co., 1949. It's a wry thought that Orwell's "Big Brother" will not look so kindly on "biological activity" as Mumford does.

"The Factory"

"The Factory," or "the Machine," as it is sometimes referred to in terms of abstract allegory, has often been the object of moral criticism and indignation since the factory riots in England in the early 19th Century. At times it has been feared that mass-production processes, especially when mechanized, would cause unemployment. And it is true that technological advance has certainly caused many skills to become obsolete; it has undoubtedly led to unemployment among those trained in the displaced skills. Obviously, there are moral overtones in the problem of technological displacement and unemployment of blameless men, and critics have not failed to point them out. But the kernel of the moral criticism against "the Factory" lies elsewhere; and this criticism is not abated even in times of full employment.

The grounds for the essential *moral* criticism of "the Factory" would still remain, even if the problem of full employment were solved once and for all. They would remain even if the stream of production were directed by an enlightened and benign private enterprise — or, presumably, even by a system of social control, for that matter — which fully provided for all spiritual as well as material needs. They would remain even under a free system in which individuals were permitted to live by whatever values they freely and individually chose — esthetic, ascetic, materialistic, mystical, intellectual, "biological," social, misanthropic, Christian, or what have you. For the essence of this criticism is directed at "the Factory" with its mechanized, mass-production processes, *as such* — as a method of organizing the work of human beings. It is not, at least not necessarily, concerned with the ability of "the Machine" to provide employment for all, nor at what it makes, nor at who owns it.

Critics say that technological advance on the side of production results in downgrading a large fraction of the population, the workers. They say it takes away elements of richness and responsibility from jobs, and insinuates in their stead elements of drudgery — or, at any rate, monotony — and irresponsibility.

As long ago as 1835–1840, Alexis de Tocqueville, author of the classic, *Democracy in America,* saw in "the Factory" the seed of a potential evolution away from democracy and toward the re-establishment of aristocracy. This, he feared, might be the consequence of a widening gulf between those who organized and planned factory work and those who actually did it. Beyond this political danger, "the Factory" harbored a *moral* danger, the dehumanization of the human being.

Because of the minute division of labor and the routinization of work in "the Factory" and the management problems entailed, the scope of the job of the planner and manager comes to resemble more and more that of "the administrator of a vast empire." But the effect on the worker is the opposite. In making his point de Tocqueville turned the tables on Adam Smith. Smith had extolled the productivity of mass-production techniques. He illustrated his point in a famous passage which describes how many more pins can be made by men using factory methods in contrast to handicraft methods. In turning this around, de Tocqueville asked:

> . . . What can be expected of a man who has spent twenty years of his life in making heads for pins? and to what can that mighty human intelligence, which has so often stirred the world, be applied in him, except it be to investigate the best method of making pins' heads? . . . his body has contracted certain fixed habits, which it can never shake off: in a word, he no longer belongs to himself, but to the calling which he has chosen. . . . a theory of manufactures . . . assigns to him a certain place in society, beyond which he cannot go. . . .[11]

[11] See the fourth English edition (Cambridge, England, 1864), Vol. II, pp. 193–194.

While the planner and manager comes to resemble more and more "the administrator of a vast empire," what is human in the worker is "degraded." *He* comes to resemble more and more "a brute." [12]

In political terms the gulf between managers and workers threatens the end of democracy. In moral terms, it threatens the humanity and the human dignity of the workers of industrial civilization.

In these ideas, de Tocqueville anticipated by almost a century Karl Mannheim's theory as to the political consequences of "functional rationalization." [13] By that length of time, he anticipated playwright Eugene O'Neill's parable of the dehumanized "hairy ape," [14] including the latter's suggestion of social stratification, brutalization of the worker, and "class struggle."

Embedded in de Tocqueville's ideas are the outlines of the kind of moral criticism of "the Factory" which has been repeated and developed at length by numerous contemporary critics of industrial civilization, including Albert Schweitzer, Emil Brunner, and Eric Gill.

Among the forces contributing to moral and spiritual decay of industrial civilization, Albert Schweitzer — to draw upon him again — assigned an important role to "the Factory" and, in particular, to the specialization of labor which has been such an integral part of that process of production. It is interesting to note how closely his ideas parallel those of de Tocqueville:

> . . . Human labour is organized and co-ordinated so that specialization may enable individuals to make the highest and most effective possible contribution. The results obtained are amazing, but the spiritual significance of the work for the worker suffers. There is no call upon the whole man, only upon some of his faculties, and this has a reflex effect

[12] Ibid., p. 195.

[13] Described in Part II, Chapter 5, above.

[14] "The Hairy Ape" (1922), *The Complete Works of Eugene O'Neill* (New York: Boni and Liveright, 1924).

> upon his nature as a whole. The faculties which build up personality and are called out by comprehensive and varied tasks are ousted by the less comprehensive ones, which from this point of view are, in the general sense of the word, less spiritual. The artisan of today does not understand his trade as a whole in the way in which his predecessor did. He no longer learns, like the latter, to work the wood or the metal through all the stages of manufacture; many of these stages have already been carried out by men and machines before the material comes into his hands. Consequently his reflectiveness, his imagination, and his skill are no longer called out by ever varying difficulties in the work, and his creative and artistic powers are atrophied. . . .[15]

Emil Brunner's views on the impact of "the Factory" on the spirit of man is very close to that of Schweitzer, and in turn to that of de Tocqueville. Like many of the critics, Brunner compared unfavorably the spiritual satisfaction of the labor of the factory worker to the satisfaction of other less specialized, and more — what shall we say? — creative, more fully rounded, and spiritually enriching work:

> . . . More and more the machine thinks for the worker, while the share of the individual worker in the meaningful whole of the work decreases. The relation of the worker to his work becomes more and more impersonal and the meaning of his work becomes invisible. He seems to be merely an unimportant part of the machinery, whilst the meaning of what he does passes from his horizon. Much of the satisfaction felt by the farmer, in his intimate relation to natural growth, and the artisan in creating a useful object, is denied to the worker at the assembly line.[16]

The judgment which Eric Gill passed upon "the Factory" was as full of loathing as the one he passed directly on the businessman. Again, Gill's view illustrates the verve which can lie behind ideas of this sort.

[15] Albert Schweitzer, *The Decay and Restoration of Civilization,* pp. 21–22. (Quoted with the permission of The Macmillan Company.)

[16] Emil Brunner, *Christianity and Civilization,* Part II, p. 64.

> . . . The factory system itself is in itself so inhuman, subhuman and anti-human an institution for the production of things for the use of human beings that, were we not so used to it, had we not been born in it, did not so many of us derive profits or wages from it, we should, as we some day shall, find it impossible to understand the frame of mind of the nations that endure it or the writers and politicians who applaud it, and of the Christian clergy who seek every excuse to avoid condemning it.[17]

These ideas concerning "the Factory" are not too distantly related to concepts of the corporation as an authoritarian collectivism. In these ideas the notion is clearly present that, while at the very top there may be scope for a measure of initiative and self-expression, at the bottom there is none, and in between there is but little. At the bottom, people are close to being "brutes" — "hairy apes" — and do only as they're told. And above them there are mere "clerks," "agents," and "half-a-life" men.

Noting that, we now pass to the moral criticism of "the City."

"The City"

Large cities, and the concentration in them of a substantial fraction of the population are one of the most palpable aspects of big business industrial civilization. Both in itself, and as an integral part of industrial civilization, "the City" has often been the object of criticism on ethical and moral grounds. The general tenor of the criticism is that life in the city is lacking in ethical and moral values and, consequently, is

[17] Eric Gill, *Autobiography*, p. 142.

Compare: "Owing to the extensive use of machinery and to division of labor, the work of the proletarians has lost all individual character, and, consequently, all charm for the workman. He becomes an appendage of the machine, and it is only the most simple, most monotonous, and most easily acquired knack that is required of him. Hence the cost of production of a workman is restricted almost entirely to the means of subsistence that he requires for his maintenance, and for the propagation of his race." — Karl Marx and Friedrich Engels, *The Communist Manifesto* (1848).

lacking in spiritual satisfactions. This, it is said, is a profoundly demoralizing and disturbing influence on the people of industrial civilization. The human relationships of the city dweller are said to be impersonal, anonymous, and ephemeral. Accordingly, these relationships lack the spiritual content, and do not give the satisfaction, of human relationships in the country, the village, or even the small town. The relationships of the urban individual and his family to neighbors and to the physical environment are held to be merely functional or utilitarian, containing nothing of human warmth. Because of this, it is said, these relationships among city dwellers lack the spiritual qualities found in the relation of the farmer and his family to the rural community and to the land. It is often even alleged, moreover, that life in "the City" is less healthy and shorter than life in "the Country."

The following passage from the Introduction to M. G. Kains' book meaningfully entitled *Five Acres and Independence* rather summarizes this kind of criticism of urban life and the unfavorable comparison which is drawn between it and rural life:

> [The "employee" (whom Kains equates with the "city dweller" realizes] that he and his family are "cliff dwellers" who probably do not know or want to know others housed under the same roof; that his children "have no place to go but out and no place to come but in"; in short, that he and they are eking out a narrowing, uneducative, imitative, more or less selfish and purposeless existence; and that his and their "expectation of life" is shortened by tainted air, restricted sunshine and lack of exercise, to say nothing of exposure to disease.
>
> Contrasted with all these and other city existence characteristics are the permanence and productivity of land . . . the self-reliance of the man himself and that developed in each member of his family; the responsibility and satisfaction of home ownership as against leasehold; the health and hap-

> piness typical not only of the life itself but of the wholesome association with genuine neighbors who reciprocate in kind and degree as few city dwellers know how to do; the probably longer and more enjoyable "expectation of life"; but, best of all, the basis and superstructure of true success – development and revelation of character and citizenship in himself, his wife, sons and daughters.
>
> . . . . .
>
> In a poignant sense city existence is non-productive; it deals with what has been produced elsewhere. Moreover it is dependent upon "income" to supply "outgo" and in the great majority of cases has nothing to show – not even character – for all the time and effort spent. Country life reverses this order; it not only produces "outgo" to supply "income" but when well ordered it provides "surplus." Nay, further, it develops character in the man and each member of the family.[18]

I suspect that ideas of this sort strike an emotionally responsive chord in many people who in no way regard themselves as opposed to industrialism, the free enterprise system, or even to big business. But the growth of cities and the growth of industrialism have gone hand in hand. And these two developments, if not basically synonymous, have in fact been organically and reciprocally related.

It is not surprising that many of those who criticize industrial civilization on moral, ethical, and spiritual grounds should also direct some of their criticisms at "the City" as well as at "the Factory." Indeed, the attack on "the City" is very often part of a syndrome, or a cluster of ideas, the whole of which is in varying degrees antagonistic or hostile toward big business, its values, its institutions, its manifes-

[18] New York: Greenberg, 1935; also Pocket Books, Inc., 1948. (Passages cited are from pp. 4 and 5 in the "Pocket Book" edition.) Mr. Kains, when this book was published, was Special Crop Culturist, U.S. Department of Agriculture. At one time he was Head of the Horticulture Department of Pennsylvania State College. This book went through 22 printings before the first Pocket Book edition.

tations, and its works. Thus, among the critics we have already cited, Albert Schweitzer, Emil Brunner, Lewis Mumford and Wilfred Wellock, for example, express varying degrees of hostility toward "the City." The criticism may be set forth explicitly at length or in brief asides; or may be implied in the recital and extolling of the inherent — not to say, mechanistically determined — spiritual merits of rural life.

In Brunner, for instance, we find this passage:

> Modern technics does not mean merely a fantastic extension of man's power over nature: it also means millions of men working underground, uncounted millions of men massed together in soulless giant cities; a proletariat without connection with nature, without a native heath or neighborhood; it means asphalt-culture, uniformity and standardization. . . .
>
> . . . When . . . a country rejoices over the growth of a city of millions of inhabitants, this is as stupid as if someone were to rejoice over the growth of a cancer. Giant cities are merely symptoms, but they are obvious symptoms of autonomous technical growth which finally leads to destruction.[19]

In Schweitzer, we find the cities of industrial society referred to as "growing agglomerations of people who are thereby compulsorily separated from the soil which feeds them, from their own homes and from nature." In the city — he says — warm, close personal relationships among individuals are lacking:

> The normal attitude of man to man is made very difficult for us. Owing to the hurry in which we live, to the increased facilities for intercourse, and to the necessity for living and working with many others in an over-crowded locality, we meet each other continually, and in the most varied relations, as strangers. Our circumstances do not allow us to deal with each other as man to man, for the limitations placed upon

19 *Christianity and Civilization,* pp. 9–10 and 13.

> the activities of the natural man are so general and so unbroken that we get accustomed to them, and no longer feel our mechanical, impersonal intercourse to be something that is unnatural. . . .[20]

It would be a fascinating topic of research to inquire to what extent ideas of this order — intermixed with less subjective considerations — lie behind the appreciable decentralization "movement" of large corporations to build new plants in rural areas and even to move their headquarters out of a city like New York to outlying areas such as Westchester County.

But that is not our concern here. And we must not get sidetracked.

Manners, Morals, and Relationships

Accordingly, we move on to the moral and ethical criticism of the social relations and human behavior in industrial civilization. Here we encounter a veritable army of critics. For this is a kind of catch-all topic. All kinds of fault and flaw are found in the manners and way of life in modern society. The critics on these subjects are of all sorts of orientations — scientific (at least in aspiration), ideological, philosophical, moralistic, and theological. Some few, perhaps, *could* be just cranks. It seems likely that some simply have failed to relate themselves usefully to reality or with satisfaction to working and social groups, and that their writings merely represent projections of their own personal feelings of bewilderment and hostility.

Critics in this area are by no means in agreement as to what they disapprove of, nor are the intensities of their criticisms uniform. Many of the criticisms are detailed and specific — some are highly particular; some are highly abstract. Sometimes, and this is frequently true of scholarly works in such fields as sociology and economics, there is only an impli-

[20] *The Decay and Restoration of Civilization,* pp. 23–24. (Quoted with the permission of The Macmillan Company.)

cation that things "ought" or "should" not be the way they are or seem. Their moralistic basis is only implicit. Some critics seem simply to be carping at things which affront their own arbitrary personal values and preferences. Others are more serious and systematic.

There is an enormous variety of standards and values by which the critics judge. In some cases, as suggested a moment ago, the criteria seem to be highly personal preferences and prejudices. In other cases, the critics seem to be judging by what they regard as universal and absolute standards. In some cases, the criteria of judgment which are being used are set forth explicitly. And these critics make themselves clear as to what, in their opinion, is wrong about the things they deplore. In other instances, the critics themselves seem not to have anything more than an intuitive set of criteria which are, of course, not set forth. And it is not at all clear in some of these instances in what sense or for what reasons that which is observed is not acceptable.

Some of the critics have been content merely to lash out at things they don't like, and let it go at that. Some of these have been acerbly amusing and popular. Others have tried, with obvious goodwill and seriousness of purpose to trace the causes of the phenomena which shock, affront, or depress them. Depending on their orientation, the critics are inclined variously to ascribe the defects and inadequacies they perceive to different kinds of factors.

Many of them are, basically, economic or institutional determinists. They lay the distressing state of society, as they see it, to such factors as the advent of "the Factory" and "the City." Some see the cause in institutional arrangements — especially in those of the private enterprise system. Others see the cause in moral misdirection. Some in the decline of religion. Still others see the cause in a rate of technological and other change which has been so rapid that it has outstripped the growth of adequate skill to administer change.

In coming to the criticism of the social relations and human behavior of industrial civilization, we are completing a circle which began with the review of the criticism of materialism. For one uniformity which is clear in much — not all — of the criticism of social relations and behavior is the inclination on the part of many of the critics — especially secular ones — to find the causes of this behavior not in "human nature," or in such a universal and timeless proposition as "the heart of the sons of men is full of evil, and madness is in their heart while they live," [21] nor in Original Sin, but in causes having uniquely to do with *this* particular civilization. Thus, the social phenomena which are disapproved of are very generally ascribed to physical characteristics of industrialism — to "the Factory" and "the City" — to the institutions and traditions of individualism, and, basically, to the material values which are held to be supreme. And as a corollary, there appears almost universally at least the suggestion that industrial civilization is morally inferior to other societies — past, present, or future — using different techniques, and having different characteristics, institutions, and values.[22]

[21] *Ecclesiastes* 9:3; or, for further instance: — "Yet man is born unto trouble as the sparks fly upward. . . . Man that is born of a woman is of few days and full of trouble." — *Job* 5:7 and 14:1.

[22] Two illustrations should convey something of the ideas along these lines.

First, from "Man on the Earth" by Edwin C. Palmer (Responsive Reading No. 41, in *Services of Religion for Use in the Churches of the Free Spirit*, Boston: The Beacon Press, Inc., 1938; pp. 99–100): —

> Great and marvelous is man's progress
> on the earth,
> He hath discovered his strength, he
> hath wrought mighty works. . . .
>
> His machines fill the earth with
> their thunder,
> But his heart is heavy within him. . . .
>
> Drunken with wealth and with
> might,
> He driveth his soul to destruction. . . .

The range, diversity, and number of the critics in this area are so great, that no mere handful can provide "typical" samples of all the points of view. We must be content with a few samples which will be illustrative of what is to be heard.

The aversion of the late Mohandas K. Gandhi for Western industrial civilization can usefully serve as the initial example of the attacks which have been made on social relations and human behavior in our culture. The profound influence which Mahatma Gandhi's ideas and philosophy have had in India and elsewhere in the East is some measure of their proven appeal and power. And Gandhi's ideas and philosophy are by no means intrinsically or inherently Oriental. For they were derived in large measure — according to Gandhi himself and his followers — from such Western critics of the 19th Century as John Ruskin, Henry Thoreau, and Leo Tolstoy.[23] Moreover, the appearance of such a recent work as *Lead Kindly Light* by Vincent Sheean [24] suggests that the ideas and values expressed by the Mahatma are capable of completing the circle and returning to find a warm reception in the minds of Westerners. For in this book, the American author and journalist tells of his exposure to Gandhi and Gandhian philosophy and, in effect, of his conversion.

Practically all the points in the attack on Western industrialism which have been illustrated in the preceding pages

---

He crusheth his brothers to increase
his might,
His mills devour their bodies and
souls. . . .

* * *

Second: "Ours is a sensual and materialistic generation. . . . life in the twentieth century has degenerated into a man-pleasing, rather than a God-pleasing affair. . . ." – Rev. Albert L. Neibacher (St. Luke's Evangelical Lutheran Church, New York) as reported in *The New York Times,* September 15, 1952.

[23] Examples of strong moral and ethical criticism of industrial civilization could easily have been drawn from the writings of each of these men.

[24] New York: Random House, 1949.

find their counterparts more or less clearly set forth in Gandhi's writings. He consistently attacked private capitalism, and the use of machinery and mass-production factory methods. He referred to large cities as "boils or abscesses on the body politic" and termed them a symptom of the "malady" known as civilization.[25]

It has been said that all that Gandhi taught "lay in the germ" in the little book entitled *Hind Swaraj* ("Indian Home Rule") which he wrote in 1908.[26] In 1938 Gandhi reaffirmed the ideas he set forth thirty years earlier, saying "The booklet is a severe condemnation of 'modern civilization.' . . . My conviction is deeper today than ever." [27] It is in this "seminal book," as it has been called, that the passage to be quoted appears excoriating the industrial civilization of big business.

It is interesting to note, just in passing, that while Gandhi was profoundly and bitterly critical of materialism, there is a running suggestion throughout his works that he himself was disposed to give something of a materialist interpretation to human phenomena. In the following passage, or so it seems to me, there is a strong overtone of a belief that human morality is determined by the material techniques and circumstances of life rather than by, say, spiritual error for which the individual is responsible, whatever his circumstances. Be that as it may, ideas of this order are commonly encountered among those who, like Gandhi, have been influenced by such earlier critics as Ruskin and Thoreau:

[25] In this particular, Gandhi reveals that he had been influenced by Edward Carpenter, author of *Civilization: Its Cause and Cure.* [This book was published in London in 1891. It is a veritable compendium of the kind of charges against industrialism which are to be found in the writings of the Webbs and Lewis Mumford.] See *Cent per Cent Swadeshi, or The Economics of Village Industries* (Ahmedabad: Navajivan Publishing House, Third Edition, 1948), pp. 129–130.

[26] *Hind Swaraj* has gone through many editions. The one quoted was reprinted in 1946 by the Navajivan Publishing House, Ahmedabad.

[27] Ibid., p. 11.

business can take much — not all — of the credit for the passage of the required legislation.

When the number of unemployed approached catastrophic levels, critics of business, it seems to me, were more active than business leaders in seeking remedies. The fact that some of these remedies were undoubtedly themselves harmful should not obscure the fact that the business community as a whole was slow in picking up responsibility for developing something better.

These are just examples. Obviously, many others could be offered.

On a broader scope, the messages of some of the religious critics, especially the Papal Encyclicals — *Rerum Novarum* and *Quadragesimo Anno,* above all — undoubtedly inspired much useful re-examination of the modern scene. And, surely, as the Federal Council of Churches has said, human society needs constant surveillance and reminders, if all the needs of Man are to be met in a tolerable balance.

In making this acknowledgment of fact and of the contribution of some of the critics, it is not a retraction still to insist that numbers of them have done the nation great disservice through contributing absurdity, systematized hostility, confusion, distrust, and despond.

As to dismissing too hastily what the critics have had to say, there are three points I should like to make, of which the last is most important by far.

Some of the critics are obscure persons with little experience with the facts of the practical world. Their influence, beyond a small circle of impressionable people, is problematical. But there are others who are obviously persons who speak with great authority, certainly with great prestige. If for no other reason than political expediency, such critics must be taken seriously and listened to attentively. That their points may sometimes seem to be poorly taken doesn't change the fact their views may generate very real political pressures.

The second point is related to the first. It is no small matter that many of these criticisms have been obviously well received by large numbers of people. Among the critics quoted are winners of the Nobel and Pulitzer prizes and internationally acknowledged leaders of the intelligentsia. A number of their works have been in the best-seller class.[19] The extent to which these works have created opinion is difficult to say. But that they strike a popular responsive chord is pike-staff plain. The administrators of big business can scarcely ignore the fact that in the minds even of many members of the present Congress affiliation with big business comes close to being a cause for disqualification for high public trust and office. In short, a lot of what the critics say seems to make sense to a large fraction of the American people.

This brings us to the third item. This I regard as being of such great importance that I have made it the focal point of what I have to say in the next, and concluding, chapter.

With ample research, main force of logic, and facile pen it might well be possible to wither one after another most of the criticisms offered up. To try to do so, however, would be a tougher job than Hercules faced when he took on the Hydra. For as soon as one criticism was blasted, at least one other would spring up to take its place. For many of the criticisms stem from feelings rather than logic. When one such criticism is turned back by reason, the feelings still remain to generate further argument.[20] Besides being of little

[19] Passages from the comic-strip broadside against "Big Business," *The Life and Times of the Shmoo,* by the cartoonist Al Capp, might well have been used to illustrate an attack with great "mass" appeal. (New York: Simon and Schuster, 1948.)

[20] Many of these criticisms undoubtedly are, to use Vilfredo Pareto's concept, "derivations." (See his *Treatise on General Sociology,* especially Vol. III; New York: Harcourt, Brace and Company, 1935.) In this connection, it is probable that some of the feeling against big business stems from some pretty deep sentiments related to the fear of the too rich, the too big, the too strong, the too clever, etc. The sentiments I have in mind are the kind which are involved in the stories of King Midas, David and Goliath, Jack the Giant Killer, Reynard the Fox, and Robin Hood. Perhaps a "social-psychoanalyst" could make something of this. I have not tried to.

avail, such an effort would be misdirected. It would, I think, miss the main point.

Behind the Criticism

The main point, it seems to me, is this: Behind all the words, the frequently spurious logic, the pervasive inadequate concepts, and especially behind the widespread public response to these attacks, there is to be discerned the outlines of people's basic hopes and aspirations. In the criticism is to be seen the outlines of what people want out of life, of what they think is important. And of what they often fear they may not get. Or so it seems to me.

These aspirations, I would say, are threefold. We want material comfort and betterment. We want for ourselves and our children more of the things which are the material base for civilized, enjoyable, secure living. Not just "the perfect refrigerator." All kinds of things. Better houses, food, clothing. Automobiles, television sets, cameras, phonograph records, and books. Better and cheaper medicines. There is no need to extend the list. Market-research departments in hundreds of companies know all this full well. On this level, whatever individual shortcomings there may be, big business has served pretty well. And, apparently, most of the people are willing to admit it — as of now, at any rate.

And, ever looking ahead, we want these things with a degree of certainty. We are not happy to dwell under the threat that has not yet been banished that our jobs may vanish, or that depression may come upon us all at any time, throwing millions out of work, closing down opportunity, and reducing the standard of living of the nation.

But that isn't all we want. To us, better living means more than just better and more *things*. It is not only by its ability to produce material things that we as a people judge big business and the rest of the free enterprise method of organizing our economic activity. If that were all big business were judged by, its place would be reasonably secure — at least as of now. But there is more.

We also have political and social objectives. And beyond those we have some human, spiritual, moral ones — call them what you will. When we say we want life, liberty, and the pursuit of happiness, we do not mean we want only a high standard of living, even on a guaranteed basis. Most of us are doing tolerably well on that score already. We also want to be sure of an increasing measure of full democracy. We want the country to be run by and for *all* the people. We want opportunity for self-realization for each and every individual. And a majority of the American people, it seems, have misgivings to some degree that big business shares this aspiration.[21] This may not be a reasonable doubt, but there it is. And there are some straws in the wind that suggest that part of this feeling may stem from the fact that — just as critics say — some large companies do look pretty undemocratic from the inside and from down below.[22] If in their daily working lives, people feel they are pushed around by a corporate authoritarian system, it should not be surprising if they have some questions as to how such a system fits in with democratic political and social ideals. Anyway, it is perfectly clear that big business is judged on political and social performance as well as economic. On this, a lot of people give it a pretty poor grade.

[21] In the Introduction to Part II, we saw some statistics along this line. They are a measure of popular feelings. Doubts are also expressed in other terms. Professor Sidney Hook of New York University, for example, has wondered why it is that the support of big business is not more in evidence in matters concerning the other basic freedoms of a democracy as well as the freedom of enterprise. "Why is it," he asks, "that the fight for civil liberties, for academic freedom, for minority rights is left largely to bishops, lawyers, and professors?" He adds: ". . . on the whole it is incontestable that American businessmen have not accepted the challenge and opportunity to take or share leadership in rallying the community when outright violations of cultural and political freedoms occur." ("Bread, Freedom, and Businessmen," *Fortune*, September, 1951, p. 174.)

[22] See, e.g., Charles B. Walker and Robert H. Guest, *The Man on the Assembly Line* (Cambridge, Massachusetts: Harvard University Press, 1952), especially Chapter 12. In some important ways this is a superficial work. But there is no doubt that these researchers picked up from the workers in an automobile assembly plant a lot of unmistakable negative feelings about the company which had nothing to do with wages and hours.

The third element is more shadowy; not less real, I am sure — just harder to get hold of.

There are strong religious sentiments present in the American people. Statistics of church membership are one index of this. Lord Bryce of England — some time ago — and Mr. Charles Malik of Lebanon — just recently — especially remarked on this trait. A couple of years ago it was a consensus of the members of the "Round Table on Basic Elements of a Free, Dynamic Society" that ". . . The American society is a religious society governed by a secular state." [23]

I think the basic fact can be accepted.

It would be presumptuous to be categorical as to what follows from this fact. But, it seems to me that it at least follows that ethical, spiritual, moral values of one kind or another are important to Americans. I take this to mean that, among other things, we want a *good* society. That we want self-respect for ourselves and for the system of which we are a part. We want a way of life and a system in which the moral values we prize are taken into account in daily actions. Something like that. In particular, considering the religious streams which have been important in our history, these values stress the spiritual objectives, worth, and meaning of the individual human life. Second, they stress that the individual has moral responsibilities and duties toward his fellow men. Of course, there are other elements in these values, but the two mentioned, surely, are fundamental.[24]

It is my judgment — it would be next to impossible to prove this sort of thing — that far beneath a lot of the negative feeling about big business there lurk questions whether, indeed, the private enterprise system is a morally *good* one, and whether large corporations, in particular, are morally *good* institutions. These questions, I should suppose, would

23 Transcript published (April, 1951) by the Advertising Council, Inc., p. 12. Reproduced in the *Harvard Business Review,* Vol. XXIX, No. 6, November, 1951, and Vol. XXX, No. 1, January–February, 1952.

24 See Ernst Troeltsch, *The Social Teaching of the Christian Churches* (New York: The Macmillan Company, 1931), especially Vol. II.

be much like those raised by the critics reviewed in Part III, above: In the private enterprise system, are policies indeed formulated and decisions made without regard to moral values? Are moral responsibilities ignored? Inside the large corporation does the individual count for nothing as a person; is he just a means to somebody else's ends? The existence of such questioning, I think, can be inferred from all kinds of bits and snatches of data.

Of things which are suggestive along this line, I shall give just three samples; not by way of trying to *prove* the point, but as illustrations of the idea.

Values and ideas which are significant to people can be inferred from a lot of things. I take it, for example, that the books and plays which are successful are so because they say something that is meaningful to large numbers of people. The great reception accorded to items that raise questions as to values of life in modern times, such as *Babbitt, Point of No Return,* and *Death of a Salesman,* suggest to me that large numbers of people have preoccupations along these lines. Not everyone, of course; but a goodly number of people.

We have seen how critics attack "the Factory" as an immoral means of getting things produced. It is a fact that nowadays there is a good bit of concern with the question as to whether mass-production techniques are, or can be made, compatible with human dignity and individuality. And this concern shows up in the writings of many people who are clearly committed to the philosophy of the private enterprise system. Thus, we find Professor Geroid T. Robinson of Columbia pondering the point:

> . . . it goes without saying that under any conceivable condition much of the work of industry cannot possibly be decentralized . . . but must be carried on in large plants, by large groups of interdependent machines and large forces of operatives. It is here that the problem of maintaining the individuality of the worker arises in its most acute

> form. . . . The problem of humanizing the work process in machine industry is one for which no one has yet found an adequate solution. . . .[25]

That people who are by no means hostile to private enterprise are addressing themselves to the matter, it seems to me, lends it an extra significance.

A third fragment: Apparently it is the law that persons with official responsibilities for government contracts may not own stock in corporations which have government contracts. They must divest themselves of such stock. Logically, it can be argued that in the case of large corporations this has little practical significance. After all, no individual owns more than a very small fraction of the common stock of such a company as General Motors. In consequence, there is scarcely anything that anyone responsible for the administration of contracts could do — even if he were so minded — which would affect the earnings on his stock in this company by as much as a very few cents a share. Be that as it may, what did seem significant to me was that in the attendant discussions concerning Cabinet appointments in the Eisenhower Administration, it became quite evident that many people of all kinds of political persuasion apparently would not take for granted the good faith and integrity of administrators of big business.

I don't want to make too much of these fragments. The point simply is that the American people have, I think, a third set of objectives in life and a third standard by which they judge our institutions, including big business. And many have some question, rightly or wrongly, as to how well big business measures up on this particular test. I suspect

[25] "The Ideological Combat," *Foreign Affairs,* Vol. 27, No. 4, July, 1949, p. 357. See also Frank W. Abrams, "Management's Responsibilities in a Complex World," *Harvard Business Review,* Vol. XXIX, No. 3, May, 1951; and Edmund P. Learned, "Trends in Administration," *Harvard Business Review,* Vol. XXIX, No. 4, July, 1951.

that many of the doubts people express to the effect they mistrust big business *politically* are in fact, at bottom, doubts which have their origin on this third level.

In sum, whatever may be the logical inadequacies of the criticisms of big business, they do, I am convinced, reflect the fact that as a people we have personal and collective aspirations on three levels — the economic, the political and social, and the moral. We want results on all three. We judge performance in terms of results on all three. And, as of now, rightly or wrongly, big business seems generally to be accorded a good grade only on its performance at the first level.

To me, this is the essence of the meaning of the criticism of big business. These are the central facts coming out of all this criticism toward which the administrators of big business can, if they choose, direct their policies and their actions.

What they can do is the subject of the next chapter.

Let us . . . consider what state of things is described by the word "civilization." Its true test lies in the fact that people living in it make bodily welfare the object of life. . . . Formerly, in Europe, people ploughed their lands mainly by manual labour. Now, one man can plough a vast tract by means of steam engines and can thus amass great wealth. This is called a sign of civilization. Formerly, only a few men wrote valuable books. Now, anybody writes and prints anything he likes and poisons people's minds. Formerly men travelled in waggons. Now, they fly through the air in trains at the rate of four hundred and more miles a day. This is considered the height of civilization. It has been stated that, as men progress, they shall be able to travel in airships and reach any part of the world in a few hours. . . . Formerly, when people wanted to fight with one another, they measured between them their bodily strength; now it is possible to take away thousands of lives by one man working behind a gun from a hill. This is civilization. Formerly, men worked in the open air only as much as they liked. Now thousands of workmen meet together and for the sake of maintenance work in factories or mines. Their condition is worse than that of beasts. They are obliged to work, at the risk of their lives, at most dangerous occupations, for the sake of millionaires. Formerly, men were made slaves under physical compulsion. Now they are enslaved by temptation of money and of the luxuries that money can buy. . . . This civilization takes note neither of morality nor of religion. . . . Civilization seeks to increase bodily comforts, and it fails miserably even in doing so.

Women, who should be the queens of households, wander in the streets or they slave away in factories. . . .

This civilization is such that one has only to be patient and it will be self-destroyed. According to the teaching of Mahomed this would be considered a Satanic Civilization. Hinduism calls it the Black Age. I cannot give you an adequate conception of it. . . .[28]

[28] Ibid., pp. 25–27.

By way of views which emphasize institutional arrangements, especially those of private enterprise, as the cause of deplorable human behavior we can again take as illustrative those of Lewis Mumford. In his *Technics and Civilization,* Lewis Mumford takes a very dim view indeed of human behavior in industrial civilization. It appears to Mumford that the life of the individual, when he is not actually at work — and most of the time then, too — is largely made up of efforts to escape from, or to compensate for the spirit-crushing, soul-blasting realities of his existence.

Life in industrial civilization, according to Mumford, is highly routinized and disciplined. Time is short. The individual is seldom free to indulge his whims and personal preferences. He has to work instead of going fishing. Personal and organic relations are impaired. "Biological activity," it would seem, is not optimum. A population trained to maintain the routines imposed by industry and society, "at whatever sacrifice to health, convenience, and organic felicity" may well find that life is impossible without the most "strenuous compensations." What with all this discipline and rush, and the radio, daily newspaper, the telephone, and host of other stimuli — Mumford says — it becomes more and more difficult for the individual to cope with any part of his environment, let alone to deal with it as a whole. At the same time, and in consequence, for the individual the "inner world becomes progressively meager and formless." [29]

"The Machine," by failing to allow sufficient play to the organic in the established social pattern of social existence within the culture, has opened the way for the return of the organic in primitive forms.[30] Hence, says Mumford, the quest for "compensations." We find industrial civilization turning to primitive art — to that of the African negroes, for instance — and to primitive erotic music and dance.

[29] *Technics and Civilization,* pp. 269–273.
[30] Ibid., p. 302.

Sexual mores have been relaxed. Throughout the society we find all sorts of sexual and primitive compensations. We see the tabloids "symbolically recording the most crude and elementary states of emotion, feeling, barely vestigial thought." Mass spectator sports are a surrogate for true manliness. And in their latest forms, like air races and automobile races, they hold out morbid promise of injury, horror, and death. War, perhaps, is the chiefest compensation: it "breaks the tedium of a mechanized society." Then there are minor devices of compensation such as, "the cult of antiquarianism"—with its escape into suburban "Norman manor houses"—and the quest for mere novelty and change. Add to these a literature which has very largely become a "gigantic collective apparatus of escape," and the movies and radio—all of which provide the compensation of "surrogate lovers, surrogate heroes and heroines, surrogate wealth." [31]

To Mumford, it is foolish to try to conform our living and thinking to "the antiquated ideological system which helped create the numerous brilliant short-cuts that attended the early development of the machine." Instead an entirely new synthesis is needed. This is where the "advanced state" comes in. Failing this, "the Machine" will be able to continue only with the aid of "shock-absorbers which confirm its worst characteristics, or with the compensatory adjustment of vicious and barbaric elements which will, in all probability, ruin the entire structure of our civilization." [32]

Even more bitter and pessimistic, if possible, are the views of José Ortega y Gasset, renowned Spanish philosopher. Ortega is disposed to find the cause of the human behavior which distresses him in the general lapse, throughout industrial civilization, of the sense of morality and responsibility. His book, *The Revolt of the Masses,*[33] has made no little impression on at least three continents. This despite his many

[31] Ibid., pp. 299–315.
[32] Ibid., pp. 318–320.
[33] Op. cit.; page references are to "Mentor" edition.

crotchets, ingrained and rather universal petulance, his penchant for thinking in stereotypes, and flair for soaring generalizations.

To summarize Ortega's ideas rather freely, the social fabric and the moral code which previously existed have been undermined. True democracy has disappeared. And the "masses" [34] have acceded to political power, be it under Fascism, Communism, or whatever exterior form. Europe and the world are now largely peopled, as well as governed, by individuals and groups whose relationships to one another and to the community as a whole, and whose behavior, are characterized by irresponsibility and self-seeking, and an amorality which amounts to immorality.

Ortega, himself, summarizes his thesis in this sentence:

> . . . The world today is suffering from a grave demoralisation which, among other symptoms, manifests itself by an extraordinary rebellion of the masses, and has its origin in the demoralisation of Europe. . . .[35]

The crux of this demoralization of Europe — and, at many points in Ortega's argument it is perfectly clear that he thinks this is true of America also — does not lie in the fact that the "mass-man" has overthrown an antiquated moral code in exchange for a new one. On the contrary, it lies in the fact that

[34] Ortega's "masses" are not Marx's "proletariat"; they are not any economic or social class. The "mass-man" is a "generic *type*." He is to be found – it seems – in all walks of life. This mass-man has a number of characteristics. He seems to be, above all, a materialist with no understanding of the nature of civilization or any sense of obligation, nor, one might say, of responsibility. The mass-man, for example, and speaking metaphorically, has no doubt that motor-cars in five years' time will be more comfortable and cheaper than today; he believes in this as he believes that "the sun will rise in the morning." ". . . the common man, finding himself in a world so excellent technically and socially, believes that it has been produced by nature, and never thinks of the personal efforts of highly endowed individuals which the creation of this new world presupposed. Still less will he admit the notion that all these facilities still require the support of certain difficult human virtues, the least failure of which would cause the rapid disappearance of the whole magnificent edifice." (Mentor edition, p. 41.)

[35] Ibid., p. 134.

"at the centre of his scheme of life there is precisely the aspiration to live without conforming to any moral code." Ortega sees all groups and individuals, except a few which "imply survivals from the past" — "Christians, Idealists, the old Liberals" — manifesting only assertion of rights and denial of obligation. This denial of obligations, of any norm, is the denial of all morality; and this is "not amoral, but immoral." And it is because of the universality of the manifestations of that attitude which he sees, I take it, that Ortega holds out no hope that there is any prospect of the evolution of a real new moral code, nor, apparently, of a revival of the old.[36]

Turning to criticism which has a specifically religious orientation, we may take the views of the Popes of Rome as illustrative. We have seen that the Popes have been deeply critical of the institutions of undiluted individualism. But they are not disposed to lay blame on any particular material environment. Instead, they emphasize the departure from the moral values of religion and the enhancement of material values.

Several of the critical views of the Vatican which have already been quoted bear also upon the distressing human behavior and attitudes, and on the social relations which the Popes have seen in industrial civilization. Accordingly, here we shall look at only a few Papal observations on such matters for the sake of illustration.

In his encyclical *Ubi Arcano,* His Holiness Pius XI, for example, deplored the prevailing class warfare and struggles among political parties which — he said — stem, not from real differences of opinion concerning the public good, but from simple desire for power and for the opportunities to further private interests. He deplored the disintegration of the family. In particular, he lamented "the morbid restlessness which has spread among people of every age and condition in life, the general spirit of insubordination and the refusal to live up to one's obligations," the "destruction of

[36] Ibid., pp. 139–141.

purity among women," and the "great increase in the number of what might be called social misfits who almost inevitably end by joining the ranks of those malcontents who continually agitate against all order, be it public or private." [37]

As Pius XI looked out upon the world from the Vatican in 1922, it seemed to him that:

> . . . That blessed tranquility which is the effect of an orderly existence and in which the essence of peace is to be found no longer exists and, in its place, the restless spirit of revolt reigns. As a consequence industry suffers, commerce is crippled, the cultivation of literature and the arts becomes more and more difficult, and what is worse than all, Christian civilization itself is irreparably damaged thereby. In the face of our much praised progress, we behold with sorrow society lapsing back slowly but surely into a state of barbarism.[38]

For the final illustrative example of a point of view on human behavior and social relations in our society, we turn to the work of the late Professor Elton Mayo of the Harvard Business School. Mayo, almost alone among the critics of industrial civilization, was dedicated to an effort to bring the methods of rigorous scientific, clinical research to bear on the field of human relations. His work and goal are still viewed with suspicious misunderstanding by critics of both the traditional extreme Left and extreme Right.

Professor Mayo, drawing on the works of others and on his own extended observations, saw widespread and important *symptoms of social disorganization* in the human behavior and social relations in populous industrial areas.[39] These areas, of course, are the most representative of, and most affected

[37] Pages 6–7. [Compare with Elton Mayo's account of six "social misfits" in Australia, given in *The Social Problems of an Industrial Civilization* (Boston: Harvard University Graduate School of Business Administration, Division of Research, 1945), pp. 25–26.]

[38] *Ubi Arcano*, pp. 7–8.

[39] *The Human Problems of an Industrial Civilization* (New York: The Macmillan Company, 1933, and second edition, Boston: Division of Research, Graduate School of Business Administration, Harvard University, 1946), and *The Social Problems of an Industrial Civilization*, supra.

by, industrial civilization. He took as symptoms of social disorganization, the apparent relatively high rates, in those areas, of such phenomena as delinquency, criminality, suicide, neuroses, and the seeming appearance of *anomie* — that is, of planlessness in living and of restless movement.

Mayo was impressed, for example, by a study of delinquency, and a study of suicide, both made in Chicago. Both seemed to show scientifically that indexes of human aberration are associated with social disorganization.

Mayo was much interested in the theory which the Frenchman Émile Durkheim developed from his study of suicide, published in 1897: that a condition of *anomie* is characteristic of an industrial civilization in a state of rapid development.[40] This condition of *anomie* is a planless, restless way of life, with no meaningful criterion of value and pervaded by a sense of futility, defeat, and disillusion. Overt manifestations of *anomie* include the appearance in alarming numbers of "the melancholic, the suicide, the 'lone wolf' . . . the criminal." [41]

Professor Mayo also found interesting the works of the Frenchman Frédéric Le Play, who traveled widely over Europe as an engineer in the first half of the 19th Century. Le Play had concluded, from his observations of more and less advanced communities in various parts of Europe, that in the less industrialized communities there was stability in the social order: family and kinship relations were strong, ability

40 *Le Suicide* (Paris: Librairie Felix Alcan, 1894). Translated as *Suicide* by John A. Spaulding and George Simpson (Glencoe, Illinois: The Free Press, 1951). See, especially, Book Two, Chapter 5, and Book Three.

41 Elton Mayo, *The Social Problems of an Industrial Civilization*, p. 7. It is interesting to note, thinking back to the moral critics of materialism, that Durkheim attributed this *anomie* at least in part to economic development and to ever-expanding economic opportunities which whet ambitions which can never be achieved. (See *The Human Problems of an Industrial Civilization*, p. 130.) Durkheim had also been impressed with the disappearance of "secondary" organizations, close to the levels of daily life and work, which previously had acted to give cohesion to society. (*The Human Problems of an Industrial Civilization*, p. 149.) [Compare with the Encyclicals *Ubi Arcano*, as quoted on pp. 277–278, and *Quadragesimo Anno*, as quoted on pp. 243–244.]

to cooperate effectively was high, and general participation by all in the economic and social activities of the community was the rule. It struck Le Play that the situation in the modern, industrial community was the contrary: that the social code was ignored; ties of kinship were no longer binding; individuals were unhappy and desired novelty for its own sake; and that the capacity for spontaneous, effective cooperation had failed.[42]

Mayo shared the view that technological and other changes — economic development — were proceeding so rapidly that the older social order was being disrupted and that the social processes of adaptation were not keeping up.[43] He was deeply distressed by what he called "The Seamy Side of Progress." But, unlike many of the pessimists, Mayo did not stop there. Throughout his works, there is unflinching confidence that change *need not* disrupt society.

In Mayo's view, society *has* in fact been disrupted — primarily because of our limitations. First, we didn't understand what was going on. Second, our understanding of social relations, of sociology, psychology, and such matters was inadequate. Mayo attributed these lacks — which he thought still dangerously persist — largely to inadequate ways of thinking about human phenomena and to unfruitful research methods. Third, we lacked the social skills necessary to administer change. And over all — all along the line — we had left the matter of preserving "collaboration," which is the product of coherent and humanly satisfying social groups, to chance.[44] All these defects, he thought, were remediable.

[42] See *The Social Problems of an Industrial Civilization,* pp. 5–6.

[43] Mayo believed that a number of other factors were also involved. Among these he listed the high mobility of labor, the influx and incomplete assimilation of immigrants, defects in the educational system, and certain "eccentricities so far as the United States was concerned," of political and economic doctrine. (*The Human Problems of an Industrial Civilization,* pp. 142–143.)

[44] See *The Social Problems of an Industrial Civilization,* especially pp. xii–xiii, and Chapter I.

With greater understanding, knowledge, and skills, he firmly believed, we could help society assimilate and adapt to change. Not at one swoop. Not by abstract formulas. But over time; by very specific people — scholars and administrators — undertaking to do very concrete things.

Mayo's thinking stands in marked contrast to that of other observers we have sampled. Mayo insisted on the importance of rigorous clinical study, and of sure, but careful, even "pedestrian," progress in knowledge. He had no patience with thinking in stereotypes, nor for long chains of deductive thinking based on non-clinical, pre-scientific *a priori* assumptions. He was optimistic. And he was interested in practical, concrete measures — modest, perhaps, but constructive — which could be taken in the here and now by flesh and blood people.

Conclusion

Ideas, sentiments and feelings at this moral, ethical level may well determine the destiny of our society. People may come to be convinced — as many of them are already — that big business has made a great and unique contribution to our material well-being — that it has already done a great deal to provide the material basis which makes possible civilized life as we know it so far. They may come to believe that big business is indeed compatible with political and social democracy — not, perhaps, with certain rigid theories, but as shown by the broad facts of life and of history. Or they may not. But even when the time comes that they do, if it does come, there will remain the everlasting question: Is this a *good* society?

The three levels of thought and feeling we have been looking at may not be truly separable. But at this last level, the balance of feelings — deep misgivings and melancholy individual experiences as against a general confidence in an adequate opportunity for lives of human dignity and worth —

may color thought and feeling at the other levels. The balance here could be the decisive force in determining the course of the future development of industrial civilization.

* * *

As this survey of the criticism of big business and its civilization is brought to its end, questions so far held in abeyance now surge forth. How valid is this criticism? Can all these things be true — that big business is socially inefficient and "monopolistic"? That big business is incompatible with democracy — for the past 60 years or more running the country for its own purposes, and now threatening to bring on totalitarianism? Has big business truly produced a crassly materialistic culture in which Christian duties are neglected and even denied — a society of the spiritually starved who lead lives of noisy, even "Satanic," desperation?

That's one set of questions. Another adds up to this: What, if anything, can the responsible administrators of big business do in the face of all this criticism?

A study whose primary purpose was to present a systematic and illustrative survey of the criticism might well stop short of taking up questions like these. Such a survey as this could, so to speak, take the form of a staff survey which left to responsible administrators the problems of evaluating the data and casting up ideas as to appropriate policies and useful courses of action. But, since I do have some thoughts on these matters, I am going on to set them out. They will be the subjects of the two concluding chapters.

PART IV

Conclusions

CHAPTER 9

Critique of the Critics

THE UNITED STATES of America is not yet a *perfect* Union. Most of us, I guess, hope that our posterity will be able to look back upon us of the present with condescension — for what will then seem to them our low standard of living, our imperfect democracy, and our uncouth manners and morals — the way most of us now look back upon the Middle Ages. There *is* much to be done. And yet, as we have sampled all these critical ideas, practical man may well have exploded from time to time, "Nonsense!", "Rubbish!", or "Humbug!" And taking a look in broad perspective at America in the middle of the Twentieth Century, it is certainly not obvious to all of us that all the charges against big business and its culture must be true. At very least, *something* must be missing.

To judge from the economic criticism, one would be led to expect that over the past fifty years and more our standard of living must have been declining markedly, and that it has now reached a very low level indeed. For it is during that period that much of our economic activity has come to be characterized by that big business which has been called "inefficient" and "monopolistic." One would think, too, that such a nation, in the world community, must be very backward technologically. But as of now, relative to other countries where they organize economic activity by other means — Iceland, Ireland, Afghanistan, Ecuador, Ethiopia, India, Portugal, Norway, Brazil, or, for instance, Russia — we seem to have furthered technological innovation as well as some of the others, and our standard of living compares not too unfavorably. (That ought to be a modest enough self-appraisal.)

To judge from the political and social criticism, one might be led to suppose that in the first half of the Twentieth Century the United States must have drifted farther and farther from its democratic ideals. During the great growth of big business which took place over these decades, one would be led to conclude that we now have perceptibly less democracy than we did in 1900, 1800, 1700, or in 1620. One would think that our government, with each passing election, has come less and less to be responsive to the desires of the people at large. That fewer and fewer people have any real voice in public affairs. One would be led to suppose, too, that throughout most of the rest of the world, where big business has not yet intruded, that there must be many, many other countries where democracy flourishes far more vigorously than here. Yet the truth of these suppositions is something less than striking.

To judge from what many of the ethical and moral critics say, one would think that the spiritual level of life in America must have been sinking, sinking — decade by decade — as big business grew larger and larger. Thoreau grouched and grumped a century ago that even the people of pre-industrial rural Concord led "lives of quiet desperation." How much lower, then, must be the human, spiritual, and moral tone of life in the industrial America of the 1950's!

One would infer that the lot of the "typical worker" of a "Big 3" or "Big 4" must be more deadening to the human spirit than that of Bob Cratchit who worked for the small firm of Scrooge & Marly. Or of David Copperfield, when he worked, with a sense of "unmerited degradation," in the warehouse of Murdstone and Grinby. From what they say, it should be abundantly clear — if it is so — that life in urban, industrial America must nowadays be less humanly edifying, or even more downright brutish, than life in the Massachusetts Bay Colony under the Mathers, or than life in Florence under the Medicis. Or even than life in such small towns untouched by big business as Sinclair Lewis's "Gopher Prairie"

— or Sodom and Gomorrah. But a measure of doubt may linger that all this can be true.

The fact is, of course, that many of us feel there are ample grounds for feeling downright proud of America. We are proud of the material advances which have been made, of its innate and advancing democracy. And many of us are unshakably confident that few, if any, other peoples — past or present — have moved much closer than we have toward the ever-receding ideal of the *good* society. This is scarcely smugness, for we are also unshakably confident that in every phase of life there is still *much* progress yet to be made. The tens of thousands of national, regional, state, and local organizations for advancing this or that cause are but one kind of manifestation of our will to improve things and of our many high hopes for the future.

Surely, there must be *something* missing in much of the critical analysis. For, by and large, and on the whole, and over time, big business *must* have been a socially useful way of organizing important phases of economic activity. If it were not, with big business taking such a prominent role, technological advance and increasing productivity could scarcely have come to pass. Nor do *all* the facts of life and of history seem to support the view that big business is necessarily at odds with democracy or with a society which is *tolerably good,* even if it is far from perfect.[1]

The facts of life and of history pretty clearly do not fulfill the expectations and theories of most of these critics. Nor have the apparent eager hopes of the pessimistic and misanthropic among them been realized — as yet.

It is evident that much of the criticism has gone astray.

[1] Perhaps at this point I should make it perfectly clear that nothing in this book is intended to be derogatory of *small* business. Obviously there is overwhelming evidence all about us that small business units have played their part also in our general advance. Not only has small business played an important role in the past. So also will it have great opportunity in the future. The fact that *small* business has come in for scant mention in these pages, one way or another, is due simply to the fact that this *is* a book about "*big* business."

Over all, it doesn't seem to jibe too well with reality.[2] The reason, I believe, lies in some important errors and fallacies. It is these that we shall now examine.

Errors and Fallacies

First, we will take a look at the concept of the big business corporation which is a common fundamental building block of most of the criticism we have seen.

Throughout practically all the criticism we have reviewed there runs a curious, basically hostile, and — I am confident — an unrealistic concept of the nature of the business unit, of the corporation in particular. It is assumed, first, that the sole, the exclusive motivation of economic activity is the desire for economic gain. It is assumed that profit is the *sole* objective. It is assumed that economic expediency is the sole and exclusive relevant criterion of business judgments, decisions, and actions. Nothing else counts: At no time, according to this concept, is there ever any positive concern with the public weal or the interests of others, nor any forbearance of advantage out of moral scruples or qualms or goodwill. The business enterprise is thought to be individualistic to the point of irresponsibility. It is assumed that the human being who in ordinary life has at all times *many* motives, and who lives by a complex of *many* values, abandons all other considerations when engaged in business or in earning his living.[3]

As a corollary, it seems to be assumed that people, both as individuals and as corporations, view one another with hostility as a matter of course. That they see one another only

[2] For instance: "The modern laborer . . . instead of rising with the progress of industry, sinks deeper and deeper below the conditions of existence of his own class. He becomes a pauper, and pauperism develops more rapidly than population and wealth." — Karl Marx and Friedrich Engels, *The Communist Manifesto.*

[3] This assumption which underlies so much of the criticism is questioned by Professor George Katona of the University of Michigan in his *Psychological Analysis of Economic Behavior* (New York: McGraw-Hill Book Company, Inc., 1951).

as obstacles, as threats, as competitors for gain, and as possible objects for exploitation — not as human beings, nor even as entities with which it is possible to coexist in some harmony, or with which to work to mutual satisfaction. This assumption is what Professor Mayo called "The Rabble Hypothesis." [4]

Further, it is assumed that the administrative and working relationships in business organizations are purely and rigidly authoritarian. Under this scheme, it is assumed, the top administrator alone decides what should be done. He then issues orders. His subordinates down the line amplify these orders in increasing detail. They relay them down to lower levels. Progressively down through the organization, people have increasingly less and less discretion and initiative. They make fewer and fewer decisions about less and less. Down through the organization, people more and more do — or should do — only as they're told. At the lowest level, people decide nothing about anything. At the bottom level, the person is exclusively a sort of intricate machine which is controlled verbally, and manipulated by a more or less complex mechanism of wage incentives and penalties. (This view of the worker is consistent with this general viewpoint, since it is supposed that the sole relevant value for the worker is economic gain; just as for the "bosses," the directors, and the stockholders.) Or the worker may be coaxed, wheedled, and cozened by "human engineering." In any case, machine-like, he carries out an exactly predetermined job. Over all, according to this concept, business is run by the "Führer Principle." The bigger the company, apparently, the more true this is conceived to be.[5]

[4] See *The Social Problems of an Industrial Civilization*, Chapter II.

[5] This concept is exactly that described by "Lieutenant Tom Keefer" in *The Caine Mutiny:* "The work has been fragmentized by a few excellent brains at the top, on the assumption that near-morons will be responsible for each fragment. . . . [All the fragments are] predigested and regulated to a point where you'd have to search the insane asylums to find people who could muff the jobs . . . a master plan designed by geniuses for execution by idiots. . . ."

Notions along these lines run all through the ideas of critics as to how it is with business corporations. Sometimes these notions are on the surface. More often they lie deeply.

If the corporation did have these basic characteristics, and no other, it would truly be insufferable. The quest for "plunder" would indeed be the order of the day. Such an organization would be quite incapable of managing complex, far-flung activities. It could never solve complex technical problems. An economy and a society in which such entities played an important, integral part would, I am sure, justify fully all the strictures of the critics.

But, what if the concepts of critics as to why and how business corporations work are essentially *false?* Essentially false, because they are, at best, only a partial view of things? What then? What if business decisions and behavior are actually governed by a complex of *many* values, including the quest for profit? And, what if a substantial measure of responsibility and initiative is delegated all along the line, even to the man on the machine? What if it is possible for people in a corporation to have faith and confidence in one another?

What judgments would critics reach if they had a different basic concept of the corporation?

To come back to the two major aspects of the critics' concept of the corporation, their ideas as to its values and its motives, and as to the nature of organizational relationships within it: We do not know nearly as much about the corporation as we should. Our libraries contain more concrete, clinical detail on distant primitive tribes — their motives, value systems, and methods of organizing activity — than on the corporations in our midst. Only in recent years, has material stemming from close, firsthand observation of business organizations become available on a significant scale.[6]

(By Herman Wouk; Garden City, New York: Doubleday & Co., Inc., 1951, p. 97.)

[6] See, for example, Fritz J. Roethlisberger and William J. Dickson, *Management and the Worker* (Cambridge: Harvard University Press, 1939); and Melvin T. Copeland, *The Executive at Work* (Cambridge: Harvard Uni-

But already the data published so far show clearly that motives and values, and administrative philosophies and practices in corporations are in fact, as might be expected, at least as rich, complex, and varied as those of primitive groups.

The modern corporation is not described with even approximate accuracy by the oversimplified, the stereotyped concepts outlined above. These concepts do not flow out of efforts to comprehend a wealth of clinical observations which have been made at first hand. They are merely *a priori* assumptions.

Critics, generally, misconceive the nature and the functioning of one of the most distinguishing features of modern society — the business corporation. The basic misconception stems from the fact that although many of them aspire to be social *scientists,* they are not, in fact, active in research directed toward verifying the assumptions which are basic to their thinking. From this beginning, it is not surprising that they so often reach conclusions which must sound bizarre to practical experienced people.

The second source of error, as I see it, that many of the critics have fallen into is that they attempt to understand and interpret human affairs in terms of a mechanistic, materialistic philosophy. This is a big matter, and we can only

---

versity Press, 1951). See also the following publications of the Division of Research of the Harvard University Graduate School of Business Administration: John Calhoun Baker, *Directors and Their Functions* (1945); Melvin T. Copeland and Andrew R. Towl, *The Board of Directors and Business Management* (1947); Edmund P. Learned, David N. Ulrich, and Donald R. Booz, *Executive Action* (1951); Harriet O. Ronken and Paul R. Lawrence, *Administering Changes* (1952). See also, John D. Glover and Ralph M. Hower, *The Administrator, Cases on Human Relations in Business* (Chicago: Richard D. Irwin, Inc., Revised Edition, 1952).

There are other, and earlier works. The works cited are a few of the recent results of the continuing efforts of the Harvard Business School to develop a firmly based and growing body of knowledge as to why and how business organizations work, through close, firsthand observations and case material.

See also Chester I. Barnard, *The Functions of the Executive,* and *Organization and Management* (Cambridge, Massachusetts: Harvard University Press, 1938 and 1948, respectively); William B. Given, *Bottom-Up Management; People Working Together* (New York: Harper & Brothers, 1949).

scratch the surface of it. But even that should be useful in trying to understand why so much of the criticism has the ring of unreality and leads to unfulfilled expectations.

Universally among the economic critics, very generally among the political and social critics, and even frequently among the moral critics, there appears the idea that human behavior is determined by organization structures and material environment. Thus, for example, economic critics are led to believe that the intensity and quality of competition in an industry is governed by the *number* of competitors. In their view, a "Big 3" *must* be less competitive than a "Big 10," or than a "Small 50." The behavior of the competitors — the way they compete — is determined by the "structure" of the industry and not by human variables. Thus, it is contrary to their scheme of things that because of differences as to human attitudes, traditions, and skills, the degree of competition within some particular small group could be far more intense than within a much larger, but moribund, group. Structures, not human beings, govern human affairs.[7]

[7] When confronted by evidence which suggests the facts of life are more complex than their simple concept, structural determinists have no alternative but to shrug it off. Being unable to understand or to explain complex reality in terms of their simple concept, they dismiss any concrete case that doesn't fit as an "exception." Case in point: the following interchange, during the hearings of the "Celler Committee," between Congressman Kenneth B. Keating of New York and Professor Walter Adams of Michigan State College:

Mr. Keating. You mean there is no competition between these big companies that make the same product? In the automobile business there is no competition between General Motors and Chrysler, for instance?

Mr. Adams. Well, let us take the cigarette industry as an example.

Mr. Keating. I was taking the automobile industry.

Mr. Adams. Well, I think that perhaps is an example of one of the more progressive industries that we have in the oligopoly group. But cigarettes, there the case is quite clear.

Mr. Keating. How many are in that oligopoly in the automobile industry that you are talking about?

Mr. Adams. Well, you have the Big Three dominating the industry, General Motors, Chrysler, and Ford.

Mr. Keating. What about this Nash car that has just come out and says that it is the best car on the market at the lowest price?

Mr. Bryson [Congressman from South Carolina]. Hudson has just reduced its price.

Political critics we looked at hold that real democracy cannot exist unless the structures of power and political institutions follow some particular pattern. Given this way of thinking, if the actual structures they observe depart from the given ideal, it must follow that the substance of the political and social order is not democratic.

These critics are inclined to interpret history as the working out of vast, impersonal forces and movements. For them, human will and limitations, the deep-seated traditions of peoples — human hope, faith, charity, and will — count for little, if anything. Similarly, the moral and human quality of relationships in a small business are seen as necessarily superior to those in a big business — because of the difference in *structure.* From the individual firm to the nation at large, human relationships and behavior — they would have us believe — are governed by organizational and institutional structures.

Many of the lay moral critics — and even, let it be noted, some of the formally religious critics — attribute particular moral aspects of human behavior to particular ways of life, especially to its material circumstances. Thus, a rural, agrarian way of life is held to be *intrinsically* superior from a moral point of view to an urban, industrial way. Homespun is morally superior to machine-woven material. Travel on foot superior to travel by train or plane. A static society to a dynamic one. Human immorality is blamed on "the Factory," "the Machine," "the City" or, partly completing a circle back to political and social criticism, on "Capitalism," private property, and unequal wealth and power.

In this scheme of the universe, Man is an object controlled, moulded, buffeted about by the impersonal forces of organiza-

---

Mr. Keating. Mr. Kaiser has gone into the business.

Mr. Bryson. How about Studebaker?

Mr. Keating. You do agree with us?

Mr. Adams. I think the automobile industry is an outstanding exception. . . .

(*Study of Monopoly Power,* Part 2-B, pp. 1319–1320.)

tion structures and the impersonal power inherent in Things. Man is not responsible for his destiny, his triumphs, or shortcomings. Not even for his own sins. There is a destiny that shapes his ends, rough-hew them as he may. His faults lie not in himself but in his stars. Human variation, human will, human action, human responsibility become trivia or even irrelevancies. Man, himself, becomes a Thing, acted upon but not acting.

As conceived by these mechanistic theories, the business firm, the political and social atom, "the Worker," "the City Dweller" — all such — become truly tragic characters. They lose all responsibility for themselves. Human will and struggle avail naught. Nor does even individual human weakness bring on disaster. They are as powerless against the forces of organization structures and material environment as the heroes of Greek tragedy were against the forces of destiny set in motion by the gods. They have no more responsibility nor scope for action than Oedipus, Electra and Orestes, Agamemnon, or Medea. Given the implacable and irresistible will of the gods, the tragic heroes and heroines of Sophocles, Aeschylus, and Euripides were caught up and carried along willy-nilly to their ordained ends. Human strivings and failings added only pathos and irony to the circumstances of these characters, for the outcome could not be swayed by anything they did nor did not do.

The parallels between institutional and materialistic determinism and the determinism of the pagan drama are profound.

Faced with problems, real and imaginary, some determinists can think only of tinkering with structures. If only the structures can, somehow, be perfected our problems will be solved. For the forces exerted by perfected structures will bring about perfected human behavior.[8] Or they will try

[8] Thus, for example, the economic structure of minute competing atoms supposedly having been "superseded" by one in which there are present some very large ones, Professor J. K. Galbraith (see Chapter 4, pp. 144–145, fn. 5

to control the material environment, and by this means let forces be generated which will mould and direct human behavior into predetermined patterns of activity and morality.

Then there are some who believe that great, self-generating — autonomous — forces are at work shaping the evolution of the world. They talk of inevitable trends and waves of the future. Depending on their own assumptions, they may welcome this, and even, oddly enough, attempt to lend assistance to the inevitable.[9] Or they may fall into black despair and political neutralism — like many of the intellectuals of Europe. Say, like José Ortega y Gasset or Virgil Gheorghiu. Saying that we are nearing the end, they may resign themselves to fate.

Obviously, the question of whether a philosophy of determinism is a correct view of the universe and of human affairs will not be settled here. We can only note that it stands opposed to some fundamental assumptions and beliefs of the Western World, including the idea of the dignity, free will, and individual responsibility of Man.[10]

---

above) urges that this mechanism, which he distrusts, be perfected by having there be brought into being some *more* very large atoms. This new mechanism, it seems, *will* work. On the opposite side, the Federal Trade Commission, apparently, wants to perfect the structure by breaking up big atoms, and preventing their further growth. (See Chapter 5, pp. 179 and 181–182, above.)

[9] Like Professor C. Wright Mills, who — I gather — wants to organize the "White Collar" class into a militant bloc for political action. (See *White Collar,* Chapter 15.)

[10] The belief in structural determinism, as in other kinds of determinism, can be held with the same unshakable certainty as any other religious dogma. As a matter of faith and belief, it is impervious to logical assault. It lies beyond scientific inquiry and discussion. The testimony of Professor Walter Adams before the Celler Committee provides an illustration of what is perhaps an unwittingly candid expression of pure *faith* in the *structure* of pure and perfect competition. Professor Adams had been saying, ". . . the way things stand now, a firm does not survive because it is more efficient than another firm," and, ". . . a firm survives today if it can exercise monopolistic control or oligopolistic control over the market. . . ." Representative J. Frank Wilson of Texas then put a question:

Mr. Wilson. Dr. Adams, would you not call a business pretty efficient where in 1920 they sold electric light bulbs for 45 cents, and the same bulb sells now for 12 cents?

Such ideas, it seems to me, stand squarely opposed, for instance, to the teaching, *"There is nothing from without a man, that entering into him can defile him: but the things which come out of him, those are they that defile the man."* [11]

There, then, as I see them, are two of the major errors. Moving ahead, we shall look at some others.

Biased perceptions of one sort or another are very common among the critics. That is, they may perceive things which are real enough, but they see only those things which fit in with a preconceived picture. Things which do not, are filtered out. These partial perceptions which ignore all other parts of the whole become the basis for broad critical generalizations.

Some examples:

It has happened that in the files of a large corporation a memorandum written by a minor executive to the effect that it might be profitable to suppress some technical improvement becomes the basis for a generalization that the company — indeed, that big business — has no interest in, and is incapable of, technological innovation. The episode is made much of and is cited repeatedly over the years to prove the point, despite a mass of concrete evidence to the contrary. Looking at the business community, critics see the spectacular and often shocking behavior of "Robber Barons" — of Jim Fiske, Daniel Drew, Jay Gould, and "Diamond Jim" Brady. Such material — fifty years and more after the events — remains a basis for generalizations about big business, not the quiet, unhistoried, constructive accomplishments of hun-

---

Mr. Adams. I do not think that necessarily proves efficiency, because we do not know what would have happened in the industry if effective competition had prevailed, and it is my faith and belief that the advances made in the industry would have been greater had effective competition prevailed in the electric light industry.

In other words, nothing that an "oligopolist" can do can prevail against "faith and belief" in the *structure* of atomistic competition, even where there are no data for that faith to go on. (See *Hearings before the Subcommittee on Study of Monopoly Power . . .*, Serial No. 14, Part 2-B, pp. 1321–1322.)

11 *The Gospel According to St. Mark,* 7:15.

dreds and thousands of other men who have made real contributions to our welfare and advance.

An outstanding example of a critic given to biased perceptions is Lewis Mumford. He looks upon the United States and perceives things which displease him. It is easy enough for anyone to do, in a dynamic society of 160,000,000. But somehow, all the things which hearten other observers escape him. Nowhere does he see the democracy, the charity, and the promise which so deeply moved Walt Whitman, Lord Bryce, Carl Sandburg, Robert Frost, or — more recently — Charles Malik, the representative of the Republic of Lebanon in the United Nations.[12]

Biased perceptions show up in the way critics often romanticize the past, agrarian life, "Small Business" — as a stereotype — and the "Small Town" to the disadvantage of their opposites. Overlooked are the aspects of life in the past which would make it a horror to most of us now living.[13] Overlooked, for example, are all the actions brought by the Federal Trade Commission itself against businesses which are small for unethical trade practices.[14] Overlooked is the fact that few objects have more often been the butt of attack than small town life.[15]

Proponents of the past and of simple agrarian life seem to overlook the possibility, which other observers have suggested, that country churchyards, also, may be peopled with mute inglorious Miltons, men in whom the genial current of

12 See *War and Peace,* A statement by Mr. Malik before the Political Committee of the General Assembly of the United Nations, November 23, 1949. (Stamford, Connecticut, The Overbrook Press [for the National Committee for Free Europe], 1950.)

13 See, for example, G. G. Coulton, *The Medieval Village* (Cambridge, England: Cambridge University Press, 1925); G. G. Coulton, *Friar's Lantern* [London: Watts & Co. ("The Thinker's Library"), 1948]; Lord R. E. P. Ernle, *English Farming, Past and Present* (London: Longmans, Green & Co., 1922); and Bertrand Russell, *The Impact of Science on Society* (New York: Columbia University Press, 1951), especially pp. 52–53.

14 See, for example, T.N.E.C., *Final Report,* Exhibits 2802, 2803, and 2321.

15 See, for example, Harry Hartwick, *The Foreground of American Fiction* (New York: The American Book Co., 1934), especially pp. 256 ff.

the soul was frozen by chill penury; men who, tilling the soil, lived stolid and stunned, brothers to the ox; who, living, were dead to rapture and despair. They seem unable to appreciate the amount of drudgery and monotony that has been taken over by "the Machine." They seem unable to conceive that one of the great blessings of industrial civilization is, precisely, that in it untold numbers of far greater opportunities for the whole man have been opened up.

Critic after critic does not perceive — in any case, does not report — a balanced, realistic picture which has many *pros* as well as *cons* along with a host of imponderables.

Somewhat related to bias in perception is the propensity of many critics to see and describe the world in terms of stereotypes. Thus, we find them casting up images of the Financial Tycoon, the Factory Worker, the City Dweller, the Mass Man — even the Glamorous Wife of the Big Business Executive. We are told in all seriousness about how the "typical" citizen thinks, behaves, spends his time, and about how he relates himself to members of his family and the people he works with.[16]

The most pretentiously "scientific" stereotype, of course, is the "oligopolist." This disembodied entity has no individual characteristics whatever. Large corporations are not viewed as human groups which, like other human groups, exhibit all manner of characteristics. Each is an "oligopolist." It — the "oligopolist" can scarcely be called "he" — it is so far

[16] The late Harold Laski's book *The American Democracy,* for example, bristles throughout with stereotypes. His stereotype of "*the* American businessman" is sketched in considerable detail. (See pp. 169–171, *et passim.*) Mr. Laski even had a stereotype for *the* American *child.* He even cast one up to cover all 160,000,000 of us – "*The* American."

Speaking of Laski, I could have drawn quotations from almost any page of *The American Democracy* to illustrate many of the kinds of criticism we have reviewed in the foregoing pages. Laski seems to have had a deep admiration, even affection for America – as an abstraction. But he saw America only through the heavy lenses of an untempered, loveless, materialist philosophy. Accordingly, there was scarcely any concrete aspect of it that he could abide, to which he did not apply the barb of his articulate, embittered pen.

from being human that it is described by mathematical functions in space. The "oligopolist" is such a rigid stereotype that, by the very definition, there is no variation. Thus, for people who think in terms of this stereotype, it is impossible to conceive that firms, which have in common the fact that they have few competitors, may differ profoundly in kind as to administrative philosophy and as to skill and interest in research and technical knowledge, or in zest for initiative and competition. Or, that they may differ in their ideas as to what social responsibilities they are willing to shoulder. No provision is made even for variations in degree. By definition, all oligopolists, for instance, are interested, absolutely and solely, in maximizing profits. No provision is made for the possibility that, from case to case, this interest may be alloyed in differing proportions and combinations with other interests. And all are assumed to be equally intelligent, calculating, and grasping.

Such a way of thinking applied to other fractions of the population and to other human groups — to Jews, Negroes, Yankees, Southern Baptists, Democrats, Republicans, or universities, for instance — would be denounced, rightly, as unscientific, undemocratic, and inhuman.[17]

The fact is — and I am going to put this very bluntly — "Big Business," as an outstanding stereotype, has served for

[17] It is interesting to note that Karl Marx, who made great claims for the scientific quality of his thinking, conceived of individuals *only* as stereotypes — as he called them, "personifications" of "categories." His philosophy, he tells us himself, views the individual *less* as a responsible *individual* than any other. For Marx, the individual is the "creature" of organizational, structural environment: ". . . here [in *Das Kapital*] individuals are dealt with only in so far as they are the personifications of economic categories, embodiments of particular class-relations and class-interests. My standpoint, from which the evolution of the economic formation of society is viewed as a process of natural history, can less than any other make the individual responsible for relations whose creature he socially remains, however much he may subjectively raise himself above them." — Preface to the First American Edition of *Das Kapital.* [See *Capital, A Critique of Political Economy,* translated from the 3d German Edition (Chicago: Charles H. Kerr & Company, 1926), Vol. I, p. 15.]

Not much room here for the individuality, free will, responsibility, and — especially — the dignity of Man.

many people the same purpose as "the Jew" served the Nazis. It has been a useful *bête noire,* or whipping boy on which to focus all kinds of hostility. Like "the Jew," it has been blamed for inflation, deflation, war, frustrated hopes for peace, overproduction, and underproduction. It has served as a sacrificial goat on which to hang responsibility for all the aberrations and personal failures of an ever imperfect but ever hopeful humanity. This stereotype, like others, has served as a substitute for thought and a focus for free-floating hostility.

There is a final uniformity which runs through much of the criticism to which I would like to draw attention: its static, even Utopian, quality. There may well be a word or a concept from logic which describes this characteristic exactly. If there is, I do not know it. But the tendency shows up clearly enough. It seems to be related to all the characteristics we have already seen.

This characteristic shows up in the static, rigid systems which many of the critics seem to have in mind as ideals. The particular ideal may be the standard against which they measure reality as they perceive it. Or this rigid, highly specified ideal may be held forth as a goal we should be progressing toward. Since part of the essence of reality seems to be change, as well as complexity and diversity, and since reality doesn't look much like any abstract, static, mechanistic ideal, it — the concrete world of reality — inevitably comes out of such a comparison as second best. And the future ideal state inevitably appears as something we should hasten toward as quickly as possible — even before we take time to try to understand the present.

In the theories of the economic critics we reviewed, there is little provision for change, growth, and development, just as there is little provision for diversity. The chief concern seems to be with how *existing* opportunities and techniques are exploited, up to an equilibrium position, not with how new ones are brought into being and old ones recede. There is, among these critics, a curious and widespread lack of understanding of, or even interest in, the concrete processes of reality — of human activity — whereby our technology and physical environment have been transformed. The transformation is all attributed to isolated individuals, to "Small Business," or to a self-generating autonomous process which seems to be just another vast, impersonal and highly abstract force — "the advance of the industrial arts." Despite the concrete evidence which abounds on every hand, critics are unable to conceive that big business through myriads of daily actions over the decades has played an important part in this evolution.

In the political theory we examined, there is little provision for the possibility that new institutional arrangements may emerge which may be just as compatible with democracy as any fixed theoretical ideal, or even more so. In the "advanced state" we are told about, there appears no provision for the possibility that the techniques, institutions, and values of national life may wax and wane and alter over time. In Gandhi's ideal India of the future it would appear that no new techniques and no new ideas are to appear which will alter the relevance and desirability for the Indian people, of village handicraft industries.

This static quality which makes no provision for the emergence of new insights, knowledge, objectives, institutions, and techniques perhaps is simply a part of the syndrome of qualities which characterize doctrinaire, pre-scientific thinking. Thus, when Hitler tells us of the "Thousand-Year" Reich which is to be established, there is no suggestion that such an idea might cease to be useful or attractive to Germans after, say, 381 years. The Marxists tell us that after the Classless Society is established, political evolution will come to an end. This, despite the fact that some still dare to hope that the human race has quite a span of time ahead of it.[18]

[18] See Charles G. Darwin, *The Next Million Years* (New York: Doubleday & Company, 1953).

In any case, many of the critics seem to be trying to understand and to judge the world of reality in terms of static conceptual schemes. And since change, development, emergence, evolution — call it what you will — seems to be an essential part of reality, it is not surprising that much of what they say seems to fall short of realism.

Not only that. Critics often judge the present by measuring it against some idealized vision of the future. As we have seen, this sort of a contrast makes the present look, at very best, drab and humdrum, even depraved. And not only that. Often, they do not put their yardstick of their envisioned future up against anything that very closely resembles present reality at all. Not even up against present reality as perceived through a heavy bias. Instead, they compare their vision of the future against rather limited, rigid — nonclinical — *theories* and *preconceptions* of what the present reality "must" be now like.

Thus, for example, in judging the motivation and behavior of corporations and organizational relationships inside corporations today, as against supposed qualities of "yardsticks" of the order of the "advanced state," the "Thousand Year Reich," or the "Classless Society," critics often seem to be applying these "yardsticks" against particular rigid theories and preconceptions relating to matters of the present day, rather than against things actually observed. Since these theories and preconceptions are poor, not to say misleading, representations of present day reality in the first place, it is not surprising that some of the final judgments have a dream-like cast to them.

This is the sort of thing I mean: According to certain theories, big corporations are ruthlessly authoritarian. Some critics who have spent no large amount of time studying organizations at first hand seem to accept these theories as accurate descriptions of reality. Against these theories — rather than against some others or against a body of clinical description — they then apply their own luminous theories as to what the world's organizations *should* look like. It is not surprising that the resulting judgments are negative, and have the odd, unworldly ring they often do.

* * *

At this point we can stop. Much else could be said. But the task, if it can be done, of refuting all this criticism and picking it to tiny pieces I leave to others who may have stomach and energy for such an enterprise. Our objective here is to understand, not to rebut. Having tried to pursue this objective as far as I think useful for present purposes I shall now pass on to other matters.

* * *

In making what, in effect, is a counter-criticism, we run the risk of two dangers which should be guarded against by all means. First, we may be led to do the critics less than full justice. Second, we may be led to dismiss too hastily what they have to say.

Thanks to the Critics

As to full justice, it must be conceded, first and foremost, that the world is far from perfect. Not just in terms of contrast to some distant scene, but in terms of what we now know and what we can now do, the one step before us in the here and now, the American society falls short. Human societies, I suppose, will always fall short.

And many of the shortcomings, of course, are indeed of the order which have been picked up for criticism. An objective reading of history — including accounts of some contemporary affairs — must certainly lead to the conclusion that some big corporations have indeed been guilty of moribund policies; persistent inefficiency; inability to adapt to, or to initiate, change; monopolistic practices; rigid authoritarian administration; economic opportunism; and social irresponsibility.

Businessmen as well as critics have also often been chargeable for static, mechanistic, deterministic thinking. Some businessmen *have* sometimes seemed to see the objective of business policy as being the exploitation, by means of given, static techniques, of given, static opportunities. Some, it seems to me, have thought that gains were to be obtained pretty *automatically* from the mere mechanism of merger, or that economies were to be had merely as an *automatic,* mechanistic consequence of size. Some seem to have thought that dynamic problems of policy formulation and administration could be solved if *only* the right organization structure could be devised.

Goodness knows there is ample "case material" to keep large numbers of energetic critics busy for generations. There are enough opportunities for competent remedial action to keep every man of good will busy indefinitely.

Second, I, for one, am quite prepared to recognize that at least some of the critics have served a useful, even indispensable function. Very concretely, to critics of business must go considerable of the credit for the adoption of legislation which had to come.

Humanity absolutely required, for instance, that employers assume as a cost of production liability for disabling injuries suffered on the job. Criticism of the sort we have looked at, in all probability, did hasten the legislation which made the shouldering of that responsibility mandatory.

Pure food and drug legislation was, I think, necessary to protect the American people from noxious products put out by a minority of irresponsible, and sometimes ignorant, businessmen. The fact that the government has sometimes become enormously embroiled in trivial litigation under these Acts should not overshadow their major purposes and accomplishments. The passage of these Acts was undoubtedly sped by the work of spirited critics.

Honest and full disclosure of financial and other material data by companies approaching the public money markets, under penalty of personal liability for company officers, attorneys, and accountants, certainly had to come. Critics of

CHAPTER 10

Prescriptions for Action

THE CONCLUSION of the preceding chapter provides a point of departure for this closing chapter. This starting point is a three-ply proposition:

First, the American people have hopes and aspirations on three distinguishable planes. We aspire to material well-being at a high and *rising* level. Simultaneously, we aspire to an increasingly democratic political and social order. And, at the same time, we want continuing progress toward the ideal of a *good* society. We want achievement, progressive achievement, on each and all of these planes.

Second, big business as one of the outstanding features of our civilization has been, and will be, judged in terms of its contributions to achievement on each and all of these three planes. Achievement, even outstanding achievement, on one alone will not suffice.

Third, a clear majority — it would seem — as of now are reasonably well satisfied with the achievements of big business only on the economic plane. Most Americans seem not to share the views of those economists who are so critical. Nor do most Americans, I guess, share the views of the more extreme political and social and moral critics. However, there do appear to be widespread misgivings as to the achievements of big business on the political and social plane and on the moral one. It may well be that these feelings of misgivings are unjustified. Be that as it may, that they *exist* is a *reality* confronting the administrators of big business.

In this chapter we shall take up the question, What can the administrators of big business do to meet the situation outlined by this proposition?

In taking up this matter of action, we shall first look at the action implications seen by the critics. For this will round out our understanding of the criticism. And it will also make clear the varying kinds of challenge which they lay down. Following this, I shall discuss some lines of action which seem to me especially appropriate and significant for efforts by big business to meet the situation.

Action Implications as Seen by the Critics

First we shall take up the action implications seen by those critics who trace the shortcomings *they* see to institutional, structural, and organizational defects. Critics in this vein are led, naturally enough, to think of remedial action in terms of recasting economic, political, and social structures so that they will correspond to some ideal. That is, those of them are, who are not plunged into despair by the thought that such a task is too great or complex to be done, or by the thought that it is too late, and who are not content to wait quietly for vast and inevitable waves of the future to settle matters automatically.

This line of thinking leads some of the critics to look for remedy to political action by various "classes" and militant parties. By political action, new institutional structures will be erected which will control us all by the mechanistic forces which they will set in motion. Or, by political action, an élite of some kind will be put in office to direct, by authoritarian decree, the nonautomatic workings of a controlled society.

The action envisioned to improve the state of things is not of the sort which looks to widely diffused initiative and individual discretion and responsible action in ordinary daily life. A machine is going to act, or a remote anonymous "they" somewhere. The action is of the sort which proceeds at a high level of abstraction — the level of vast "forces," of ideas, plans, and programs. It is not the sort of action which proceeds at the most concrete level of human behavior — the level where millions of flesh and blood people endeavor to improve countless particular situations by working with concrete people and concrete things. For the mass of the people will have no rôle of initiative or responsible action. They will merely respond to structural forces. Or do as they're told — or else.

In particular, the more thoroughgoing of these critics visualize no rôle of responsible, purposive action for the administrators of business. Obviously, they will have no rôle if private enterprise is "extirpated" or even quietly nationalized.

But even far short of any such bright, antiseptic new society, where the mass of mankind is to be relieved of the burdens of free-will, initiative, discretion, and responsibility, many of the critics can visualize no conscious, broad, socially useful rôle of action for the administrators of business. Not even in the here and now — let alone in some ideal new society — can they conceive that the administrators of business might play an active rôle in serving society's broad purposes by dealing constructively with the situations with which they are connected.

The inability to conceive of a socially useful, active part for business to play even under the present state of things stems from two sources: first, from the stereotype of the corporation; second, from faith in mechanisms and distrust of human discretion. Actually, these two streams of thought, when they are combined, create a logical dilemma — for critics, at any rate — which precludes the possibility of positive action by large corporations to contribute directly to the broad aspirations of the people.

In the first instance, by their reasoning, the corporation has no rôle but to pursue profit relentlessly and exclusively by whatever and all means it must. It behaves solely in accordance with the dictates of economic opportunism. For this reason, the corporation — above all, the *big*, "oligopolistic" corporation — cannot really be counted upon even to do very much by way of contributing to progress on the economic plane. Nor, especially, can the big company be counted upon to contribute to progress on the other planes. This mournful conclusion follows inevitably from the notion that the corporation has no interest in serving a multiplicity of ends and being a source of a variety of satisfactions to a variety of interested parties. This conclusion follows from the notion that the corporation, far from being a democratic institution, is ruthlessly authoritarian. It follows from the notion that the values of the corporation are exclusively materialistic and that the corporation is entirely amoral. Given ideas like this, it follows that corporations, acting in accordance with their nature, "must" ignore whole large areas of the broad interests of society. In sum, in the philosophy of such critics the corporation is debarred by its own nature, from being anything other than a piece of economic machinery—for many, an essentially antisocial piece of machinery.

In the second instance, structuralist critics tend not to *want* corporations to do anything but what is prescribed for the corporate stereotype. For, we are told, if corporations do not — by some quirk — really operate like the stereotype, they will not produce even the maximum consistent with "monopoly." That clearly is not in the economic interest of society. But there is an even worse side to the matter than this.

If corporations don't *really* operate like the stereotype, it might turn out that corporations actually have varying amounts of free-way for discretion. And it might turn out that, within those areas of freedom, they actually pursue a number of objectives and take into account a number of considerations in reaching decisions, in addition to profitability. All this in a way which is unpredictable from company to company, and somewhat indeterminate even from case to case within the individual firm. In short, it might turn out that human consciousness, will, skill, and decision — to say nothing of human diversity — have something to do with how corporations behave. This would mean that they are not just mechanisms responding mechanically to mechanistic forces. This would mean that corporations would, after all, be capable of responsible action. But above all, it would mean that they have discretion.

The possibility that corporations may have discretion is a source of apprehension to many critics. And they are led to propose various means to eliminate this discretion — by having the government take over, by extending government control, or by reconstructing the economic mechanism so that it *will* govern human activity. In short, critics of this cast do not *want* corporations which do not operate like the stereotype, mechanically and irresponsibly.

Examples of this kind of thinking occur again and again, more often than not just in fragments. Here are a few examples:

From *The Decline of Competition,* by Professor Burns of Columbia:

> . . . The ideal of service said to be developing among business managers implies that some . . . broadening of the basis of their industrial policy has occurred. Discussion of this ideal among businessmen springs more probably from a suspicion that the lack of such a viewpoint exposes them to criticism than from a willingness to adopt it. . . .
>
> The development of an ideal of social service, of course, undermines the foundation of economic thought based upon the assumption that the primary drive to economic activity is the maximization of individual income but that assumption is already open to considerable question. It is seriously undermined by the conduct of the major part of industrial activity, by corporations whose managers do not directly secure all the gains arising out of profitable policies or suffer all the losses resulting from unprofitable ones.[1]

Not much faith here in the possibility of genuine socially responsible behavior by corporations. Anyway, it seems, such

[1] Op. cit., p. 527 and footnote 1, pp. 527–528.

behavior would be incompatible with the maximization of income.

To the idea that monopolists (implicitly equated with "big business") may not actually exact from the unfortunate who have to deal with them the last full measure which lies within their power, Professor George J. Stigler of Columbia retorts:

> Should there be some big businesses that forgo the use of their dominant position, it is difficult to see what advantage accrues from private ownership, for the profit motive is already absent.[2]

Not much room here for the generous gesture or even for moral squeamishness. Certainly no room for social responsibility. Just maximum profits, by any means whatever — including utmost use of monopoly power. And if they *don't* behave that way — well, isn't that an argument in favor of public ownership?

Not even in relation to its own employees can the corporation serve the broader purposes of society. It is supposed that there can be nothing in this relationship of mutual satisfaction, good will, sense of obligation, confidence, or any of the other attributes of warm, natural relationships. This is intolerable. On the other hand, if — by some quirk — the *real* relationship doesn't actually correspond to this stereotyped concept — well, Professor E. H. Carr puts it this way:

> . . . The essence of so-called private enterprise, even when it takes the form of large-scale monopoly or oligopoly, is that it is capable of making only an economic appeal to the worker. Its practice and aim is profit-earning; its philosophy of work recognizes material gain as the sole effective stimulus. Once it departs from this premise, it becomes a public utility and had better be recognized and organized as such.[3]

[2] "The Case Against Big Business," p. 158.
[3] *The New Society*, p. 55.

There's the dilemma. On the one hand, the big, one-valued, irresponsible corporation is intolerable. (The small, irresponsible "atom" can be put up with.) On the other, a big, many-valued, responsible human institution is intolerable also. It would not operate according to the structuralist blueprint of the stereotyped, mechanistic firm.

Underlying much of this thinking is a profound fear of human initiative, discretion, and free will. What is wanted is a system, a structure, a mechanism that will govern human affairs. If only such a rule can be imposed over mankind, we can — it appears — escape from the dangers, the infinite possibilities, and the frightening indeterminacy of free human behavior. The "ideal" is a system where there is no scope for individual action — certainly not in the economic sphere. In this "ideal" structure, obviously, no place is to be found for large corporations which have a measure of discretion, some initiative, and some scope for free action.

A fundamental fear of this sort is to be found lurking even in the thinking of such a writer as Professor John M. Clark, also of Columbia, who is certainly no doctrinaire, irreconcilable critic of big business — a man, indeed, who has contributed some of the most outstandingly promising ideas to leaven the subject of economics in recent years:

> Competition is our main safeguard against exploitation. In our sophisticated civilization we dare not trust the terms of exchange to tribal custom and sense of honor, as some primitive peoples can. Under self-interest, people of our advanced stage of culture would naturally incline to give as little and get as much as possible; they would increase their gains by reducing their services, by producing less to sell for more. But competition works the simple miracle whereby each one increases his individual gains by increasing his services rather than reducing them: he makes more by producing more to sell for less.[4]

. . . . .

[4] *The Alternative to Serfdom* (New York: Alfred A. Knopf, 1948), p. 62.

> . . . a monopolist does not typically price for the utmost possible immediate profit that curves of demand and cost permit, but seeks expanding business at a profit that seems to him reasonable. It is not exactly safe to let him be the sole judge of reasonableness in his own case; in fact, it is thoroughly unsound. He will be more than human if he does not rate his risks as deserving of a higher premium than others would approve and he may lack vision and enterprise in promoting future growth. It is safe to assume that he will charge too much, even if, as a general thing, he does not consciously squeeze out the utmost profit the immediate market will afford. He may, of course, do that if it is the only way in which he can get a profit that satisfies his sense of reasonableness. But he can do plenty of harm if he uses only a third or a quarter of his monopoly power. The trouble with monopoly is not that it always leads to the kind of pricing which theory assumes, but rather that it can do so, and is virtually sure to distort pricing in that direction, leaving the monopolist too wide a range of arbitrary discretion.[5]

People, it seems, cannot be trusted with discretion, and responsibility. Hence, the "ideal" system seems to be one in

[5] Ibid., pp. 65–66. (Professor Clark's assumptions, in this particular passage, as to the "natural" inclinations of humanity are as unflattering and cheerless as Adam Smith's. Professor Clark, be it said, is by no means always this pessimistic.)

A dour, a pessimistic, a misanthropic set of assumptions regarding humanity, often expressed in nonclinical, pre-scientific generalizations as to "natural" human motivation and behavior and as to human relationships, goes logically hand in hand with a faith in mechanisms, structures, and "forces." It is an interesting philosophical question, which is hen, here, and which is egg?

Just by way of another glimpse of this dark generalized picture of human nature – from a statement by Stephen J. Spingarn, until recently a member of the Federal Trade Commission: ". . . There is a general tendency in human beings to let well enough alone, to form habits, to crystallize these habits into social institutions, and thus to live in a society which shows a minimum of change. . . ." (*Monopoly and Cartels,* Hearings before a Subcommittee of the Select Committee on Small Business, 82d Cong., 2d Sess., Part I; p. 9.) See also *Monopolistic Practices and Small Business,* Staff Report of the Federal Trade Commission for the Subcommitee on Monopoly of the Select Committee on Small Business, United States Senate Committee Print. (Both items published in Washington: Government Printing Office, 1952.)

which there is no discretion or free-way in behavior, in which behavior is totally and precisely determined by exterior, mechanical forces.

In sum, to draw this matter to a close, structuralist and mechanistically inclined critics visualize no active responsible rôle for big business in the struggle of humanity to better itself along a broad front. In the first instance, according to them, this is precluded by the corporation's very nature which admits of no discretion for departure from intolerably narrow and rigid economic opportunism. In the second instance, if — by some quirk — there really *is* some discretion, this really ought to be eliminated or controlled.[6]

Critics inclined to a mechanistic, structuralistic interpretation of human affairs, especially a good many economic and social theorists, see no action implications for the business corporation — except, perhaps, for it to break itself up voluntarily into as many and as small pieces as it possibly can. These people look for remedy and progress to changes in institutional structures and to government action. In effect, the challenge which these people lay down to the administrators of big business is, "There is nothing for you to do."

Passing on to the religious critics, their theory of action to remedy the shortcomings which they see in society is essentially simple: It is for mankind to return to established doctrines, principles, and values of religion. Of course, there are deep differences among the leaders of religion. But they do, for the most part, view human action as a matter of the free-will, discretion, and responsibility of the individual. Their concept of remedial action, consequently, is primarily a matter of individual application of the ideals of religion in individual life. That is, their remedy is to be put into effect

[6] The fear of discretion does not always extend to discretion in the hands of government agencies. I suspect, if I may offer a theory of my own, that this is because "government" is likely to be regarded just as another bloodless, impersonal mechanism – the sort of *thing* in which it is proper to have faith. "Government" seems not to be viewed as a group of human beings who would, "naturally," be inclined toward antisocial behavior, along with the rest of the human race.

concretely in the ordinary daily doings, choices, and decisions of individuals.

Their appeal for action is addressed to all individuals. Religious critics seem not to lay any especial burden of action upon the administrators of big business. They, along with the rest of mankind, apparently are equally charged with guiding their lives, decisions, and actions by the prescribed tenets. The businessman is not appealed to as such, but only as another human being. The only special charge for action seems to be directed at ministers of religion who have the responsibility of leading the laity to the correct view of things.

Religious critics generally seem not to concern themselves greatly with the matter of economic progress. They do, of course, often concern themselves with the question of the *distribution* of wealth, for in this they may see moral questions of justice involved. They do also, from time to time, express concern over the need to increase the material standard of life in backward areas of the world. But on the whole they seem not to attach any great weight to general economic progress, certainly not in the United States.

Accordingly, the popular aspirations in which they are greatly interested are largely those of the social and moral planes. And, for them, progress on these planes, as already suggested, is primarily a matter of the total sum of the actions of individuals. In any case, the strictly religious critics do not look to institutional mechanisms and structures to solve the problems of the human race.[7]

For action, religious critics look, in sum, primarily to individual action, to action which will express in each individual life a more moral ordering of values. Their injunc-

[7] Some of the religious criticism, as we have seen, sometimes sounds as though it is believed that certain ways and conditions of life are inherently more moral than others — agrarian, rural life being superior to industrial, urban life, for instance. But such ideas do not appear to be of the essence of the *religious* outlook as such. Indeed, such a view may be something of a materialist heresy.

tion to all humanity, including the administrators of big business, runs to the effect: "Broaden and re-order your values, your objectives, and the criteria of your decisions."

We come now to the theory of action of those who, like the late Professor Elton Mayo, attribute the shortcomings of industrial civilization primarily to inadequate social skill — lack of administrative competence — and to inadequate *scientific* knowledge of human relations.

These ideas as to action stand in especial contrast to those of critics, like R. H. Tawney, who view the defects *they* observe in industrial civilization as manifestations of "the sickness of an acquisitive society." Critics like Tawney trace the cause of malady to a wrong ordering of values. Given this diagnosis, the remedy naturally seems to be to change the system of values. Up to this point, the diagnosis and the therapy are reminiscent of religious thinking. However, Tawney and the Webbs and others of like bent wish to accomplish the re-ordering of values through change in institutional structures and in the political system, rather than through individual will, conversion, or re-dedication.[8] Against this thinking, Mayo put forth an entirely different diagnosis, and his theory of action was equally divergent.

In opposition, Mayo argued, "Actually the problem *is not that of the sickness of an acquisitive society; it is that of the acquisitiveness of a sick society*. The acquisitiveness [Tawney] selects for such unsparing condemnation is itself no more than a symptom of the failing integration which invariably accompanies too rapid social change." [9] People "have relapsed upon self-interest when social association has failed them." [10]

[8] Such an idea poses a nice and an old philosophical — or is it theological? — question: In a world where there are no obstacles to virtue and no temptations, can there *be* any virtue? Or does human virtue consist, precisely, of overcoming obstacles and temptations?

[9] *The Human Problems of an Industrial Civilization,* p. 153. (Italics in original.)

[10] *The Social Problems of an Industrial Civilization,* p. 43.

In a period of rapid and ineptly administered technological change, with consequent rapid and chaotic social change, the lives of large numbers of individuals have come to lack satisfying "social association" at work, in the community, and at home. Not only is the satisfaction of social association lacking; circumstances are such that it is hard for the individual to come by, even when he actively seeks it. *Because* of this vacuum, to Mayo's way of thinking, modern society has been marked by a general preoccupation with materialistic objectives and antisocial behavior.

The base of Mayo's position was that our social skills have not advanced in proportion to our technical skills. Especially, we have not learned as well as we must how to administer change. Hence, the human and social problems of industrial civilization. From this point of view, tinkering with institutional arrangements misses the essential problem. For, whatever the institutional system, human affairs have to be organized and administered by human beings. So long as we do not know how to administer change so that it will not be a disrupting factor, we shall have serious human and social problems.

Nor is human *will* enough. We need *skill.*

From this standpoint, a major line of action called for is the practice of greater social skill and more skillful administration in ordinary affairs, in all human organizations, and from the topmost level all the way down. Not "skillful" in a Machiavellian, manipulative sense; but in the sense of technically competent and socially responsible administrative action which will enable society — beginning with individual human groups at work — to assimilate, and adapt successfully to the realities of technological and social change, and to *initiate* change. That is one line of action which clearly appears not only to be available, but necessary.

Since knowledge places a limitation on what can be practiced, a second line of action is called for — more and more pedestrian, clinical research into the realities of human relations. Indeed, in Mayo's opinion, the prime purpose and direction of the social sciences should be to contribute to the necessary increase in our social, administrative skills.

The objectives of these two lines of action are manifold: To make it possible to solve in more useful ways the problems of society — including technological problems of development and production — at the concrete level. To enable society more easily to assimilate and adapt to change in ways which preserve its coherence, meaning, and opportunities for satisfying associations for the individual.

To this way of thinking, as I interpret it, there is unlimited opportunity and need for widely diffused competent, responsible administration in all human organizations, and at every level — nowhere more than at the top of large corporations. Because of the positions of influence they occupy, the administrators of big business are seen as having a special opportunity, and a special responsibility for the kind of action which will permit society to make the broad advances desired by the American people on all three levels: economic, political and social, and moral.

Prescription for Positive Action

I now move on to set out the areas of action for the administrators of big business which seem to me to be especially appropriate and significant for meeting the situation outlined at the beginning of this chapter.

Not because they are of any particular interest to the reader, but in order to avoid misunderstanding, I should like, at this outset to make my own position clear. I am no pessimist. I reject, as narrow and unrealistic, the philosophies of materialism and determinism manifested in so much of the criticism of big business. Facts — it seems to me — teem about us on every side to attest the great contributions that big business has made to American life. Big business deserves much of the credit — not all, by any means — for our unequalled technological advance and standard of living.

It seems to me that no reasonable man, looking objectively at the facts, can believe that big business runs the country, nor that it is pushing us, willy-nilly, into totalitarianism. In fact, it ought to be perfectly obvious that if there is any real threat of this sort, it comes from those who desire, by authoritarian political action — by the power, and ultimately by the force of the State — to remake the country to correspond to some fixed ideal of their own, or to push us back into some never-never Golden Age.[11]

I do not believe that large corporations do, or can, solve the fantastically complex problems of modern technology and production in the authoritarian ways supposed by critics. I believe, on the contrary, that large corporations have necessarily created large numbers of opportunities for individual self-realization in jobs calling for high degrees of social skill, technical competence, and responsible participation. I believe that the moral climate in the general run of large corporations and the moral quality of their actions does not compare unfavorably with the general moral climate of the country and the quality of the actions of its citizens.

On the other hand, I do not believe that we have achieved the millennium. We still have a *long* way to go. We cannot yet rest confident that depression cannot come again. And, being human institutions large corporations are not likely often to achieve perfection. Like other human institutions, they *are* sometimes chargeable on grounds of social inefficiency, irresponsibility, and immoral acts. These lapses are not the norm. It is simply that, in common with the rest of mankind, they, too, have a long way to go.

[11] Item: Professor Benjamin Higgins' recent plea that an élite of benign, wise and – anticlimactically – *certified* economists should be given *power* to run the economy. See, *What Do Economists Know?* (Melbourne, Australia: Melbourne University Press, 1951; and New York: Cambridge University Press, 1952.) (Query: Who is to certify the certifiers?) This is merely another of the many guises in which the hoary authoritarian dream of Plato is trotted out, from time to time, as the solution to mankind's problems – the dazzling, or perhaps more exactly, the *blinding* vision of the dictatorship of the philosopher-kings.

In sum, big business — even though far from perfect — has rendered great service to the United States. And I am confident that in the future large corporations can, and will, make significant contributions to the continuing progress which Americans want — on the economic plane, on the political and social plane, and on the moral plane.

Accordingly, even though, on the whole, big business has done well by the United States there is ample room for constructively intended suggestions as to possible ways in which it can do ever more toward meeting the threefold aspirations and standards of the American people.

Probably the most obvious contribution big business can make to America in the decades before us is to be an ever more efficient instrument of our economic life. That goes without saying.

And this, of course, will call for business policies and actions that are creative, dynamic, and aggressive in every dimension, touched with a vision that sees beyond the years — policies and actions that first release, then harness, continuous technological and administrative innovation. Such a contribution as this — it also goes without saying — will not be brought forth out of business policies that brood over "vanished frontiers" and the gloomy — not to say presumptuous — myth that technological progress has reached its ultimate dead-end, and that America is now foredoomed, willy-nilly, to secular stagnation. Such a contribution will not issue from business policies preoccupied with maintaining a static share of a static market for a static product.

Having said this much on an obvious point, I now move on to other matters.

As I see things, there are four other major areas for action. First, the administrators of big business can clarify their own thinking as to the basic nature of the corporation. In particular, they can move to free business thinking from the error it sometimes falls into of accepting the very same unrealistic stereotype of the corporation which is basic to the hostility of critics. Second, they can explicitly broaden their concept of corporate objectives and policies so that recognized corporate goals will more clearly include accomplishments on more than just the economic plane. Third, by administrative skill and competence, they can see to it that these broadened policies are, in fact, converted into concrete realities. Finally, they can contribute to a more realistic understanding of the large corporation by sponsoring research directed toward extending our social skills and administrative capacities, and by making opportunities for self-education available to educators and others, that they may at first hand learn something of the realities of how large corporations operate.

Business Thinking about Business

To the first of these four areas. The logical starting point for effective action by the administrators of business to meet *all* the aspirations of the American people — and, incidentally, to meet much of the criticism of "big business" — is for them to clarify their own thinking about the fundamental nature and purposes of large business organizations. To the extent that this is not done, all other efforts to meet American aspirations are likely to be confused and ineffectual.

In the first place, the administrators of business can jettison from their *talk* about big business all implications which suggest that they, too, accept the stereotyped concept of the corporation. It is surprising and ironical, that, to judge by what businessmen often *say,* one would think that they, too, agree that the nature of business corporations is exactly and precisely what critics say it is; namely, that the corporation has no other purpose, and recognizes no other criterion of decision except profits, and that it pursues these profits just as single-mindedly and irresponsibly as it can.

When administrators of big business sometimes seem to share the same fundamental premise as to the nature of business enterprise, it cannot be surprising if critics take their statements as confirmation that the concept which is basic to their hostility is a valid one. The result is confusing to all — to the administrators of big business no less than the rest.

Consider the annual reports of corporations. It is not unnatural that people — critics, for example — should infer from what corporations report of their activities what it is they consider to be relevant and important to the companies and their stockholders. Even today, some companies report nothing but financial and technical operating data. This information, of course, is essential. But these companies do not also report, for instance, "We are glad that in the past year we were able to offer opportunities for their first self-supporting jobs to 537 young people."

If a corporation in reporting its accomplishments for the year fails to mention anything of *human* or *social* consequence, it should not be surprising if an outsider — say, a critic — infers either that there were no such accomplishments or, if there were, that the officers of the corporation considered them to be irrelevant.[12]

A number of factors lie behind communications of the sort which carry suggestions that administrators of big business have only the narrowest of concepts as to purposes and values. One can only guess what they are and how important

12 The late Professor Thomas H. Sanders of the Harvard Business School in his study, *Company Annual Reports to Stockholders, Employees, and the Public* (Boston: Harvard University Graduate School of Business Administration, Division of Research, 1949), was of the opinion that explicit self-vindicating statements as to motives were not appropriate material for annual reports. In Professor Sanders' words, the corporate administrator "must confine himself, in his annual reports, to telling of his problems and his efforts to deal with them as directly and convincingly as he can, and hope that a plain tale truly told will do the job. . . . It is reasonable and constructive to use the annual report to describe the problems which confront him and his efforts to cope with them, and to steer clear of expressions about motives, so likely to be misunderstood." (Page 7.)

In recent years, of course, the annual reports of many corporations clearly have been carrying the message that important accomplishments and achievements of the year include a variety of things *in addition* to the net income earned or the net loss suffered. Such reports may provide at least the suggestion that corporations are not, after all, the single-valued and single-purposed bodies the critics say they are.

each is. But some of them, at least, are appropriate objects for remedial effort if the thinking of these business leaders about the nature of the corporation is to be clarified.

For one thing, it is probable that some objectives of corporate policy and some of the considerations which actually enter decisions are so much taken for granted that they are not even mentioned. For example, in many companies it seems to be *taken for granted* that, in all its dealing with suppliers, customers, employees, and others, "the company" will endeavor to be generous, honest, sincere, and responsible. Yet it sometimes seems difficult for people to talk about things like this — to concede, for instance, that one of the major objectives of the company *is* to be a *good* company. Perhaps it is because that is entirely taken for granted. Perhaps it is because, in our culture, people are sometimes "ashamed" or embarrassed to talk of such things. It has been urged that such considerations should not be passed over as "taken for granted." [13] It could also be urged that businessmen would do well to try to get over any "shame" or embarrassment they have in such matters.

Another factor which may account for the curiously narrow concept of the purposes and values of the large corporation that often seems to come through to the public may be that business enterprise has, as yet, no systematic rationalization that takes into account these other "taken-for-granted" factors. The only systematic rationalization we have is that which stemmed out of a materialistic, mechanistic philosophy. Possibly, these ideas have buried themselves so deeply in our thinking that many people, when they come to rationalize about business, have only these traditional concepts with which to think and to talk about it. It is too much to expect that the administrators of big business should soon come up with a new full-fledged systematic rationalization. But at least a beginning can be made.

[13] Donald K. David, "Business Responsibilities in an Uncertain World," *Harvard Business Review,* Vol. XXVII, No. 3, Supplement, May, 1949, p. 8.

In any event, it is probable that these two considerations account for the fact that in their talk and in their rationalizations, businessmen sometimes do *sound* just like the stereotype cast up for them by the critics. Some businessmen seem emotionally as well as intellectually unable to admit that they do govern their actions by something more than economic expediency and that they are, in fact, at least no less responsible and less good citizens than others in the community. This tendency — perhaps less common than it used to be — is undoubtedly a good part of the explanation of why it is that business has failed to get much of whatever credit it has deserved for breadth of objectives and acts of social responsibility.[14]

This leads right on to the next point. The administrators of large corporations can take the lead in trying to re-cast the concept of business enterprise which lurks behind much of the legal thinking about corporations. For many purposes of the law, the business corporation is conceived to be the very same bloodless, heartless, opportunistic, selfishly calculating entity depicted by its critics. Much of the legal rationalization of business enterprise bears an obvious kinship to the traditional rationalization which has been picked up by critics as being an accurate description of reality. This concept of the business corporation in the law plays directly into the hands of the critics.

This stark concept of the corporation shows up nowhere more clearly than in decisions in suits concerning the power of corporations to make contributions and in de-

14 "Years of listening to businessmen talk about their businesses creates the feeling that in many cases their own words do them less than justice. Particularly is this true when they employ phrases like 'Our purpose is to make a profit.' This expression is not so prevalent in annual reports as it used to be, but its appearance in the public utterances of company officials continues to color the reception accorded to their annual reports, which constitute a principal medium of business self-expression. . . . [The businessman] need not belittle his own efforts by declaring that profit is his primary motive, when it is plain to all that his days are filled with constant care and arduous exertion, and that his achievement is his real satisfaction." (Thomas H. Sanders, *Company Annual Reports* . . ., pp. 5–6, and 7.)

cisions as to what are "ordinary and necessary" business expenses.[15]

A leading case in this field is the English case of *Hutton* v. *West Cork Railway Co.*[16] In this case, a company *in liquidation* had voluntarily made additional severance payments to employees who were being discharged and who had been paid their regular wages in full. In the stockholders' suit over this matter, the judge accepted the argument that the stockholders of the company could receive no benefit in return from these additional payments. That is, they could receive no pecuniary return. He therefore ruled that the directors exceeded their powers in making such terminal payments.

Revealing the concept of the corporation as a chilled entity quite unresponsive to feelings of warmth, obligation, or responsibility, the judge held that the directors exceeded their powers in making these payments, because they were not *businesslike,* but *charitable.* He laid down the rule that, "Charity has no business to sit at boards of directors *qua* charity." [17]

The judge went on:

> There is, however, a kind of charitable dealing which is for the interest of those who practice it, and to that extent and in that garb (I admit not a very philanthropic garb) charity may sit at the board, but for no other purpose.[18]

The judge, if he had had a different concept of business and of the corporation, might have viewed these payments simply as a warm act flowing from a feeling of obligation — the kind of act that people individually and in corporate

[15] Some of the quotations and citations in the next few paragraphs come from a private memorandum, *Power of Corporations to Make Charitable Contributions,* prepared by Mr. Stuart Marks, an associate of the firm of Davis, Polk, Wardwell, Sunderland & Kiendl. The interpretations and recommendations, of course, are all entirely my own.

[16] 23 Ch. D. 654 (1883).

[17] Ibid., p. 673.

[18] Ibid.

bodies engage in every day in the normal carrying on of business. Had he had such a concept, the judge might well have held that making such payments was well "within the ordinary scope of the company's business." [19] He did accept the idea, however, that since there was no pecuniary return to the stockholders, the act was not an act of *business,* but — and the categorical contrast is a deeply invidious one — an act of "charity."

In this thinking is disclosed a further facet of the corporate stereotype as conceived by the law. Revealed also is a wondrously inverted rule of corporate morality as opposed to ordinary morality. For in effect, the judge is saying that a warm, human act, even an act of charity pure and simple, engaged in for its own sake and with no calculated ulterior selfish motive, is *not* a permissible corporate act. The reason that it is not permissible is that it is not — by the concept — consonant with the nature of the corporation. By the rule laid down, such an act is not "reasonably incidental to the carrying on of the company's business for the company's benefit."

On the other hand, a *seemingly* charitable act can be justified if it can be shown that it was *really* motivated only by the ulterior intent of furthering the corporation's own interest in a calculated way. For that *is* in accord with the assumed nature of the corporation, which is to direct all its actions to furthering its own interests.[20]

This very principle is clearly implicit in the decision of the United States Board of Tax Appeals in the *Sprunt* [21] case

[19] Ibid., p. 672.

[20] In the application of this rule, it is apparently an act beyond the lawful powers of the corporation – an *ultra vires* act – for an insurance company to pay claims which it is not enforceably bound to do *under the letter* of a contract, if its reason for so doing is simply that that is an honorable, responsible, natural thing to do. If, however, it does the same *apparently* natural and responsible act, but is *really* acting out of the ulterior motive of attracting business to itself, then it is all right. (See *Hutton* v. *West Cork Railway Co.,* p. 665.)

[21] *Alexander Sprunt & Son, Inc., petitioner,* v. *Commissioner of Internal Revenue, respondent,* 24 B.T.A. 599 (1931).

which bore on the question, What deductions can be claimed by a business enterprise as "ordinary and necessary" expenses in computing net income? In this case, a business firm engaged in the international cotton trade contributed $5,000 toward a fund which was raised by cotton exchanges and cotton merchants to combat the boll weevil. The Commissioner of Internal Revenue questioned whether this was an allowable deduction against net income as an "ordinary and necessary" business expense. The Board of Tax Appeals held that it was. But what is intriguing here is the Board's reasoning, and the light that throws on the law's concept of the corporation:

> . . . In making the contribution there was *no thought of charity or philanthropy; the motives of the petitioner were purely mercenary,* its expectation being that its business would be benefited proportionately to the degree of success attendant upon the campaign of eradication or control of the pest. . . . The question always is whether balancing the outlay against the benefits to be reasonably expected, the business interests of the taxpayer will be advanced.[22]

In other words, the test of an act, as to whether it is the sort of thing a corporation might ordinarily and necessarily do in carrying on its business, is whether the motivation is *purely mercenary.*

In the inverted morality of corporations — as laid down for them by the law — any act in which there enters a thought of charity or philanthropy, or any imponderable feelings of business responsibility and obligation, is not the kind of thing corporations can be expected ordinarily to do. The reason, of course, is that the corporation is conceived to be single-purposed and irresponsible. The norm of corporate behavior is what such an entity as this might do — not what a normal group of people might do.[23]

[22] Ibid., 617. (Italics added.)

[23] Corporations, of course, do make substantial contributions to charitable, educational, and like organizations. Since 1944, the recorded contri-

This concept of the business corporation in law, and the rule which flows from it, results in corporation lawyers cooking up, for formal resolutions to be adopted by boards of directors, the most far-fetched kinds of reasons to rationalize as calculating acts for gain what were simply normal acts of people trying to exercise ordinary judgment. In fact, the rule *drives* lawyers to insist upon the invention of elaborate ulterior reasons for decisions which are actually made on the basis of ordinary, common-sense judgments. Corporations are compelled, for the record, to malign their own motives.

One of the most useful things that the administrators of big business could do in meeting the criticism is to sponsor a full re-examination of whether this concept, so deeply embedded in the law, is realistic and useful, or libelous and misleading. With such a concept having full legal status, it should not be surprising if people take it as being an accurate representation of the fact.[24]

---

butions of corporations in the United States "have each year exceeded the total collections of all community chests." (F. Emerson Andrews, *Corporation Giving*, New York: Russell Sage Foundation, 1952, p. 15.) But, in order that such outlays may be regarded as proper business actions — *intra vires* acts — there is the feeling on the part of many lawyers that boards of directors must be prepared to show that they acted out of the direct, calculated interest of the corporation, not out of feelings of philanthropy, obligation, or responsibility.

The absurd length to which legal thinking can be carried in the endeavor to ascribe cynical, ulterior, calculating motives — hence, *permissible* motives — to what are really simple acts is sometimes breath-taking. For example, an Attorney General of the State of New York ruled that savings banks in the State could contribute to the Red Cross fund raised on the occasion of the great Japanese earthquake. His reason was *not* that such a contribution was a simple, understandable, and normal act of humanity, but that it was in the banks' own selfish interest, what with "the interdependence of nations" and the "delicate adjustment of our financial machinery in its relation to foreign affairs." (1923 *Op. N.Y. Atty. Gen.*, p. 317.) See also *Armstrong Cork Co.* v. *H. A. Meldrum Co.*, 285 Fed. 58 (Western District of New York, 1922).

[24] In the recent case of *The A. P. Smith Manufacturing Co.* v. *Ruth F. Barlow, et al.*, the Supreme Court of the State of New Jersey affirmed the power of a New Jersey corporation to make a contribution to a university. In reaching this decision the court, significantly, had the benefit of the favoring testimony of Messrs. Frank W. Abrams, chairman of the board of Standard Oil Company (New Jersey) and Irving S. Olds, chairman of the board of the United States Steel Corporation.

This first area for action has been dwelt upon at considerable length because it is the key to all else. If action at this level of basic ideas is not effective, little can be expected from anything else that might be done. If, on the other hand, these ideas are crystallized, many other aspects of action will fall easily into place and be carried through successfully.

This brings us to a final point related to the need for the

In handing down its opinion, the court gave voice to an impliedly somewhat broader and more realistic idea of the nature of the business corporation. But the justification of the corporate act of giving still rested *primarily* on the traditional rationalization of self-interest: ". . . Princeton emphasizes by precept and indoctrination the principles which are very vital to the preservation of our own democratic system of business and government, particularly vital at this time when alien ideologies seek to impose themselves upon our habits and our dreams for the future. I [Judge Albert Stein] cannot conceive of any greater benefit to corporations in this country than to build, and continue to build, respect for and adherence to a system of free enterprise and democratic government, the serious impairment of either of which may well spell the destruction of all corporate enterprise."

The university is also recognized as a source of future scientific and executive talent for the company. Also the Court reasoned, a corporate gift may result in public esteem for the donating corporation.

The Judge did go on to state that, in his view, it is also a "solemn duty" for corporations to contribute to a cause which is "intimately tied into the preservation of American business and the American way of life."

"Solemn duty" is obviously not on the same plane as self-interest. But this thought, with its implications that corporations may act out of a sense of *duty,* as well as out of pursuit of self-interest, was not expanded upon.

What the Court here recognized and gave only the scantest mention as a *secondary* justification for the contribution, the company's directors — in their own resolution to make the gift — had put in *first* place: *They* said, ". . . corporations which in their own capacities enjoy many of the benefits of citizenship are under an obligation, greater in times of prosperity, to assume their part of the burdens of citizenship, one such burden being the support of voluntary charity, including the privately supported universities and colleges. . . ." In this view, the implication is perfectly clear that corporations — or, to put it differently, human beings acting corporately — are not necessarily devoid of a moral, even altruistic sense to which they may and do properly respond in managing their affairs.

It is a pity that the Court missed the opportunity to give express and clear sanction to this simple truth. It could have taken a big and certain, rather than a small and faltering step toward bringing the law's idea of the corporation into closer accord with reality. Perhaps other courts might have followed its lead.

(See Superior Court of New Jersey, Chancery Division, Essex County, Docket No. C–1274–51; decided May 19, 1953.)

administrators of big business to begin action by clarifying their own thinking. Up to this point, the discussion has, of course, been going along on the proposition that the basic concept which critics have as to the nature of the corporation is essentially a false and misleading one. Generally speaking this proposition is well-founded. The opinions of those who have studied corporations closely at first hand bear out this idea.[25]

Needless to say, however, there are many instances of corporate behavior which seem clearly to give the lie to this idea. There have been many acts which — by their appearance, at least — seem to bear out the hostile concept of the most enthusiastic critics.

It is quite likely that such actions reflect business thinking which may be clear enough, but is exactly in the opposite direction from what is needed if the broad aspirations — and demands — of the American people are to be met. What is needed in such cases is not clarification of thinking, but *new*, different, broader, more responsible thinking. In this connection, a number of large corporations, either by themselves or with outside assistance, from time to time even now review their policy objectives and methods of operating to ascertain whether these make sense in terms of meeting *all* the objectives they have set for themselves, including their broad social responsibilities.

With this thought, we pass to the second area in which the administrators of big business can act.

Broader Business Policies

The business community has been well advised that it should develop a concept of the objectives and responsibilities of business enterprise which is broader than the traditional one — broader, that is, than the concept which is held

[25] See, for instance, John C. Baker, *Directors and Their Functions*, pp. 14, 130, and 138; and Melvin T. Copeland and Andrew R. Towl, *The Board of Directors and Business Management*, pp. 7 and 151.

by the critics along with some businessmen. The parallel between this advice and the injunctions of the religious critics is obvious.

One such person to set forth such a broader concept of business policy was Owen D. Young, one-time chairman of the board of the General Electric Company. As long ago as 1929, Mr. Young professed the belief that in his capacity as chairman of the board he was a "trustee" for the several groups who have an interest in the company:

> . . . One is the group of fifty-odd thousand people who have put their capital in the company, namely, its stockholders. Another is a group of well toward one hundred thousand people who are putting their labor and their lives into the business of the company. The third group is of customers and the general public.
>
> Customers have a right to demand that a concern so large shall not only do its business honestly and properly, but further, that it shall meet its public obligations and perform its public duties . . . in a word, vast as it is, that it should be a good citizen.[26]

Another person who has urged a similar view is Frank W. Abrams, then chairman of the board of Standard Oil Company (New Jersey):

> The job of professional management, as I see it, is to conduct the affairs of the enterprise in its charge in such a way as to maintain an equitable and workable balance among the claims of the various directly interested groups. Business firms are man-made instruments of society. They can be made to achieve their greatest social usefulness — and thus their future can be best assured — when management succeeds in finding a harmonious balance among the claims of the various interested groups: the stockholders, employees,

[26] "What is Right in Business," an address delivered at the Park Avenue Baptist Church, New York. Quoted by John H. Sears, *The New Place of the Stockholder* (New York & London: Harper & Brothers, 1929), p. 209; by John C. Baker, *Directors and Their Functions,* p. 6; and by George B. Hurff, *Social Aspects of Enterprise in the Large Corporation* (Philadelphia: University of Pennsylvania Press, 1950), p. 113.

customers, and public at large. But management's responsibility, in the broadest sense, extends beyond the search for a balance among respective claims. Management, as a good citizen, and because it cannot properly function in an acrimonious and contentious atmosphere, has the positive duty to work for peaceful relations and understanding among men — for a restoration of faith of men in each other in all walks of life.

. . . A modern corporation management, which has developed good social sense as well as good business sense, will accept the major responsibility to contribute to a satisfactory way of life for the men and women who work for it.[27]

Dean Donald K. David of the Harvard Business School has stated his concept of the needed broad policy objectives of corporate enterprise in these terms:

. . . I see the businessman as having an almost unprecedented opportunity to serve his fellow man. His opportunity is twofold: (1) Within his own business he can seek new ways and means of furnishing opportunities for men to find human satisfactions on the job. (2) He can help society determine — in a continuing and purposeful program — the most effective ways of furnishing the maximum of human satisfactions and security.[28]

Many other views of the broader concepts of purpose that corporation executives can strive for could be cited.[29] But the concepts which are presented are uniformly along the general lines sketched out by these three illustrative statements. There is a common essence to the concept of the corporation which is advanced: First, the corporation is not single-valued, looking toward profits alone. It is multi-

[27] "Management's Responsibilities in a Complex World," *Harvard Business Review*, Vol. XXIX, No. 3, May, 1951, pp. 29–30, and 31.

[28] "The Danger of Drifting," *Harvard Business Review*, Vol. XXVII, No. 1, January, 1950, p. 28.

[29] See, e.g., Benjamin M. Selekman, "Wanted: Mature Managers," *Harvard Business Review*, Vol. XXIV, No. 2, Winter, 1946, pp. 228 ff.; and Reverend Bernard W. Dempsey, S.J., "The Roots of Business Responsibility," *Harvard Business Review*, Vol. XXVII, No. 4, July, 1949, pp. 393 ff.

valued, looking toward a *number* of objectives, *including* profits. Second, the corporation is not an irresponsible entity. It is a responsible "citizen."

To these thoughts, there is little I can add except this one idea:

It is of vital importance, if big business is truly to go further in meeting the aspirations of the American people, that the corporation be conceived of as pursuing its multiple objectives *concurrently* and *simultaneously*. Put another way, the several purposes and prime values of the corporation must be conceived of as being in *co-equal rank*. If these multiple objectives, however many a corporation may state for itself, are thought of and acted upon as being of different priorities, there is grave danger that it may fail in this larger mission. There is danger in thinking, for example, that the *first* objective of the corporation is to make a profit, and that *secondarily* it has other objectives, such as being a "good citizen" or a "good society," or serving its customers well, and that, *thirdly,* it has some other objective, and so on.

In the first place, to conceive of these objectives as being of different priorities runs the danger that the ones of lower rank may come to be thought of — and acted upon — as being essentially *in opposition* one to another, especially in opposition to the *prime* objective. An outstanding and common example of this danger is the idea that running the corporation at a profit is *one* thing — a first objective — and maintaining a good society is *another* — a secondary objective. This is the danger [30] of thinking that "Producing an article at a profit and maintaining good employee relations are . . . antithetical propositions." There is, in fact, in this case, much clinical evidence to show that, far from being opposed, "these two sets of problems are interrelated and interdependent." [31] To think of these two particular objec-

[30] This danger is pointed out by Fritz J. Roethlisberger and W. J. Dickson in *Management and the Worker,* p. 552.

[31] Ibid.

tives, for example, as being opposing or even different goals runs the risk of confusion both in thinking and in action.

It may well be, of course, that at particular times in particular situations these various objectives actually may be in opposition. But a general *a priori* assumption that there is an inherent, necessary, conflict between them is not realistic, hence, not useful.

In the second place, to conceive of these objectives as of different priorities and essentially in opposition may set up a subtle and confusing presumption in the minds of administrators that their own policy objectives are basically opposed one to another and that, accordingly, their objectives are essentially inconsistent. Such a confusion may lead the corporation to be administered *as though* it had inconsistent objectives. Such management is likely to lead, in fact, to a pattern of inconsistency. A pattern of this sort is hardly compatible with effective management and the atmosphere of general confidence and trust in which communication and problem solving are easy. Actions will look, and will be, capricious and arbitrary.

In the third place, to conceive of these objectives as having different priorities runs the danger that the ones of lower rank may come to be thought of — and acted upon — simply as means to an end, the *real* end in itself being that objective which is given first rank. Such a point of view and such action may well lead to confusing opportunism as managers try to figure out whether or not "this time" it furthers the basic objective to take into account objectives of lower priority.

For example, some people tend to be in favor of good human relations not because they think this is a desirable objective in its own right, but merely because, as they conceive the matter, good human relations are profitable. In the general run of cases, perhaps they are. At least a general presumption is justified that the ability to produce at a profit and the state of employee relations are interrelated. But the idea here not only sets up a separation between what are parts of an organic whole, but it tries to subordinate one of them to the status of a simple means to the other. It justifies on grounds of expediency an objective which is probably more effectively pursued when it is conceived to be self-justifying as part of a system of interrelated goals. This is the kind of thinking that leads to confusion and opportunism.[32]

Saying that a corporation's several objectives should be conceived of as being in co-equal rank does not mean they are equally relevant and weighty in each and every administrative situation. In fact, the weights attached to the several policy objectives and the different criteria of decision will, in fact, vary from situation to situation. The skill of the administrator turns in large measure on his ability to give weights which are in some fashion appropriate to the various considerations in each individual case.

The point is, that while the importance of each of the corporate objectives in fact varies from case to case, there is *no general prejudgment* apart from cases that one or the other of the objectives is *necessarily* to be given greatest weight. Many particular actions will, in fact, be taken with little or no thought as to whether they are profitable. Indeed, actions will be sometimes taken which are demonstrably unprofitable, and with no ulterior motives, simply because some other objective, hence some other criterion of decision, is of overriding importance in the particular situation.

Administrators of big business can help to assure that their companies will do even more to meet American aspirations by being multivalued in their actions if they recognize explicitly, and let it be known, that they pursue their several objectives *concurrently* and not in *sequence*.

This brings us to the third area of action.

[32] Compare Sir George Schuster, *Christianity and Human Relations in Industry* (London: The Epsworth Press, 1951), p. 19.

Policy in Action

The third general point is that — obviously — much hard-headed thinking, professional zeal, and management skill will be needed if the administrators of big business are to make significant progress in converting these broad objectives into concrete realities. Day-to-day decisions and actions — not just laudable formal resolutions as to policy — are the things which will ultimately determine whether large corporations will actually do more to meet America's aspirations on all three levels — especially on the second two.

This point in no way minimizes the indispensability of clear vision and sound choice as to policies and criteria of decision. The practice of the highest degree of skill is not likely to produce meaningful results in the absence of clear thinking as to *what ends* and *why* the skills are being employed. This is especially true as concerns accomplishments which are meaningful at the second and third levels.

While there is much more to be learned about the administration of large organizations, the level of skill which is already common in many big companies is such as to assure that much can be, and will be achieved beyond what has been attained heretofore. And, there is a growing body of advancing firm knowledge about these skills — knowledge which stems from close, clinical observation of facts at first-hand. A number of these contributions have already been referred to.[33] There also has appeared on the subject of administration, alas, a good bit of utter rubbish — some of it apparently quite plausible. The thoughtful administrator is too wise, however, to be led astray by such items.

Obviously, the problem of what is involved in so administering an organization that worthy and sound policies and ob-

[33] In this connection, two further works should be cited in addition to those already mentioned: Myles L. Mace, *The Growth and Development of Executives,* and A. Zaleznik, *Foreman Training in a Growing Enterprise,* both published by the Division of Research of the Harvard University Graduate School of Business Administration, 1950 and 1951.

jectives are converted into concrete realities is far too great to be dealt with even superficially here. However, there are two points which can be made which are especially pertinent to the actions of top administrators themselves.

First, they can, if they choose, ask themselves, quite frankly, a number of questions of this order: What *are,* in fact, our objectives as a company? What *are,* in fact, the criteria by which we make our decisions, at this level and down through the organization? What responsibilities, if any, *are* we prepared to admit as regards making opportunities available to our people for their fullest self-realization? What *does* our company look like from inside and from down below? What does it look like from the *outside?* From a social point of view, are we *truly* efficient in our use of resources and in the development of improvements? What, in fact, have been the consequences of the operations of this company this past year *besides* its production and financial results?

The frank answers to frank questions like these will suggest further action.

Second — Whether worthy and sound policies will ever be translated into realities at the level of concrete situations, things, people, and events depends — as is well known — very largely upon the daily *actions* of the top administrators themselves. Unfortunately, the examples sometimes actually given by the daily actions of top administrators, and the pressures which, intentionally or otherwise, the top administrators generate on levels down below, result in behavior which in fact negates the desired objective.

Two examples should illustrate the point.

Over the last few years the top management of a certain large company has adopted as a formal policy the intention that the independent dealers who handle the company's products are to be treated as indeed independent businessmen. The top management desires — with complete sincerity it would seem — that in all relationships between the dealers and various departments of the company there is to be cordial respect, and that the true independence of the dealer in running his own business is never to be questioned by word or deed. This is the kind of policy that ties directly in with criticism and aspirations at the political and social level.

In fact, however, in this company, as the management is well aware, there are many instances where sales personnel and others in the company treat dealers like "hired hands," even going so far as to imply the threat that their franchises may be revoked if they don't do as they are told or "get into line." Such behavior is by no means the norm in the company. But it happens with sufficient frequency to distress the top management.

Ironically, one of the reasons these events occur, it seems clear, is because of the behavior of the top management itself. By daily actions, the top management signals its great interest — certainly a well-founded one — in volume. It generates enormous pressures, especially on the sales organization, by its systems of budgets and quotas. Daily actions of the top management do not, however, equally often signal — through praise, promotion, and the like — an equally great concern for good relations with dealers. A salesman, for instance, whose behavior gives rise to dealer complaints may be admonished, and quite severely. But the salesman who has trouble meeting budgets and sales quotas is very likely to get fired. In short, day-to-day actions of the top management unwittingly frequently generate pressures down below which lead to direct violations of the desires of the men at the top that dealers shall be treated as completely and entirely independent businessmen with whom the company desires mutually cordial and respectful relations.

The pressures that may be set up on production organizations by variable budgets which are slavishly regarded as ideals and firm expectations, rather than as useful goals and analytical tools, often result in the failure of companies to move as well as they might toward meeting the realities of competition and cost and *at the same time* to move toward the objective of good and satisfying human relations in the plants.[34]

The personal administrative skill and day-to-day behavior of the top management may well set the pattern of the administration of the company in determining what it actually accomplishes.[35]

While focusing here on the job of top administrators, I do not mean to slight the opportunities for useful action by managers down the line. The skills and actions of managers on lower levels, of course, have much to do with how well the organization down under them stacks up on each of the three planes of performance we have been discussing.[36]

Perhaps this point has been overly elaborated. But a few managements show something of a tendency to look to systems, devices, structures, "gimmicks," plans, and other factors beside their own day-to-day actions for getting policies translated into reality. This, of course, is not the administrative skill necessary to meet broad objectives.

At this point, it may be necessary again to re-emphasize that large corporations, taking the very thinnest along with the thick, have done a good job. Their day-to-day administration has enabled them to accomplish what they have. It is a question of continued progress.

We come now to the fourth and final area of action.

[34] See John D. Glover and Fritz J. Roethlisberger, "Human Reactions to Standards and Controls" in *Controllership in Modern Management,* T. F. Bradshaw and C. C. Hull, editors (Chicago: Richard D. Irwin, Inc., 1949); and Chris Argyris, "Human Problems with Budgets," *Harvard Business Review,* Vol. XXXI, No. 1, January–February, 1953, pp. 97 ff.

[35] For a stimulating expression of this thought, see the statement by John S. Tomajan, president of The Washburn Company, "It Begins with Me," in *Individual Initiative in Business,* George H. Allen, editor (Cambridge, Harvard University Press, 1950), pp. 101–106.

[36] See, for example, *Teamwork and Labor Turnover in the Aircraft Industry of Southern California,* by Elton Mayo and George F. F. Lombard (Boston: Harvard University, Graduate School of Business Administration, Bureau of Business Research, 1944).

Toward Better Understanding of Big Business

The administrators of big business can do much to help meet one of the great needs of our time: A better understanding of the real nature of large corporations and of how things really get done and are done in these organizations.

By this, it is not suggested that the administrators of big business should start in motion a great "public-relations" campaign to convince the people that "What helps business helps you," or that "The large corporation is indispensable to the well-being of America." On the contrary, few things could be designed which would less effectively attain the desired result. The intellectual critics of big business — including Supreme Court Justices, Congressmen, professors, and ministers of religion — cannot be moved from their positions by slogans coined by "hucksters." Nor can the public at large be led, by self-serving *words,* to exchange those elements of basic mistrust which are in their feelings for elements of faith. For the long-haul *actions* will have a greater educational impact than words.

To say this is to say nothing new. Many people, including many businessmen, entertain the same idea. But, lest there be misunderstanding perhaps it is just as well to make the point.

In the meantime, while actual deeds are taking place in everyday life where people can see them at first hand, there are two especially constructive things the administrators of big business can do by way of contributing to the education of us all as to how big business operates, and why, and with what results.

The first is an obvious course of action, and can be disposed of quickly. That is for large corporations to contribute to the financing of painstaking studies by social scientists into the nature and functioning of large corporations. A number of large corporations are doing just that already. It will be a pity, though, if such studies, instead of being increased, are pushed aside by the obvious need to finance technical research during a period of unremitting, and seemingly interminable international danger.

The second thing they can do by way of contributing to the education of us all in the realities of big business is to make many, many opportunities available to educators and others to come into their organizations *to see for themselves* what a big business really looks like and how it really works. Large corporations can do much to make it financially possible, as well, for such people to do this.

Again, an obvious remark should be made. The point in doing this is not to wage a "public relations" campaign to "prove" that big business is without fault or flaw. The fact, of course, is that despite all that has been done, there is still much yet to be done and things to be undone also.

The purpose in making such opportunities available is to permit these people to engage in a process of *self*-education: To let them see at first hand that the standard concepts and stereotypes of big business are an inadequate basis for realistic and really constructive thinking. It must be remembered that many Doctors of Philosophy in university departments — including, of all places, economics — have never spent so much as a *single day* "in the clinic" actually studying closely and scientifically at first hand the anatomy and physiology of a single large corporation. This does not discourage them from making diagnoses at a distance or from prescribing drastic therapies. The nation would not long tolerate *medical* doctors so trained. That there is this gross blind spot in their training is not necessarily their fault. Many of them would, long since, have welcomed such opportunities if they had been made available.

An illustration will highlight the need for this kind of self-education. Not long ago, a young professor had the opportunity to spend several days talking with members of the top management of a large corporation. This was probably not so effective as actually watching them at work. But it was better than nothing. This man came away *amazed* that top management people, including members of the board of directors, were obviously *technically competent* and familiar with the operating problems of the company. This *amazing* fact shattered a deeply entrenched preconception — perhaps developed through overexposure to the writings of Thorstein Veblen. Up to that time, the only images he had of the top levels of big business were of "manipulators," "plungers," and "riggers" who made, and who could make, no real contribution to the technically complex substantive operations of large companies.

This man, in all probability, was not "won over" by a few hours of first-hand contact with big business. But he may now be started on a line of self-education and independent re-examination of some of his ideas.

Here, the point should be re-emphasized that the purpose of making these opportunities for self-education is *not* to "win friends and influence people." It is, simply, to make opportunities for self-education available to independent, intelligent people. It may well be that some who come to observe will have their worst fears confirmed. Most likely this will be because deep rooted preconceptions prevent the whole reality — the thick along with the thin — from being observed and registered. But, in some cases, it may also be because the facts justify the conclusion. To be aware of the possibility of such "failure" in making these opportunities available and yet to go ahead, requires an act of faith — a faith that most people are well intentioned and can improve their own ideas, given the opportunity.

For some, such an act of faith may come hard. For some, it may be impossible. Not long ago, a professor was urging an officer of a large corporation to propose to the rest of the management that the company adopt and finance a program to make it possible each year for, say, ten or a dozen educators to spend a few days, or more, freely observing any part of the company that particularly interested them. The company man was hesitant. He noted that such a program would cost in the neighborhood of x thousand dollars a year. He was somewhat reassured when the professor pointed out that this amount represented less than $\frac{1}{10}$ of 1% of the company's annual advertising budget. But he threw up his hands when he came to realize, with the professor's assistance and concurrence, that a "*no* pressure" campaign like the one they were talking about, could not be guaranteed to result in all these people being "won over." He was so sure — or was he just so timid? — rightly or wrongly, that the top management wouldn't buy such an "impractical" idea that he never even raised the question with them.

But "*no* pressure" programs of this sort are exactly what are called for. In all likelihood, of course, some critics will remain critical — critical of big business per se — as a stereotype, that is. This is probably inevitable. The others may be better enabled to turn their critical talents to practical use. If they are helped and encouraged to address these talents to analyzing and dealing with the problems of reality, they may be enabled to make really useful contributions. These contributions may be directly to the more useful and harmonious operation of larger corporations. Perhaps their contributions may be of the order which are broadly useful to society as a whole — through conveying to the community at large a better understanding of realities. Their contributions may come out of their participating in the formulation of more realistic, more useful, and more effective policies of government toward business. In any case, we should all be better off.

If even a quarter of the critics who have spent recent decades in carping at figments could have spent their time, effort, and undoubted talents in trying, first, to understand and, second, in trying to improve *real* and *concrete* situations, we should all be considerably further advanced toward the goals that most Americans have in mind. The administrators of big business can hang out the latch-string.[37]

* * *

This brings to an end the discussion of what administrators of big business can *do* to try to meet the aspirations of the American people — a line of action which is of greater importance than any direct effort to counter the criticisms of big business. The ideas taken up are very modest. They are, most obviously, not the only ideas worth considering. But they are practical, and they are to the point.

Ideas like these avoid two important pitfalls which courses of action at this level recommended to businessmen often fall into. First, they are pedestrian ideas. They do not envision any ultimate state of things in which all growth and emergence come to an end. They are ideas addressed to a here and now which is a dynamic precursor of a dynamic future in which all things may change.

Second, such ideas are not addressed to a business élite — or any other kind of élite — which is going to run everybody and be responsible for everything.[38] There are, clearly, many, many people in the nation, in many callings of life, who are sincerely interested in the nation's welfare and who, too, have *their* responsibilities and competence for useful action — whether it be in the workings of government agencies, labor unions, universities, or whatever, or whether it be for formulating the constructive criticism which we shall always need if we are to keep progressing, maintaining all the time a tolerably good balance in all the factors that make for worthwhile and meaningful life.

These ideas on action are merely addressed to the adminis-

37 That new insight and better understanding can flow from first-hand observation of big business is dramatically illustrated by David E. Lilienthal's experience, described in his book, *Big Business: A New Era* (New York: Harper & Brothers, 1953).

38 See Josef Winterschuh, "Young Businessmen and Germany's Future," *Harvard Business Review,* Vol. XXIX, No. 3, May, 1951, pp. 35 ff.

trators of big business, who, among others in the nation, have especial and immediate responsibilities for the economic, the political and social, and the moral performance and appearance of American civilization.

* * *

As some of the advocates of big business foretold half a century ago, big business has served us well. While we have not yet arrived at the point where we can ever and always be sure that jobs will be available for all who seek opportunity and employment — and we *must* make progress on that score — still in no other nation is there an equal freedom from want. This we have achieved in a system free from the fear of heavy knocks on our doors in the hour before dawn. Freedom of speech, we have, and freedom of faith. And freedom of self-realization.

When — where — in the world have people been so free from the limitations of conditions and circumstances outside themselves to seek their own greatest potentialities, and had so much material wherewithal to help them on their way? Never. Nowhere.

And our own industrial revolution has scarcely yet begun, as human history goes.

But no matter how far we progress, critics we shall have with us always. To criticize is human. Besides, there will always and forever be imperfections to be pointed out, premises to be questioned, and acts of irresponsibility to be decried. To *need* criticism is just as human.

And critics we *must* have with us always. For progress takes place in an atmosphere of tension — the tension of the free competition of differing ideas and differing objectives. Only in the complacence of universal orthodoxy, of decay — in a mausoleum — is there no tension. It is out of the stresses of tension of everlasting action, criticism, countercriticism, and further action, that progress comes.

So what we need now is more and ever broader action by big business. And more criticism.

Some of the criticism of big business will continue yet, for some time to come, to be of a reactionary, reminiscent cast, searching, groping, backward a century and more to find its ideal way of life. Some will gaze toward a millennial, static Utopia. Those kinds of criticism will get in the way and distract.

But there will be also, as there have been in the past, critics who, with charity, clarity, and resolution, will compel inward re-examination, who will point out concretely some next few steps forward to be taken in the here and now.

The winnowing of time will blow away the chaff. The wise administrator will gather up the grain.

APPENDIX

Excerpts from the testimony of Henry O. Havemeyer,
President, American Sugar Refining Company,
before the Industrial Commission, June 14, 1899.

* * *

It is my opinion that corporations are under no obligations whatever to any of the States for their existence. Quite the reverse; the States are under obligations to them.

* * *

. . . when Spreckels came in with his enormous capacity we either had to fight or make no dividend; we concluded to fight and that is what we are doing now.

Q. When were you fighting against him?

A. [Mr. Havemeyer] That fight lasted in the neighborhood — lasted until we got his refinery — that is about the length of it.

* * *

. . . by buying up all the refineries, burning them up, and concentrating the meltings in four refineries and working them full, you work at a minimum cost. That enables us to pay a dividend on the common stock.

* * *

. . . We maintain that when we reduced the cost we were entitled to the profit, and that it was none of the public's business; we took it and paid it out to our stockholders; it may be business policy to share that with the public sometimes; we did not do that then; we have done it since. We had to increase the

Source: Industrial Commission, *Preliminary Report on Trusts and Industrial Combinations* (Washington: Government Printing Office, 1900), Vol. I, Part II, pp. 103–136. [See, further, testimony by Mr. Havemeyer, *Report and Proceedings of the Joint Committee of the (New York) Senate and Assembly Appointed to Investigate Trusts* ("Lexow Report"), Albany, 1897, pp. 109–112.]

output; we could injure our competition by reducing our margin. This is business policy again, not philanthropy.

* * *

Q. Suppose, for instance, these competing sugar refineries were put on this table to take in. You would not take them in?

A. I would take them in pretty quickly, and get out of them all I could. As long as I do not restrict, or the Government interfere with them, anybody can get into the business. Why is not that a good business proposition? What is harmful in it? That is the way business has been done from the year one, and always will be.

* * *

Q. Is it for the benefit of the consumer that prices are temporarily put down when competition enters the field until you can crush out that competitor, as I gather from your testimony? Is it for the advantage of the consumer, if, when that competition is crushed out, you put up the prices immediately thereafter to such a margin of profits as will cover all these expenses and others – that is, the expenses of the fight, the wear and tear, the buying out refineries, and all that? I would ask you if that is for the benefit of the consumer?

A. Well, I do not know. You would have to find out what the figures were in order to determine whether it was just or not. I think the consumer would have to be subject to such a condition of things if it was a trade condition.

* * *

Q. . . . Now, I want to know if you think – you stated that the consumer received the benefits of this consolidation of industry – it a fair ethical proposition, independent of the business view you put on it, that the consumers should pay dividends on this $25,000,000 of overcapitalization?

A. I do not care two cents for your ethics. I do not know enough of them to apply them.

Q. Well as a business proposition, is it right?

A. As a business proposition, it is right to get all out of business that you possibly can. If you get too much of a profit, you get somebody in competition.

* * *

. . . We had to consider whether we should furnish this sugar to the consumer at a cheap price and get out of it a suitable dividend for the stockholders, or maintain all the different organizations and keep all the men employed. We naturally closed many of the refineries, concentrated the meltings in a few, and achieved the results we sought. But there were a great many men undoubtedly that were left out of employment and had to seek other employment. It is pretty hard. . . . It looks like cold blood, but when you come to analyze it it is one of those conditions of trade that there is no human way to prevent.

* * *

Q. You think, then, that when a corporation is chartered by the State, offers stock to the public, and is one in which the public is interested, that the public has no right to know what its earning power is or to subject them to any inspection whatever, that the people may not buy this stock blindly?

A. Yes; that is my theory. Let the buyer beware; that covers the whole business. You can not wet nurse people from the time they are born until the time they die. They have got to wade in and get stuck, and that is the way men are educated and cultivated.

Q. Then, you think that they have a right to charter corporations and allow them to offer stock to the people – to the whole community – and that the community then has no right to a knowledge of what the earning power of that stock is?

A. Precisely.

* * *

Q. Is there no way to ventilate the works so as to prevent the men working in such intense heat as they do?

A. That is very much exaggerated. The normal heat of a refinery is 90°; there are places where the sugar is dried where it runs up to 110°. They rather like that heat; they perspire freely and do not feel it. They drink a great deal of beer, and that tends to promote perspiration.

* * *

Q. You own your own brewery?

A. No. We buy beer of a certain standard, sell it by weight, and give it to the men at cost. Otherwise they would be running out to saloons and getting drunk, and be away from their work, and gambling their money away. We do it as a business proposition again.

* * *

Q. You are aware that there is a notion in the country that these companies and combinations are very much in the character of commercial conspiracies; that is the general opinion about trusts?

A. Yes.

Q. You take this view of it, do you not, that as a business proposition a trust, or combine, or great capitalized association is simply the survival of the fittest in business?

A. Precisely.

* * *

Q. One thing further. Did you pay the last dividends out of the earnings or out of the surplus?

A. I did not mention that.

Q. Do you mean to say you would not like to answer that?

A. I mean to say that I did not mention it.

Q. Do you refuse to answer that question?

A. I think it had better remain as it is, Mr. Chairman.

* * *

ADDITIONAL SELECTED BIBLIOGRAPHY

Books

Abell, Aaron I. *The Urban Impact on American Protestantism, 1865–1900.* Cambridge: Harvard University Press, 1943.

Adams, Brooks. *Theory of Social Revolutions.* New York: The Macmillan Company, 1913.

Adams, James Truslow. *Our Business Civilization.* New York: A. & C. Boni, 1929.

Arnold, Thurman W. *Bottlenecks of Business.* New York: Reynal & Hitchcock, 1940.

Ballinger, William J. *By Vote of the People.* New York: Charles Scribner's Sons, 1946.

Beard, Miriam. *A History of the Businessman.* New York: The Macmillan Company, 1938.

Bellamy, Edward. *Looking Backward.* New York: Vanguard Press, Inc., 1926.

Brandeis, Louis D. *Business — A Profession.* Boston: Hale, Cushman & Flint, 1933.

—— *The Curse of Bigness.* New York: The Viking Press, Inc., 1937.

Bryce, James. *The American Commonwealth.* New York: The Macmillan Company, new edition, two volumes, 1920.

Casson, Stanley. *Progress and Catastrophe.* New York: Harper & Brothers, 1937.

Cavan, Ruth Shoule. *Suicide.* Chicago: University of Chicago Press, 1928.

Chamberlin, Edward H., Editor. *Monopoly and Competition and Their Regulation.* New York: St. Martin's Press, 1954.

Childs, Marquis W., and Douglass Cater. *Ethics in a Business Society.* New York: Harper & Brothers, 1954. (Also Mentor Books, 1954.)

Cochran, Thomas C., and William Miller. *The Age of Enterprise.* New York: The Macmillan Company, 1943.

Cole, G. D. H. *Introduction to Economic History, 1750–1950.* London: Macmillan & Co., Ltd., 1950.

Corey, Lewis. *The House of Morgan.* New York: G. Howard Satt, 1930.

Cournot, Augustin. *Researches into the Mathematical Principles of the Theory of Wealth.* 1838. Translated by Nathaniel T. Bacon, with a bibliography of mathematical economics by Irving Fisher. New York: The Macmillan Company, 1897.

Demant, V. A. *Religion and the Decline of Capitalism.* New York: Charles Scribner's Sons, 1952.

Dexter, Chester M. *American Radicalism, 1865–1901.* Menasha, Wisconsin: Collegiate Press, 1946.

Epstein, Abraham. *Insecurity.* New York: Random House, Inc., 1938.

Faulkner, Harold Underwood. *The Quest for Social Justice, 1898–1901.* New York: The Macmillan Company, 1930.

Gabriel, Ralph. *The Course of American Democratic Thought.* New York: The Ronald Press, 1940.

George, Henry. *Progress and Poverty.* San Francisco: W. M. Hinton & Co., printers, 1879.

Hobson, John A. *The Evolution of Modern Capitalism; A Study of Machine Production.* London: George Allen & Unwin, Ltd., and New York: The Macmillan Company, revised edition, 1926, reprinted 1949.

Hopkins, Charles H. *The Rise of the Social Gospel in American Protestantism, 1865–1919.* New Haven: Yale University Press, 1940.

Hunter, Floyd. *Community Power Structure: A Study of Decision Makers.* Chapel Hill: The University of North Carolina Press, 1953.

Josephson, Matthew. *The Robber Barons.* New York: Harcourt, Brace & Co., Inc., 1934.

Keyserling, Hermann Alexander. *America Set Free.* New York: Harper & Brothers, 1929.

Laidler, Harry W. *Concentration of Control in American Industry.* New York: Thomas Y. Crowell, 1931.

Lloyd, Henry Demarest. *Wealth against Commonwealth.* New York: Harper & Brothers, 1894.

Lynd, Robert S. and Helen M. *Middletown.* New York: Harcourt, Brace & Co., Inc., 1929.

Lynd, Robert S. and Helen M. *Middletown in Transition.* New York: Harcourt, Brace & Co., Inc., 1937.

McCloskey, Robert Green. *American Conservatism in an Age of Enterprise.* Cambridge: Harvard University Press, 1952.

Marcel, Gabriel. *Man against Society.* Chicago: Henry Regnery Company, 1952.

Mason, Edward S. *Explorations in Economics.* Article on "Industrial Concentration and the Decline of Competition." New York: McGraw-Hill Book Company, Inc., 1936.

May, Henry F. *Protestant Churches and Industrial America.* New York: The Macmillan Company, 1949.

Minnegerode, Meade. *Certain Rich Men.* New York: G. P. Putnam's Sons, 1927.

Montgomery, R. H. *The Brimstone Game.* New York: The Vanguard Press, Inc., 1940.

Morris, William. *News from Nowhere.* Boston: Roberts Brothers, 1890, and London: Reeves & Turner, 1891. ("Pocket Edition," London: Longmans, Green and Co., 1912.)

Mumford, Lewis. *The Culture of Cities.* New York: Harcourt, Brace & Co., Inc., 1938.

Nettleton, A. B. *Trusts or Competition?* Chicago: The Leon Publishing Company, 1900.

O'Brien, Edward Joseph Harrington. *The Dance of the Machines. The American Short Story and the Industrial Age.* New York: Macaulay Publishing Co., 1929.

O'Rahilly, Alfred. *Social Principles.* Cork, Ireland: The Cork University Press, 1948.

Parrington, Vernon L. *Main Currents in American Thought.* New York: Harcourt, Brace & Co., Inc., 1930.

Rauschenbusch, Walter. *Christianity and the Social Crisis.* New York: The Macmillan Company, 1907.

Ross, Edward A. *Sin and Society,* with introduction by Theodore Roosevelt. Boston: Houghton Mifflin Company, 1907.

Ruml, Beardsley. *Tomorrow's Business.* New York: Farrar & Rinehart, Inc., 1945.

Ruskin, John. *Time and Tide.* London: Smith, Elder & Co., 1867.

Ryan, John A. *Social Doctrine in Action.* New York: Harper and Brothers, 1941.

Schumpeter, Joseph A. *Theory of Economic Development.* Cambridge: Harvard University Press, 1934.

Shaw, Clifford R. *Delinquency Areas.* Chicago: University of Chicago Press, 1929.

Simons, Algie M. *Social Forces in American History.* New York: The Macmillan Company, 1911.

Smith, James Allen. *The Spirit of American Government.* New York: The Macmillan Company, 1907.

Stearns, Harold E., Editor. *Civilization in the United States.* New York: Harcourt, Brace & Co., Inc., 1922.

Steindl, J. *Small and Big Business.* Oxford: B. Blackwell, 1945.

Toulman, H. A., Jr. *Millions in Mergers.* New York: B. C. Forbes Co., 1929.

Tugwell, Rexford. *Industry's Coming of Age.* New York: Harcourt, Brace & Co., Inc., 1927.

Veblen, Thorstein. *Absentee Ownership and Business Enterprise.* New York: B. W. Huebsch, Inc., 1923.

von Beckerath, Herbert. *Modern Industrial Organization.* New York: McGraw-Hill Book Company, Inc., 1933.

Walling, William. *Progressivism and After.* New York: The Macmillan Company, 1914.

White, H. G. *Social Thought in America.* New York: The Viking Press, Inc., 1949.

Articles

Amlie, T. R., "Program for Big Business," *The Nation,* Vol. 157, November 27, 1943.

Berge, W., "Monopoly and the American Future," *Virginia Quarterly Review,* Vol. 23, No. 4, October 1947.

Boulding, Kenneth E., "Does Large-Scale Enterprise Result in Lower Costs? – Discussion," *American Economic Review,* Vol. 38, No. 2, May 1948.

Dean, Joel, "Does Large-Scale Enterprise Result in Lower Costs? – Cost Structure of Enterprises and Break-Even Charts," *American Economic Review,* Vol. 38, No. 2, May 1948.

"Facts About Big Business," *New Republic,* Vol. 115, September 2, 1946.

Homan, P. T., "Trusts," *Encyclopedia of the Social Sciences.* (New York: The Macmillan Company, Vol. 15, 1931.)

Houghton, Harrison F., "The Progress of Concentration in Industry – The Growth of Big Business," *American Economic Review,* Vol. 38, No. 2, May 1948.

Hower, Ralph M., "Is Private Enterprise Undermining Our Citizenry – and Itself?" *Harvard Business School Alumni Bulletin,* Vol. 26, No. 4, Winter 1950.

Jacobs, W., "Our Economic Straight Jacket; Monopoly Gnaws at Our Economic Vitals," *Vital Speeches of the Day,* Vol. 11, August 15, 1945.

Johnson, R. W., "Break It Up; American Business Should Be Decentralized," *Saturday Evening Post,* Vol. 218, January 5, 1946.

Johnson, V., "Monopoly on the March Again," *American Mercury,* Vol. 63, December 1946.

Lewis, H. Gregg, "The Economic Theory of Imperfect Competition, Oligopoly, and Monopoly – Some Observations on Duopoly Theory," *American Economic Review,* Vol. 38, No. 2, May 1948.

Mason, E. S., "Methods of Developing a Proper Control of Big Business," *Proceedings of the Academy of Political Science,* Vol. 18, June 1939.

—— "Price and Production Policies of Large-Scale Enterprise," *American Economic Review,* Vol. 29, No. 1, March 1939 supplement.

Mayer, Kurt, "Small Business as a Social Institution," *Social Research,* Vol. 14, No. 3, September 1947.

Means, Gardiner C., "The Large Corporation in American Life," *American Economic Review,* Vol. 21, No. 1, March 1931.

Morgenstern, Oskar, "The Economic Theory of Imperfect Competition, Oligopoly, and Monopoly – Oligopoly, Monopolistic Competition, and the Theory of Games," *American Economic Review,* Vol. 38, No. 2, May 1948.

Mund, V. H., "Monopolistic Competition Theory and Public Price Policy, *American Economic Review,* Vol. 32, No. 4, December 1942.

O'Mahoney, J. C., "Big Business Needs Big Government," *Commercial and Financial Chronicle,* Vol. 169, April 21, 1949.

—— "Is Big Business Too Big?" *Reader's Digest,* Vol. 54, April 1949.

Outman, R. E., "Small Business Fights for Life," *Atlantic Monthly,* Vol. 117, April 1946.

Pius XII, Pope, "The 'Depersonalization' of Modern Man," *Vital Speeches of the Day,* Vol. 19, No. 7, January 15, 1953.

Robertson, N., "What Do You Mean, Free Enterprise?" *Harper's,* Vol. 197, November 1948.

—— "Monopoly Tightens Its Grip and Congress Helps," *New Republic,* Vol. 115, July 8, 1946.

Roosevelt, Franklin D., "State of the Union Message," *New York Times,* January 4, 1936.

Rose, Lisle A., "Bibliographical Survey of Economic and Political Writings," *American Literature,* January 1944.

"Round Table on Monopolistic and Imperfect Competition," *American Economic Review,* Vol. 27, No. 2, June 1937.

Scitovsky, T., "Ignorance as a Source of Oligopoly Power," *American Economic Review,* Vol. 40, No. 2, May 1950.

Stigler, George J., "The Extent and Bases of Monopoly," *American Economic Review,* Vol. 32, Supplement, June 1942.

Government Documents

Smaller War Plants Corporation. *Economic Concentration and World War II.* Report to the Special Committee to Study Problems of American Small Business, 79th Cong., 2d Sess. (Washington: Government Printing Office, 1946)

U. S. Congress. House, Select Committee on Small Business, Staff Report to the Monopoly Sub-Committee. *U.S. vs. Economic Concentration and Monopoly,* 79th Cong. (Washington: Government Printing Office, 1946)

U. S. Congress. Senate, Special Committee to Study Problems of American Small Business. *Independent Business. Its Struggle for Survival,* 81st Cong., 1st Sess. (Washington: Government Printing Office, 1949)

Supreme Court Cases

American Tobacco Co. et al. vs. *United States.* 328 U.S. 781 (1946)

United States vs. *Socony-Vacuum Oil Co., Inc. et al.* 310 U.S. 150 (1940)

Name and Title Index